DATE DUE

~~JV 2 '93~~			
~~JA 7 '94~~			
~~MR 4 '94~~			
~~RENEW~~			
MR 25 '94			
JY 6 '95			
~~NO 9 '95~~			
~~DE 18 '95~~			
MR 29 '99			
~~AP 21 '99~~			
JA 28 '03			

DEMCO 38-296

The Generalizability of Critical Thinking

Multiple Perspectives on an Educational Ideal

The Generalizability of Critical Thinking

Multiple Perspectives on an Educational Ideal

edited by
Stephen P. Norris

TEACHERS COLLEGE PRESS

Teachers College, Columbia University
New York and London

Published by Teachers College Press, 1234 Amsterdam Avenue, New York, N.Y. 10027

Copyright © 1992 by Teachers College, Columbia University

Library of Congress Cataloging-in-Publication Data

The Generalizability of critical thinking : multiple perspectives on
   an educational ideal / edited by Stephen P. Norris.
       p.   cm.
    Includes bibliographical references and index.
     ISBN 0-8077-3173-0 (alk. paper). — ISBN 0-8077-3172-2 (pbk. :
  alk. paper)
     1. Critical thinking. 2. Transfer of training.   I. Norris,
  Stephen, P.
  BF441.G42 1992
  153.4'2—dc20   91-39406

ISBN 0-8077-3173-0
ISBN 0-8077-3172-2 (pbk.)

Printed on acid-free paper
Manufactured in the United States of America
99 98 97 96 95 94 93 92   8 7 6 5 4 3 2 1

This book is dedicated to my friend and mentor,
Robert H. Ennis

Contents

Preface

One of the most healthy controversies in the critical thinking movement centers around the question of whether or not, and, if so, to what extent and in what ways, critical thinking is generalizable. The generalizability question has catalyzed some of the most significant advances in the understanding of critical thinking. The stance adopted on this issue affects how critical thinking is taught, how it is tested, and how research on critical thinking is conducted. Thus, given the perceived importance of critical thinking to education, the generalizability question must be tackled with vigor.

This volume is divided into four sections: (a) an introductory chapter that poses the generalizability question in its various forms, and shows what is at stake given various possible answers to it; (b) a set of chapters that clarifies many of the central concepts and issues involved in the debate and proposes directions for further research; (c) chapters that defend the generalizability position from a number of viewpoints; and (d) a set of challenges mounted against several of the tenets of generalizability.

The chapters are written from two broad perspectives, that of philosophy and psychology. This is appropriate, since much of the debate turns on whether the generalizability question is essentially a conceptual problem, and hence within the domain of philosophy, or an empirical problem, and hence within the domain of psychology. The issue is even more subtle and vexing, since, as becomes apparent early in this volume, domains of knowledge are difficult to demarcate operationally. Hence, the possibility exists that the generalizability question involves interconnected conceptual and empirical issues that must be resolved simultaneously.

The central purposes of the book are to introduce the major aspects of the generalizability question and to provide a foundation of knowledge and concepts for exploring the question further. The book should be useful as a supplemental text for courses in critical thinking, philosophy, philosophy of education, and educational psychology. Also, the book highlights a large number of unanswered and unexplored questions about critical thinking generalizability that researchers in the area will find valuable.

Acknowledgments

I thank Memorial University of Newfoundland for granting me the time and the facilities to produce this manuscript. I especially thank all the contributing authors for their diligence and faithfulness to deadlines, Judy Blundon for her usual adroitness in taking care of administrative matters, and Jackie Pitcher-March, Clare Dwyer, and Ann Hollett for help in producing the manuscript.

This book is the result of a conference held at Memorial University of Newfoundland in St. John's, September 22–24, 1989. The conference was supported by grants from the Social Sciences and Humanities Research Council of Canada (Grant Number 443–89–0083) and from the Canadian Educational Researchers' Association. I am grateful to both organizations.

I am also grateful to the American Educational Research Association for granting permission to reprint with modifications the following copyrighted materials:

1. Ennis, R. H. (1989). Critical thinking and subject specificity: Clarification and needed research. *Educational Researcher, 18*(3), 4–10.
2. McPeck, J. E. (1990). Critical thinking and subject specificity: A reply to Ennis. *Educational Researcher, 19*(4), 10–12.

The chapter by Harvey Siegel was written originally for this collection. It has also appeared in the journal, *Educational Philosophy and Theory, 23*(1), 18–30, 1991.

The Generalizability of Critical Thinking

Multiple Perspectives on an Educational Ideal

1 Introduction: The Generalizability Question

Stephen P. Norris
Memorial University of Newfoundland

Critical thinking is generalizable to the extent that four conditions are satisfied: (a) the idea of thinking-in-general, that is, thinking abstracted from the particulars that are the objects of thought, makes sense (for example, while it clearly makes sense to speak of the deductive reasoning involved in solving the equation $2x - 7 = 11$, it must also make sense to speak of deductive reasoning separate from the content of a particular mathematical problem, or problem in any other subject or topic); (b) at least some commonality exists in the critical thinking needed from field to field, subject to subject, topic to topic, concern to concern; (c) critical thinking provides a significant fund of resources for dealing effectively with each of these various fields, subjects, topics, and concerns; and (d) the ability to think critically as learned in one field, subject, topic, or concern has a positive influence on thinking critically in other fields, subjects, topics, and concerns.

Whether or not condition (a) is satisfied is primarily a question for conceptual analysis. Whether or not condition (d) is satisfied is primarily a question for psychology. About categorizing these two tasks there is, I believe, little controversy. How to determine whether conditions (b) and (c) are satisfied, however, is open to debate. Some believe that whether or not (b) and (c) are met is an epistemological issue. Others believe it is an empirical psychological one. For reasons that will become clear later in this chapter, the issue raises conceptual, epistemological, and empirical questions that must be addressed before the satisfaction of conditions (b) and (c) can be determined.

In this chapter, I shall first address the significance to educational practice of the question of critical thinking generalizability. Second, I shall reveal some of the unanalyzed implicit assumptions about critical thinking generalizability in various critical thinking theories. Third, I shall explore the act of defining "critical thinking," and explain three options that are available for categorizing this term among the nouns of our language. Fourth, I shall argue that disagreements over the proper way to categorize "critical thinking" give rise to much of the debate over critical thinking generalizability, although this connection is not always recognized. Fifth, I shall sketch some research on the nature of critical thinking that might be pursued, given the recognition that the generalizability debate is largely a debate over how to define "critical thinking."

SIGNIFICANCE FOR PRACTICE

Concern with the generalizability of critical thinking is motivated often by a number of questions about educational practice: (a) Are there dispositions of thought that are teachable and, if so, are they as important to teach as critical thinking abilities? (b) Should critical thinking be taught separately or as part of traditional school subjects? (c) Can the quality of students' critical thinking be evaluated, and, if so, how can this be done? (d) Is there a need to teach critical thinking in all subjects? and (e) Does it make sense to hold critical thinking as a goal of education?

The question of whether critical thinking is generalizable has a bearing on each of these questions. Consider, for instance, the question of whether dispositions or abilities should be emphasized more. Since in education we strive to promote things of general intellectual significance, the answer depends on the extent to which the four conditions for the existence of critical thinking generalizability are satisfied by critical thinking dispositions and abilities. If, for instance, dispositions tend to satisfy the conditions more than abilities, then there may be more educational significance in fostering the dispositions. Similarly, whether or not critical thinking should be taught as a separate school subject depends upon whether there are aspects of critical thinking that apply to all or most subjects, and upon whether separate instruction in critical thinking proves useful for students in areas in which they do not receive instruction. Whether critical thinking can be evaluated depends upon whether critical thinking can be abstracted from various subject matters. If critical thinking cannot be abstracted, then critical thinking tests cannot be conceived, let alone designed. Finally, if critical thinking is not generalizable, it makes less sense to hold it as a goal of education, since one of the reasons for holding it as a goal is to make what is taught in school generally relevant to inside-of- and outside-of-school activities.

UNEXPLORED IMPLICIT ASSUMPTIONS

Until recently, the generalizability question usually was not formulated explicitly in the critical thinking literature. Instead, many theorists assumed implicitly that critical thinking is generalizable, and many others equivocated on the matter—at one time implicitly assuming generalizability, while at another time implicitly assuming its denial. Dewey, for instance, seems to have been a generalist about both critical thinking abilities and dispositions, accepting the conceptual possibility of generalizability as well as its epistemological and psychological soundness. Concerning abilities, he said: "The various ways in which men *do* think can be told and can be described in their general features" (1933, p. 3). Concerning dispositions, Dewey said: "There is such a thing as *readiness* to consider in a thoughtful way the subjects that do come within the range of experience—a readiness that contrasts strongly with the disposition to pass judgment on the basis of mere custom, tradition, prejudice, etc., and thus shun the task of thinking" (1933, p. 34).

Black, on the other hand, seems to equivocate on the issue. For instance, in his introductory chapter, he speaks about a distinction between good and bad reasoning, as if such a distinction could be made without regard to subject matter: "To be in a position to improve reasoning means to be in a position to distinguish good reasoning from bad" (1946, p. 7). Yet, on the same page, he says that "the critic's judgment of the value of a piece of music (or an omelet, or a piece of reasoning) is grounded in knowledge of principles and standards appropriate to the subject matter" (1946, p. 7), suggesting the epistemological view that what counts as good and bad reasoning depends upon the subject.

The Harvard Committee, formed in 1943 by the president of Harvard University, James Conant, to develop objectives of a general education in a free society, also equivocates. At one point the committee talks about effective thinking as comprising "certain broad mental skills" (Harvard Committee, 1945, p. 66). However, being more explicit about the different kinds of thinking needed in different fields, the committee claims that "the three phases of effective thinking, logical, relational, and imaginative, correspond roughly to the three divisions of learning, the natural sciences, the social studies, and the humanities, respectively" (1945, p. 67). According to this latter statement, good thinking would seem to vary from subject to subject.

Hullfish and P. G. Smith (1968, pp. 43–44) offer a description of the general phases of all reflective activity, and B. O. Smith (1953) describes general things that can be done to improve critical thinking, such as focusing on meaning and distinguishing observations from inferences. However, in contrast to many people writing on this topic prior to about 1980, B. O. Smith directly addresses condition (d), the psychological dimension of generalizability, saying that "we should expect our students to use their improved habits of thinking generally, provided we have taught these habits in a variety of subject matters and situations" (1953, p. 133). Thus, he recognizes that generalizability along the psychological dimension cannot be taken for granted, but must be promoted directly through instruction. However, he seems to assume that condition (b) is satisfied, namely, that there is some commonality to critical thinking across "a variety of subject matters."

Within the last decade or so, there have been several direct and unambiguous challenges to the generalizability view. Psychologists have offered evidence to show that knowledge of subject, and not some generalized ability to think well, is what differentiates experts from novices in a variety of fields (Carey, 1985; Glaser, 1984; Larkin, McDermott, Simon, & Simon, 1980). Some philosophers have argued that different things count as good reasons in different fields (for example, McPeck, 1981), and thus that thinking well differs from field to field. Furthermore, evidence has been presented to show that teaching general, context-independent thinking strategies does not help outside the specific domains in which they are taught (Perkins & Salomon, 1989). Thus, recent challenges are directed toward both the epistemological and psychological dimensions of generalizability.

These challenges have started a considerably energetic debate. The vigor is due to the high stakes: to challenge generalizability is to challenge what many educators take to be one of the fundamental justifications for schooling—that the habits of mind and methods of thinking fostered by schooling transcend the specific content, much of which becomes obsolete. The debate's outcome promises to have profound impact on the theory and practice of education. It could mean, at one extreme, the abandonment of critical thinking as an educational ideal. At another extreme, it could mean the unifying of the curriculum under the single umbrella of critical thinking.

DEFINING "CRITICAL THINKING"

Questions about the meaning of "critical thinking" are at the heart of the generalizability question. This fact is apparent if one considers that at least eight authors of the remaining chapters in this volume deal explicitly with the definition of critical thinking before they begin to outline their theses on critical thinking generalizability. Furthermore, of those authors in this volume who do not deal with the definitional issue, most have dealt with it thoroughly in their other writings and refer here to that other work.

In addition to what "critical thinking" means, presuppositions about how we ought to go about defining "critical thinking" affect the generalizability question. For instance, it is presumed by some theorists that critical thinking is an educational value, and that we should define it so as to best promote our educational goals. Other theorists believe that the meaning of critical thinking should be based upon the evidence from empirical research about how people think when faced with different kinds of tasks.

In this section, I shall try to explain why individuals may hold different presuppositions about how to go about defining "critical thinking" by outlining a view that groups the nouns of our language into three categories: nominal kind terms, strict natural kind terms, and nonstrict natural kind terms. My outline borrows heavily from Schwartz (1979). I shall contend that much of the difference in responses to the generalizability question arises from different presuppositions about where "critical thinking" and "critical thinker" fit into this category system. Thus, my analysis is meant to provide a partial understanding of the "deep structure" of the generalizability question, of what lies beneath its surface, and, hence, a deeper understanding of the divergence of views represented in this book.

Nominal Kind Terms

Certain common nouns, exemplified by "bachelor," "sister," "table," "triangle," and "key," are terms whose meaning is explained well by a theory that has been advocated for at least three centuries. According to this theory, all common nouns have associated with them an *intension* and an *extension*. The intension of a term, sometimes called the *concept* associated with it, contains a list of properties that determines the referents of the term. The set of referents makes up the extension. The properties listed in the intension of "bachelor," for example, might include being male, being unmarried, and being of marriageable age. Having each of the properties in the list is severally necessary and jointly sufficient for being an entity in the extension of the term. Thus, *intension determines extension;* if Frank has all the properties listed in the intension of "bachelor," then he is a bachelor. Since the extension of a term is the set of entities that have the properties listed in the intension, the extension of a term is determined empirically through a procedure of matching the properties listed to entities in the world.

The properties that constitute the intension of a term depend upon the conventional meaning of the term. Thus, the intension is *semantically* associated with the term. If a community of language users alters the properties listed in the intension of a term, then it has altered its meaning.

An attraction of this theory is that it explains how words acquire a purchase on the world: they do it via the reference relation, which is determined empirically. Common nouns refer to those entities that possess the properties listed in their intensions.

Another attraction of the theory is that it allows us to distinguish between analytic and empirical truths associated with terms. (I note that, in advancing this attraction, I am ignoring the Quinian [Quine, 1953] challenge to the analytic/synthetic distinction—a challenge I find compelling.) "Bachelors are unmarried" is true analytically, that is, by definition, because "being unmarried" is a property listed in the intension of "bachelor." "Bachelors earn greater than average-sized incomes" is, if true, true empirically, that is, according to whether or not it corresponds to what occurs in the world, because "earning greater than average-sized income" is not part of the intension of "bachelor."

Because of its simplicity, explanatory power, and promise to clarify the grounds for the truth of various statements, this theory of the meaning of common nouns has received wide acceptance. Unfortunately, the acceptance has been too wide, because it has been applied to the meaning of all nouns but does not work for all. I shall call the nouns for which the theory does work *nominal kind terms*. Schwartz (1979) proposes that terms for artifacts ("chair," "book," "hammer"), distinctions of rank ("president," "corporal," "assistant professor"), relations of people ("sister," "nephew," "sibling"), and legal and ceremonial use ("contract," "ordination," "will") are examples of nominal kind terms.

Consider, however, the proper name "Shakespeare." Paralleling the analysis of "bachelor," we might think that there is an intension and extension (in this case an extension containing one entity) associated with this term, and that the intension determines the extension. For example, we might associate with Shakespeare the property that he wrote the play *Hamlet*.

However, the parallel with common nouns breaks down when we consider the statement, "Shakespeare is the author of *Hamlet*," and ask whether the statement is analytically or empirically true. If the theory outlined for common nouns is correct, then the statement must be analytically true, since being the author of *Hamlet* is part of the concept associated with the term.

However, a theory of noun meaning that yields this result must be an incorrect theory of the meaning of proper names. We can well imagine, for instance, learning some day that Shakespeare (that very same person to whom we now refer) did not write *Hamlet* at all. We may learn that Francis Bacon wrote the play. Since this is a conceivable outcome, unlike the outcome of finding a married bachelor, being the author of *Hamlet*, if it is associated with the proper name "Shakespeare," must be contingently associated with it. Furthermore, finding out that Bacon did write *Hamlet* would not change necessarily the referent of "Shakespeare." The name might still refer to that English poet and dramatist who lived between 1564 and 1616.

Are these latter properties part of the intension of "Shakespeare?" Again, they are not, since they are, if true, empirical truths, not truths by definition. We can conceive of discovering that Shakespeare was born or died on different dates, or that he was not English but French, and had moved to England from France as a child. Upon analysis, it can be seen that proper names do not have meanings in the sense of common nouns. That is, they do not have concepts associated with them; there are no analytic statements associated with proper names that determine the entities that fall into their extensions. Proper names have associated with them, instead, a set of *identifying descriptions* that are empirically defeasible. We might say that these descriptions form a *concep-

tion, rather than concept, of the entity named. The conception is used to *help pick out* the referent, but not to determine it. In most cases, through the triangulation afforded by the use of multiple descriptions, a unique entity can be identified. This, too, is a contingent fact, and one that goes a long way towards making the world a manageable place in which to live. If, however, in a given case, enough of the identifying descriptions associated with a proper name are found to be false, then the referent of the name may be called into question. It is conceivable, for instance, that "Shakespeare" refers to Bacon.

Strict Natural Kind Terms

There is also a set of common nouns, exemplified by "tiger," "gold," "water," and "human," that cannot be explained by the theory of nominal kind terms, but behave rather like proper names. Consider "gold," and its possible intension. Plausible candidate properties are: yellow, malleable, metallic, electrically conductive, and valuable. However, contrary to the case of "bachelor" and the properties of being male and unmarried, none of these properties are semantically associated with the term. It is conceivable that a type of gold could be found or created that has none of these properties: it may not be metallic, but rather some other structural form; we may someday be able to produce forms of gold that are not malleable or not electrically conductive; it is already known that when finely divided gold may be black, ruby, or purple. Therefore, yellowness, malleability, conductivity, and so on are identifying descriptions, and not part of the concept, of gold, just as the author of *Hamlet* is an identifying description, and not part of the concept, of Shakespeare. For something to be gold, it must not necessarily, by definition, have these properties. The descriptions are used to pick out gold, but they do not define what it is. Hence, "gold is malleable" is not analytically true. *If* true, it is an empirical truth.

"Carbon" is another interesting example. Carbon is very soft *or* very hard, black *or* colorless, opaque *or* transparent, electrically conductive *or* electrically insulative, depending upon its allotropic form—graphite or diamond. Having a set of disjunctive properties such as this does not fit the traditional theory of the meaning of nominal kind terms. The case of carbon shows that, for a particular class of entities, phenomenal properties can be misleading indicators of their nature. If "carbon is very soft" were analytically true, then it would be impossible to discover that carbon also can be very hard, just as it is impossible to discover a married bachelor. It would also have been impossible to have discovered recently (as has been done) a third allotropic form of carbon that has yet another set of phenomenal properties.

Rather than take "gold" or "carbon" to be terms with associated concepts that pick out their extensions, we might take them to be singular referring terms, like "Shakespeare." But, to what do they refer? One answer is that they refer to a certain *underlying trait,* which it is the job of physics to determine. The current view is that gold is a substance composed of atoms of atomic number 79, which are characterized by having particular numbers of electrons, protons, and neutrons. If gold has this underlying trait (I say "if," since the trait is defeasible), it *must* be out of *empirical* necessity, because with any other structure it would not be gold, but some other substance. Again, if gold has this trait, the extension of "gold" consists only of those entities that have the trait. This is why instances of both graphite and diamond (and the new form of carbon) fall into the extension of "carbon": they all have the same underlying trait—atoms of atomic number 6—even though they have contradictory phenomenal properties. If these current beliefs change about the traits that underlie gold and carbon, the extensions of "gold" and "carbon" need not change, just as the extension of "Shakespeare" need not change if our beliefs about Shakespeare change. Common nouns whose extensions are determined by the presence or absence of underlying traits shall be called *strict natural kind terms.*

Nonstrict Natural Kind Terms

In addition to nouns that derive their extensions via semantically related properties and empirically related underlying traits, there are those that derive their extensions via both routes. An example is "gander." A gander is a male goose. Maleness is semantically associated with "gander," so the statement "ganders are male" is analytically true. However, webbed feet, bills, and feathers are identifying descriptions of ganders, and thus are empirically, but not semantically, related to "gander." We could imagine ganders that do not have webbed feet, or any feet at all for that matter, do not have bills, and do not have feathers. These imagined ganders may, for instance, be the offspring of geese that are exposed to nuclear fallout. However, once we identify the underlying species trait of ganders, presumably something about the structure of their DNA, then ganders have that trait out of empirical necessity. Common nouns whose extensions are determined by both semantically related properties and empirically related underlying traits shall be called nonstrict natural kind terms.

Categorizing "Critical Thinker"

Into which of these categories might "critical thinking" and "critical thinker" be placed? Churchland has argued that "thinker" is "quite possibly, bordering on probably" (1982, p. 236), a strict natural kind term. Further, he postulates that thinkers are probably the same natural kind as are living things, and that the underlying trait of this kind is defined by the physics of nonequilibrium thermodynamics: "a living thing is a dissipative system, a semiclosed local entropic minimum, whose internal negative entropy filters out further negative entropy from the energy flowing through it" (1982, p. 233). While the precise meaning of this trait description may not be grasped by most of us, the fact that someone has suggested an underlying trait for the entities that fall into the extension of "thinker" is what is important here.

Churchland's postulation helps us to see the importance of asking whether the properties that are commonly associated with critical thinkers (open-mindedness, disposition to seek reasons, ability to judge credibility, and so on) are properties semantically related to a nominal kind term, identifying descriptions empirically related to a natural kind term, or underlying traits possessed by the entities to which a natural kind term refers. Alternatively, are there some properties semantically related to "critical thinker," other empirically related identifying descriptions, and, somewhere, an underlying trait? That is, does "critical thinker" function in the language mostly like "bachelor," mostly like "gold," or mostly like "gander," and, perhaps more importantly, how *ought* it to function in our educational theorizing? These are nontrivial and theoretically important questions.

If "critical thinker" is a nominal kind term, then theorists might differ over its meaning according to their individual programmatic agendas. Under this scheme of things, the properties associated with "critical thinker" would be associated semantically with it. Changing the list of properties would amount to changing the concept related to the term, and thus the class of individuals that fall into its extension; and deciding on the list of properties would be a matter of how we wanted language to be used. This decision would be influenced primarily by language users' values. Depending upon their agendas, individuals would disagree over who should be classified as critical thinkers.

If "critical thinker" is a strict natural kind term, assigning individuals to the class would not be strictly a value issue. The extension of "critical thinker" would not be determined by a set of negotiable, semantically related, conventionally agreed properties. The extension would include only those individuals who had the trait that underlies critical thinkers. This trait would be nonarbitrary, and the task of science to discover. Differences in view would arise over scientific matters.

As the final option, it is possible that "thinker" is a strict natural kind, as Churchland has postulated, but that "critical thinker" refers to a negotiated division within that kind, much like "gander" refers to a negotiated division of geese. If "critical thinker" is a nonstrict natural kind term of this sort, then there will be properties associated with "critical thinker" that are negotiable according to value orientations, but an underlying trait that is the task of science to discover.

THE GENERALIZABILITY DEBATE

I wish to propose that much of the debate over critical thinking generalizability occurs because individuals hold different presuppositions about where "critical thinker" fits into the category system previously outlined, and because many individuals have not settled in their own minds where they stand on the issue. Let us consider the stance of four of the contributors to this volume. Some of the ideas that I discuss are not contained in their contributions to this volume, but are found in other works. However, an examination of these ideas provides a backdrop for the ones they do present herein. Furthermore, the discussion of these four contributors provides a perspective to keep in mind when reading the other contributions.

Ennis (1981) provides a long list of abilities and dispositions that critical thinkers have. Does saying that critical thinkers have these abilities and dispositions express a series of analytic truths according to Ennis? If so, and if for Ennis this is all there is to the meaning of "critical thinker," then "critical thinker" would be a nominal kind term for Ennis. On the other hand, does his list provide a set of identifying descriptions of critical thinkers that, if true, are empirical truths? If so, and if Ennis believes there are no properties semantically related to "critical thinker," then "critical thinker" would be a strict natural kind term for Ennis. Finally, does the list entail analytic truths about critical thinkers, while allowing that critical thinkers have some underlying trait that is their nature? If so, then "critical thinker" would be a nonstrict natural kind term for Ennis.

I find it difficult to answer these questions about Ennis's ideas, but I am inclined to think he believes that "critical thinker" is a nominal kind term about which we can reach agreement on conventional meaning. I do not mean to say that Ennis believes that he has provided a set of severally necessary and jointly sufficient conditions for being a critical thinker, since he has explicitly denied having done so (Ennis, 1980). However, it seems that this is the aim of his theorizing. I remember Ennis answering, to a question about how he decided when to stop adding items to his list, that he included all that came to mind. The implication is that, if he thought of more things, he would add them, and that others should feel free to add; the aim is to have a complete list. Aiming for a complete list does not suit the task of choosing identifying descriptions for a natural kind term, because all that is needed is a set sufficiently discriminating to home in on the desired referent.

What about Siegel; how would he classify critical thinkers, whom he sees as persons "appropriately moved by reasons" (1988)? Unlike Ennis, Siegel does not provide long lists of abilities and dispositions held by critical thinkers. I believe that Siegel takes critical thinkers to be at least a nonstrict natural kind. He claims that "a critical thinker *is*... a certain sort of person....Just as sugar has the disposition to dissolve in water while still in the sugar bowl, so does the critical thinker have the dispositions, habits of mind and character traits we have considered while not engaged in reason assessment" (1988, p. 41). It seems fairly clear from this statement that Siegel believes that critical thinkers have underlying traits characteristic of them, and that only critical thinkers have those traits. Whether or not Siegel also believes that there are characteristics that are semantically related to "critical thinker" is unclear to me at this time.

How about McPeck? It seems clearer than in Ennis's case that he takes "critical thinker" to be a nominal kind term. McPeck (1990) charges Norris, writing in the following passage about "reasoning" as a natural kind term, with confusing philosophical and scientific questions:

> The first question [whether "reasoning" denotes a particular process, per-formance or type of achievement, or a variety of them] would concern the denotation of "reasoning," which would involve the same sorts of explo-ration used to determine the denotation of any natural kind term. It would be necessary to carry out scientific investigations into the underlying nature of reasoning. (Norris, 1990, p. 71)

While Norris clearly states his position that "reasoning" (and by implica-tion "critical thinking," since that was the context of the discussion) is a natu-ral kind term, McPeck just as clearly states his position: "the denotation, *qua* denotation, of common terms like 'reasoning' is a *conceptual* question *par excellence,* and has nothing whatsoever to do with scientific investigation" (McPeck, 1990, p. 92). To take the denotation of "reasoning" to be a concep-tual question is to adopt the view that, once the concept is delineated, the extension of the term is determined. This is the nominalist stance. McPeck overlooked the alternative view that denotation can also be determined via underlying traits, which seems to be the route Norris assumed was appropriate for "reasoning."

On reflection, given this sampling of contributors and the discrepancy in their views over this fundamental issue of the nature of critical thinking, it should not be surprising that there is considerable debate over critical think-ing generalizability represented in this volume. According to the generalizabil-ity thesis, critical thinkers have abilities and dispositions that are generaliz-able across subjects. But how is this characteristic related to critical thinkers? If it is true that critical thinkers have generalizable abilities and dispositions, is it true analytically, because of a semantic relation between the property of generalizability and the term "critical thinker"? On the other hand, if it is true that critical thinkers have generalizable abilities and dispositions, is it true empirically, because of a contingent relation between generalizability and crit-ical thinkers? These are central questions for which there are currently no set-tled answers.

A SKETCH FOR FUTURE RESEARCH

Some theorists see "critical thinker" as a nominal kind term (McPeck, possibly); some see "critical thinker" as a strict natural kind term (Norris, possibly); some see "critical thinker" as a nonstrict natural kind term (Siegel, possibly); and some take a position that makes them difficult to categorize (Ennis, possibly). However, few theorists have taken an explicit stance on this issue, and no theorist has linked this issue to the generalizability question and then brought the issue in that form to the table for resolution. Hence, it lurks in the background of much of the current dialectic over critical thinking, including the dialectic over critical thinking generalizability contained herein.

However, it is not a matter of taste with no consequences for educational practice which position on the definition of "critical thinker" is adopted. One purported aim of critical thinking theorizing is to make school students better critical thinkers, that is, to effect change in the world. In this regard, we can expect some practices to work and others not to work, but, it seems to me, those that have the poorest chance of success are those that are based on inadequate theories of human learning. A minimal condition of adequacy for a theory of human learning is that its central terms refer. For instance, the adequacy of a theory of learning that used as a central term, "innate intelligence," would be reduced if innate intelligence does not exist. A central term of many critical thinking learning theories is "thinking disposition." The adequacy of these theories is reduced if thinking dispositions do not exist.

The strict nominalist stance, with its antiempirical approach to determining denotation, seems to be the approach to defining "critical thinker" that is least likely to meet this minimal condition of a critical thinking learning theory. Virtually all major theories of meaning assume that empirical research is necessary for determining denotation. In 1892, Frege (1892/1974) showed us that conceptualization alone would never have led to the truth that "the morning star" and "the evening star" denote the same entity. In 1905, Russell (1905/1956) showed that determining the truth value of "The King of France is bald", depends upon determining whether there is an entity that possesses the property of being the King of France. In 1966, Donnellan showed that the meaning of definite descriptions depends upon empirically checking whether the descriptions are attributing properties to entities or merely referring to entities. Thus, if we want the term "critical thinker" to denote, which is necessary if we want any theory that employs the term as a central concept to have anything to do with educating people, then its definition cannot be derived using solely conceptual analysis.

The demand for denotation by the central terms in a theory of critical thinking learning, in particular the term "critical thinker," seems to point us, then, towards natural kind terms. At the same time, since "critical thinker" is a term that is intended for the prescription of educational goals and practices, it cannot be treated as a strict natural kind term. Philosophers must have some conceptual leeway to build into the concept of critical thinker features that are valuable to education. For instance, Ennis (1980) once proposed that thinking critically implies thinking morally, while Martin (this volume) argues that too much critical thinking takes place that violates moral standards. It seems to me that this is not the sort of issue that can be settled by empirical research. It depends upon how we want the concept of critical thinker to operate in our educational prescriptions.

Thus, my current thinking is that "critical thinker" is a nonstrict natural kind term—one that is constrained by the psychology of human beings and also by educational values. My intuition is that we have the conceptual leeway to build into the concept of "critical thinker" features that we value, but that we do not have complete control, because critical thinkers are limited by human psychology. If this is so, the implication is that both philosophical and empirical research are needed to clarify the meaning of "critical thinker" and to answer the generalizability question. We may have certain conceptual leeway in attaching the property of generalizability of abilities and dispositions to the term "critical thinker." However, if we want people to be contained in the extension of the term, then the psychology of human beings must be taken into account!

I cannot justify adequately my speculation about the nature of "critical thinker" in this introduction. Instead, I shall suggest some issues that might be pursued. It seems to me that we need a thorough examination of extant conceptions of critical thinkers such as provided by Johnson in this volume, and ask whether there are properties cited that we wish to be semantically related to the term. If such properties exist (open-mindedness, for example, might be one candidate), then we shall have to ask whether these properties are realized and realizable in individuals. The clear implication if they are not is that these properties do not help determine an extension for the term, and may not contribute to a term that has practical educational value.

A further complication is that most of the properties of critical thinkers exist as a matter of degree. For example, individuals can be more or less open-minded, and, hence, more or less critical thinkers. This means that falling into the extension of the term is not a straightforward matter of having or not having the appropriate properties. Current theories of meaning do not deal effectively with this complication.

We might decide to take certain properties as semantically related to the concept. Then we might look to the world with the help of this conceptualization of critical thinkers, and search for characteristics of the individuals picked out that are empirically related to their critically thinking. Finally, some sort of amalgamation of the resulting sets of semantically and empirically related properties might be fashioned. This is probably the biggest task, since there is no theoretical framework that describes how properties that are semantically related and those that are empirically related to a term can work together to determine the extension of that term. However, from an educator's perspective, both sets of properties are likely to be important.

CONCLUSION

I invite the reader to take my analyses of the generalizability question and of the semantics of "critical thinker" and use them to help organize the discussion presented in the following chapters. The chapters are written from two broad perspectives, that of philosophy and psychology. The links between these disciplines, the generalizability question, and the semantics of "critical thinker" should by now be clear. If "critical thinker" is a nominal kind term, then philosophy, and in particular conceptual analysis, should have the primary role in clarifying its meaning and in answering the generalizability question. If, on the other hand, "critical thinker" is a strict natural kind term, then psychology should be of primary importance. If, finally, "critical thinker" is a nonstrict natural kind term, as I think it is, then cooperative effort between philosophy and psychology will be needed.

REFERENCES

Black, M. (1946). *Critical thinking*. Englewood Cliffs, NJ: Prentice-Hall.

Carey, S. (1985). Are children fundamentally different kinds of thinkers and learners than adults? In S. F. Chipman, J. W. Segal, & R. Glaser (Eds.), *Thinking and learning skills* (Vol. 2, pp. 485–517). Hillsdale, NJ: Erlbaum.

Churchland, P. M. (1982). Is thinker a natural kind? *Dialogue, 21*, 223–238.

Dewey, J. (1933). *How we think*. Boston: D. C. Heath.

Donnellan, K. S. (1966). Reference and definite descriptions. *The Philosophical Review, 75*, 281–304.

Ennis, R. H. (1980). A conception of rational thinking. In J. R. Coombs (Ed.), *Philosophy of education 1979* (pp. 3–30). Normal, IL: Philosophy of Education Society.

Ennis, R. H. (1981). Rational thinking and educational practice. In J. F. Soltis (Ed.), *Philosophy of education* (pp. 143–183). Chicago: National Society for the Study of Education.

Frege, G. (1974). On sense and reference. In F. Zabeeh, E.D. Klemke, & A. Jacobson (Eds.), *Readings in semantics* (pp. 117–140). Urbana, Il: University of Illinois Press. (Original work published 1892)

Glaser, R. (1984). Education and thinking: The role of knowledge. *American Psychologist, 39*, 93–104.

Harvard Committee. (1945). *General education in a free society*. Cambridge, MA: Harvard University Press.

Hullfish, H. G., & Smith, P. G. (1968). *Reflective thinking: The method of education.* New York: Dodd, Mead, & Company.

Larkin, J., McDermott, J., Simon, D., & Simon, H. (1980). Expert and novice performance in solving physics problems. *Science, 208,* 1335–1342.

McPeck, J. E. (1981). *Critical thinking and education.* New York: St. Martin's.

McPeck, J. E. (1990). *Teaching critical thinking.* New York: Routledge.

Norris, S. P. (1990). Thinking about critical thinking: Philosophers can't go it alone. In J. E. McPeck (Ed.), *Teaching critical thinking* (pp.67–74). New York: Routledge.

Perkins, D. N., & Salomon, G. (1989). Are cognitive skills context-bound? *Educational Researcher, 18* (1), 16–25.

Quine, W. V. O. (1953). From a logical point of view. Cambridge, MA: Harvard University Press.

Russell, B. (1956). On denoting. In R.C. Marsh (Ed.), *Logic and knowledge* (pp. 41–56). New York: Capricorn Books. (Original work published 1905)

Schwartz, S. P. (1979). Natural kind terms. *Cognition, 7,* 301–315.

Siegel, H. (1988). *Educating reason: Rationality, critical thinking, and education.* London: Routledge.

Smith, B. O. (1953). The improvement of critical thinking. *Progressive Education, 30*(5), 129–134.

SECTION I

Clarifications and Directions for Research

Robert H. Ennis, in Chapter 2, analyzes the confusing topic of subject specificity, which is the antithesis of critical thinking generalizability, and outlines some needed research. He makes several crucial distinctions, including one among the empirical, epistemological, and conceptual versions of subject specificity. It is this distinction that allows us to see the various dimensions along which critical thinking generalizability can extend. Ennis cautions that these distinctions, though conceptually clear, are continua with borderline cases. In Ennis's view, conceptual subject specificity is too vague. However, the other two versions incorporate valuable insights: both emphasize the importance of background knowledge, epistemological subject specificity maintains that what constitutes a good reason varies from field to field, and domain specificity notes the importance of deliberate teaching for transfer and the use of examples in many different areas.

Ennis also proposes a broad agenda for research on the topic. He calls for studies of whether specific aspects of critical thinking developed in one or more topics are applied to others. Concomitant with this research, he would like to see increased attention to clarifying the concept of domain as it is used in transfer research. He calls for long-term studies in realistic situations of the effectiveness of the four approaches to critical thinking instruction: general, infusion, immersion, and mixed. Finally, he urges an examination of the degree of commonality of the critical thinking found in the different disciplines.

In Chapter 3, Ralph H. Johnson argues that whether or not critical thinking is generalizable depends upon what critical thinking is. Johnson concentrates his attention on definitions offered by members of what he calls the "Group of Five" (Ennis, Lipman, McPeck, Siegel, and Paul), and raises a number of questions based on his examination:

1. Does critical thinking affect action as well as belief?
2. Do critical thinkers have a certain moral character?
3. What is the relationship between critical thinking, problem solving, rationality, rational thinking, and metacognition?
4. Is critical thinking by definition a good thing? (Since Johnson notes that all definitions of critical thinking are stipulative, we should also ask whether stipulating a definition of critical thinking is the proper approach, given that stipulation would seem most appropriate for nominal kind terms as discussed in Chapter 1.)

Johnson argues that a theory of critical thinking should answer these questions as well as make it plain what is important about criticism; should yield assessment tools, and, more generally, lead to empirically testable hypotheses; and should not assume, a priori, a connection with other cognitive operations.

In addressing the question of the generalizability of critical thinking in Chapter 4, Robert S. Lockhart examines the case of memory generalization, and in so doing makes the implicit assumption that "critical thinking" is at least a nonstrict natural kind term as defined in Chapter 1. Remembering can be taught as a generalizable skill, in the sense that it transfers from one area to another. For instance, mnemonic techniques are known to work, and the explanation of why they do is available: they exploit the properties of the rememberer's existing knowledge to structure the material that is to be remembered. Given this explanation, Lockhart argues, we should expect that remembering techniques exploiting content-specific knowledge structures would be less generalizable, and they are.

Lockhart wonders whether there is a direct analogy to critical thinking? The basic problem in making the extension is the problem of abductive access. In short, the generalizability of critical thinking might hinge more on factors that determine the thinker's access to rules than on the generality of the rules themselves. Access to certain rules may be bound to particular content, impeding access to the rules in the context of other content. Lockhart points out that the access relation between content and rules is governed by abductive remembering.

Thus, many examples of poor critical thinking may arise because of how the content and the context affect the thinker's abductive memory. Lockhart looks here to analogical reasoning research. Experimental work in this area repeatedly has shown that practice at using a concept in one problem-solving context helps little in other problems, unless the initial context lays down memory cues that will be activated by the subsequent problem. That is, whereas transfer of memory is governed by similarity of thematic content, transfer of effective thinking strategies is governed by the similarity of conceptual structure. This means that to increase the transfer of effective thinking, the effectiveness of different forms of content in cuing those structures must be increased.

Lockhart concludes that the view that reasoning is virtually completely content dependent is probably too pessimistic. It is not the reasoner's specific knowledge and experience that is critical, it is whether the content of the situation activates appropriate reasoning. Expert reasoning consists in being able to discern from the surface features of a problem which general forms of reasoning are likely to be effective in solving it. This fact should provide an opening for the training of generalizable thinking skills.

It is often suggested, as by Ennis in Chapter 2, that empirical study of the reasoning actually employed in different fields is needed before the generalizability question can be settled. This is certainly true if critical thinking is a natural kind. James Ryan attempts in Chapter 5 both to begin this research, by studying a debate over a particular scientific theory, and to propose a model for how similar research might be done either on other debates in science or in other disciplines.

Ryan proposes that a useful model for characterizing much of the thinking in various fields is a modified Kuhnian good reasons model that focuses on the reasons expressed in the arguments and counterarguments over some issue. He proposes that we use such a model to examine debates within a field in search of data relevant to the question of interfield variation and generalizability of thinking.

Ryan singles out the debate surrounding the theory of continental drift. He claims, first, that a careful reading of the historical record shows that arguments to accept or reject the theory were not made on the basis of reasons usually cited by philosophers, for example, that the theory did or did not explain more of the relevant data. Instead, he shows that the arguments were over such issues as whether the match of the coastlines of continents across present oceans could serve as credible scientific evidence, and whether or not there was a plausible mechanism to explain how continents moved. Concerning this last issue, different views were represented by those who were willing to accept the drift hypothesis on the assumption that a mechanism would be found later, and by those who would accept the drift hypothesis only if a mechanism that could produce drift were known beforehand.

Ryan suggests that such differences in view about how to treat causal hypotheses might be sought in other disciplines. He reasons

that, if the antigeneralizability view is true, then the strategies and
lines of reasoning that occurred in the debate over continental drift
should look unique to geology, or at least to science, and would not be
found elsewhere. He concludes, however, that this is not the case. The
strategies and lines of reasoning are found in debates in various fields,
disciplines, and areas of everyday concern. In Ryan's view, this finding
helps to shift the burden of proof to the antigeneralizability proponents, and demonstrates that the empirical analysis of thinking in a
field can shed light on the generalizability question.

2 The Degree to Which Critical Thinking Is Subject Specific: Clarification and Needed Research

Robert H. Ennis
University of Illinois at Urbana-Champaign

Perhaps the most controversial issue within the critical thinking movement these days is whether critical thinking should be taught separately (the "general" approach), be infused in instruction in existing subject-matter areas (the "infusion" approach), result from a student's immersion in the subject matter (the "immersion" approach), or—an oft-neglected possibility—be taught as a combination of the general approach with infusion or immersion (a "mixed model" approach, to use Sternberg's term; 1987, p. 255). I shall elaborate these approaches after sketching the general plan for this chapter, the context of which is this basic issue about which approach to use. I shall not attempt to resolve this basic issue. Rather the goal is to make a conceptual contribution to its resolution, paving the way for more research of the sort that is needed to help resolve the issue, and facilitating interpretation of this research.

In addition to the practical political, economic, and administrative aspects of the basic issue, one significant unresolved theoretical aspect is whether critical thinking is subject specific, that is, specific to subjects. Subject specificity is a confusing idea that has not received adequate attention, and is my principal concern in this chapter. I shall attempt to clarify this confusing notion, offer some distinctions, note some pitfalls, and suggest needed research.

There are three principal versions—empirical, epistemological, and conceptual—of the view that critical thinking is subject specific. Norris (1985) has introduced a distinction between the first two versions in his enlightening discussion of abilities—including critical thinking ability. Distinguishing and elaborating these versions of subject specificity is important, since the arguments for them, and the reasonableness and implications of them, differ. To this task I shall devote most of my attention in this essay. But before directly addressing these three versions of subject specificity, I shall offer some preliminary clarification.

PRELIMINARY CLARIFICATION

Critical Thinking and Thinking

I assume critical thinking to be *reasonable reflective thinking focused on deciding what to believe or do,* a concept I have elaborated elsewhere (Ennis, 1985, 1987). The ideas in this essay, however, apply to other concepts of critical thinking, including "the correct assessing of statements" (Ennis, 1962, p. 82) and "the propensity and skill to engage in an activity with reflective scepticism" (McPeck, 1981, p. 152). They also apply to other concepts of thinking, such as higher order thinking, problem solving, and metacognition.

The General Approach

By the "general approach" I mean an approach that attempts to teach critical thinking abilities and dispositions separately from the presentation of the content of the existing subject-matter offerings. Examples of the general approach usually do involve content. Local or national political issues, problems in the school cafeteria, or previously learned school subject matter, for example, could provide content about which the critical thinking is done, but the primary purpose is to teach students to think critically, using nonschool-subject contexts.

However, the concept of the general approach does not require that there be content. For example, logic instruction can be formulated in terms of relationships between variables. The following principle has no content in this sense: *"All A's are B's" implies that if something is not a B, then it is not an A.* Teaching it is like teaching *(A x B) = (B x A)* in mathematics. Under the general approach, the appropriate balance between emphasis on principles that are applied to content and emphasis on abstract principles depends at least on the nature of the content, the critical thinking dispositions and abilities being promoted, and the students. This balance must be determined empirically.

General critical thinking instruction could take place in separate courses (such as an informal logic course in college, or a critical thinking course in secondary school), in separate instructional units in the elementary school, or as a separate thread in an existing subject-matter sequence (just as writing is a thread in language arts and English). Among the ways of implementing the general approach in secondary schools, the separate critical thinking thread within an existing subject sequence is probably the most feasible politically. Examples of the pure general approach are described in several summaries, including those by Kruse and Presseisen (1987); Nickerson, Perkins, and Smith (1985); Sternberg (1984, 1985); and Sternberg and Kastoor (1986).

Infusion and Immersion

Infusion of critical thinking instruction in subject-matter instruction is deep, thoughtful, well-understood subject-matter instruction in which students are encouraged to think critically in the subject, and in which general principles of critical thinking dispositions and abilities are *made explicit*. On the other hand, *immersion* is a similar thought-provoking kind of subject-matter instruction in which students do get deeply immersed in the subject, but in which general critical thinking principles are *not made explicit*.

Proponents of the infusion approach include Glaser (1984, 1985), Resnick (1987), and Swartz (1984, 1987). Proponents of the immersion approach include McPeck (1981).

The Mixed Approach

The mixed approach consists of a combination of the general approach with either the infusion or immersion approaches. Under it there is a separate thread or course aimed at teaching general principles of critical thinking, but students are also involved in subject-specific critical thinking instruction. There are many possibilities for such combinations, but presumably the general thread would facilitate articulation among the various efforts and would help fill gaps that are left as a result of practical exigencies that develop. Proponents of the mixed approach include Ennis (1985), Sternberg (1987), Nickerson (1988), and Perkins and Salomon (1989).

Table 2.1 sets forth the major characteristics of the four basic approaches to teaching critical thinking that provide the context for the subject-specificity

Table 2.1 Characteristics of the Four Basic Approaches to Teaching Critical Thinking

Approach	Makes General Principles Explicit?	Uses Content?	Uses Only Standard Subject-Matter Content?	Uses Standard Subject-Matter and Other Content?
General				
a. Abstract (only)	Y	N	N	N
b. Abstract (also)	Y	Y	N	Perhaps both
Mixed	Y	Y	N	Y
Infusion	Y	Y	Y	N
Immersion	N	Y	Y	N

issue. These should be viewed as idealized types. In practice, combinations and deviations are not only possible but likely.

Ambiguity of the Word, "Subject"

It is often noted that critical thinking is always about some subject (McPeck, 1981; Adler, 1986). This seems obviously true if by the word "subject" one means "topic." But one must beware of slipping back and forth between two significant uses of the word "subject" when considering the implications of the statement that critical thinking is always about some subject. Sometimes the word "subject" is used to refer to some subject taught in school. Sometimes it refers to the topic under consideration. There are of course many topics which are not school subjects and are not included in the study of the school subjects to which a person considering these topics is exposed. For example, the topic stabbing, which was considered in a murder trial for which I was on the jury, was not part of any school subject that any of us had studied in school or college. Yet, that was a topic about which we were supposed to think critically.

It is tempting, but a mistake, to infer from the fact that critical thinking is always about some subject (that is, topic) to the conclusion that critical thinking teaching can take place only in school subjects.

Assuming these distinctions and definitions, I shall elaborate the three basic versions of subject specificity.

DOMAIN SPECIFICITY: A POPULAR EMPIRICAL VIEW

The use of the word "domain" instead of "subject" tends to avoid the equivocation I have just described, though it suffers from a vagueness problem that I shall discuss presently. Since the word "domain" is commonly used by cognitive scientists in discussing subject specificity, I shall use it as part of the name of an empirically based subject specificity, characterizable by three principles:

1. *Background Knowledge.* Background knowledge is essential for thinking in a given domain.
2. *Transfer.* (a) Simple transfer of critical thinking dispositions and abilities from one domain to another domain is unlikely; however, (b) transfer becomes likely if, but only if, (1) there is sufficient practice in a variety of domains and (2) there is instruction that focuses on transfer.
3. *General Instruction.* It is unlikely that any general critical thinking instruction will be effective.

Most cognitive scientists hold at least the first two principles. All three principles together constitute what I shall call "strong domain specificity." If true, it would support the infusion-only approach to teaching critical thinking. Proponents appear to include Glaser when he urged: "abilities to think and reason will be attained when these cognitive activities are taught not as subsequent add-ons to what we have learned, but rather are explicitly developed in the process of acquiring the knowledge and skills that we consider to be the objectives of education and training" (1984, p. 93). As I read this statement by Glaser, the general approach provides "add-ons," so he appears to endorse the third principle.

The first two principles constitute what I shall call "moderate domain specificity." Proponents include Resnick (1987), who appears to be agnostic about the third principle, but supports an infusion approach, because it assures that at least "something worth while will have been learned" (p. 36). Other proponents appear to feel that the third principle is wrong, including Nickerson (1988), who supports a mixed approach to teaching critical thinking. I shall consider the three principles of domain specificity, exhibit traps and pitfalls, and urge caution and further research.

Domain-Specificity Principle 1

Background knowledge is essential for thinking in a given domain.

That knowledge about a topic is ordinarily a necessary condition for thinking critically in the topic seems obvious and is shown by a number of studies, including several cited by Glaser (1984) in support of his infusion-only position. However, we must beware of inferring carelessly from this that subject-matter knowledge is a sufficient condition for good thinking. There are at least three problems with making such an inference:

1. An experienced person can become so well informed about and embedded in an area that the person stops thinking, becoming inflexible and, for example, unable to conceive of and consider alternatives.
2. Subject-matter knowledge often consists of a mass of rotely memorized subject matter that is not understood deeply enough to enable a student to think critically in the subject. Students are often taught and tested in a way that makes this a likely result. At least the first phases of E. D. Hirsch, Jr.'s (1987) cultural literacy, the ones on which he places the most emphasis, appear to be this sort of learning.
3. If the domain-specificity transfer principle is correct, immersion in a subject-matter area, which, let us assume, includes ability to think in the area, probably will not lead to critical thinking in everyday life

(except perhaps for gifted students), since immersion is not accompanied by explicit attention to general principles of critical thinking. I am assuming that critical thinking in everyday life is an important goal of the schools, and that explicit attention to general principles of critical thinking is the way to focus on transfer. (Focusing is required by the transfer principle.)

This is not to suggest that anyone would state explicitly that a necessary condition is thereby a sufficient condition, and thus risk the difficulties I outlined. Rather, unconsciously doing so is a trap for the unwary.

Domain-Specificity Principle 2

   1. Simple transfer of critical thinking dispositions and abilities from one domain to another domain is unlikely.
   2. Transfer becomes likely if, but only if, (a) there is sufficient practice in a variety of domains, and (b) there is instruction that focuses on transfer.

Vagueness of the concept, domain. The application of Parts 1 and 2(a) of the transfer principle requires us to be able to distinguish domains. Otherwise we cannot tell whether we are going from one domain to another instead of staying within the same domain, and we cannot tell whether we are working with a variety of domains, or just one. But the concept, *domain,* is vague, because of the ease with which we can draw different boundaries for domains.

To see the vagueness, try to decide which of the following four topics is in the same subject-matter domain as one or more of the others: (a) the degree to which a straight rod will bend (a standard Piagetian topic), (b) the degree to which a spring will stretch, (c) the impact of a sphere that rolls down a ramp, and (d) a person's judgment about the credibility of a source of information. Assume that the critical thinking ability involved is judging causal hypotheses in an experimental situation and justifying one's judgment.

All four examples conceivably could be classified under the same domain, science. But science itself is divided into many areas. The first three might come under natural science (or progressively more narrowly, physical science, or physics, or mechanics—which should we choose?) and the last under social science (or psychology, or social psychology, or speech communication—which?). So, are the four topics in different domains, or the same domain (that is, science)? Why?

Furthermore, within mechanics the first two might come under statics and the third under dynamics. So the first two could be in different domains from the third, but also in the same domain as the third: mechanics (or physics, etc.). Which is it?

Linn, Pulus, and Gans (1981, p. 443) found that there was a content effect for these first three topics in the area of hypothesis judging and justifying—with the rods and springs (both within statics) being about as distant from each other in tested hypothesis-judging and hypothesis-justifying achievement as the springs (statics) and ramps (dynamics) topics were from each other. So here is a case in which the difference in domains, if statics and dynamics are the assumed domains, did not appear to make a difference. (It was just as large within them as between). But if rods and springs are assumed to be in separate domains, then the difference in domains appeared to make a difference. There does appear to be a content effect, but we have no prior ground for classifying rods and springs into separate domains. We have no basis in the domain-specificity position for predicting the result, because of the vagueness of the concept, *domain.*

Furthermore, although there is some difference among these three in the Linn, Pulus, and Gans study (1981), we do not know whether there is a practical difference among them. As with most variables involving human beings, there appears to be a continuum.

A possible definition. The only reasonable attempted definition of "domain" by a domain specificist that I have found was offered by Carey (1985), for which she credits Dudley Shapere, a philosopher of science: "[Shapere] characterized a domain as encompassing a certain set of real-world phenomena, a set of concepts used to represent those phenomena, and the laws and other explanatory mechanisms that constitute an understanding of the domain" (p. 487). This broad definition, if accepted, would probably help us to apply the transfer principle in making predictions about whether learning in the last area will then be applied in the others. This is because the concepts, laws, and explanatory mechanisms used by scientists in studying the things that affect people's judgment about the credibility of sources are not the ones (such as inertia and impact) used in studying rods, springs, and inclined planes. However, the definition does not tell us whether the first three topics are in different domains from one another. We could put them together under the domain, physics—or mechanics—by starting with a broad set of phenomena and consequently a broad set of concepts and laws. Or we could even separate rods and springs (as suggested by Linn et al., 1981) by noting that the study of springs (if we try to amalgamate it with rods) invokes the concept of a spring being a spiral rod—a concept not needed in studying rods. It depends on the set of phenomena, concepts, laws, and explanatory mechanisms we choose to associate with a given example.

Another problem with this definition is that it is not at all clear that this is the concept of domain that most cognitive psychologists employ when making statements of domain specificity. So it is not clear that the existing research can be applied in terms of this definition.

Research possibilities. In order to avoid the severe vagueness of the term "domain" in the critical thinking transfer principle, we probably need to reconceive the way the principle works. One possibility is to turn the transfer principle around by using empirically determined nontransfer as one criterion for separate domains (instead of separate domains as the independently determined criterion for nontransfer). The resulting theory would employ the concept *domain* as a summarizing concept, rather than an independent variable in the research.

Then we would need much detailed exploratory research (of which Linn et al., 1981 is a precursor) that investigates the extent to which each of many aspects of critical thinking, when taught to various kinds of students in the context of single pieces or various combinations of pieces of subject matter, is likely to be successfully applied to some other particular piece of subject matter. After a good bit of this sort of exploratory research, some theorizing might well be possible, but the resulting theories would probably be more elaborate than the simple domain-specificity transfer principle.

Until we have much more information, Parts 1and 2(a) of the transfer principle are too slogan-like. The concept, *domain,* is too vague to generate predictions about whether critical thinking abilities and dispositions taught and applied in one situation will not be applied in another situation without special transfer instruction.

Domain-Specificity Principle 3

It is unlikely that any general critical thinking instruction will be effective.

For present purposes a detailed description of the research on the effectiveness of general critical thinking instruction is unnecessary. Instead, the important thing to note about the summaries that have been done is that the results are mixed. On the basis of his review of the literature, Glaser (1984) is pessimistic about the possibilities of teaching "the abilities to think and reason...as subsequent add-ons to what we have learned" (p. 93), as are Resnick (1987)—though less so—and many others. On the other hand, Holland, Holyoak, Nisbett, and Thagard (1986); Langley, Simon, Bradshaw, and Zytkow (1987); Nickerson (1984, 1988); Nickerson, Perkins, and Smith (1985); Nisbett, Fong, Lehman, and Cheng (1987); Perkins (1985); Perkins and Salomon (1989); and Sternberg and Kastoor (1986) are somewhat optimistic and have concluded that some general programs are helpful.

However, most of these more optimistic reviewers express reservations about this overall conclusion because of the difficulties in evaluating the results of the programs that have been studied. Absence of information about what occurred, conflict of interest of those who did the studies, uncertain validity of evaluation devices, vagaries of experimental design, lack of objective information, and differences in conceptual systems and jargon are some of the things that they say make evaluation difficult. But still the reviewers make guarded claims that some general thinking programs (including at least some in critical thinking) were helpful.

Needed Research and Development

Better evaluation approaches and instruments need to be developed, since our results can be no better than our evaluation devices. Ennis (1984), Arter and Salmon (1987), Ennis and Norris (1990), and Norris and Ennis (1989) have descriptions of available critical thinking tests accompanied by discussion of some problems, indicating the need for research on approaches and the development of more, better, and varied instruments. Ennis (1985), a study group chaired by Alexander (Study Group, 1987), The Review Committee of the National Academy of Education (1987), and Resnick (1987) have called for such development. Unfortunately, the Review Committee (1987) has also suggested that we limit our efforts to the development of tests that are specific to school subject-matter areas (p. 54), a mistake if the transfer of critical thinking instruction to real life is a goal of the schools. These tests would presumably not test for such transfer.

Large scale, long-term use of several variations of each of the four major approaches (general, infusion-only, immersion-only, and mixed) by schools both individually and sometimes district-wide should be compared. Careful records should be kept of the perceived difficulties and successes, and of what actually occurs in the schools. The research should be sponsored and carried out by disinterested parties able to make a long-term commitment.

After such research is done we will have a much better idea of the effectiveness of each of the approaches, including the effectiveness of the controversial general approach, the possibilities of transfer to everyday life from the infusion and immersion approaches, the advantages and disadvantages of the mixed approach, and of the practical problems involved in implementing each. The practical problems are important to know about—it might turn out that even though an approach such as the infusion-only approach is the most effective when actually implemented, the coordination, subject-matter coverage, and articulation problems that go with it are overwhelming.

EPISTEMOLOGICAL SUBJECT SPECIFICITY

The epistemological version of subject specificity holds that different sorts of things count as good reasons in different fields, so critical thinking varies from field to field. The conclusion that only the immersion approach to critical thinking instruction would be appropriate is drawn from epistemological subject specificity by McPeck (1981), who is the version's most influential proponent in education. Swartz (1984) also expresses the view, as does Resnick (1987): "Each discipline has characteristic ways of reasoning" (p. 36). But they do not draw the strong immersion-only conclusion from it that McPeck does.

Here are three principles of epistemological subject specificity, which I have abstracted from McPeck (1981, pp. 22–38):

1. *Background Knowledge.* Background knowledge is essential for critical thinking in a given field.
2. *Interfield Variation.* Since in different fields different things "constitute good reasons for various beliefs" (p.22), critical thinking must vary from field to field.
3. *Full Understanding.* A full understanding of a field requires the ability to think critically in the field.

Attractiveness of the Principles

The first principle (background knowledge) seems quite acceptable. Though based on an examination of what matters in rationally settling field-specific issues, it is like the first principle of domain specificity, which is based upon observation of the difficulties experienced by ignorant people in thinking critically. Being well informed is necessary for critical thinking, no matter which way you look at it.

The following three contrasts show the plausibility of the second principle (interfield variation): (a) Mathematics has different criteria for good reasons from most other fields, because mathematics accepts only deductive proof, whereas most fields do not even seek it for the establishment of a final conclusion; (b) In the social sciences, statistical significance is an important consideration, whereas in many branches of physics it is largely ignored; (c) In the arts, some subjectivity is usually acceptable, whereas in the sciences, it is usually shunned.

The third principle (full understanding) is also acceptable if we take the words "full understanding" to mean much more than memorization of facts and principles and some ability to apply them, and to include the ability to think critically in the field. The principle then becomes true by definition, but it does express a reasonable interpretation of "full understanding," and represents much more than students usually acquire in our schools.

Problems for the Immersion-Only Approach

If one wants to infer from these principles that the only approach to critical thinking instruction is the immersion approach, there are problems.

Vagueness of the concept, field. For one thing, the concept *field* is almost as vague as the concept *domain*. For example, is the bending rods investigation in the same field as the investigation of the impact of spheres rolling down a ramp? They are both in physics and in mechanics, but one is in statics and the other in dynamics. Are they in the same or different fields? Toulmin (1964), a philosopher who has inspired McPeck's (1981) epistemological subject specificity, has defined field in terms of the logical type of argument used: "Two arguments will be said to belong to the same field when the data and conclusions in each of the two arguments are, respectively, of the same logical type" (p. 14). Although it seems clear that arguments in mathematics (which are generally deductive) are of a different logical type from arguments in the social and natural sciences (where the form often seems to be best-explanation inference), the concept of logical type seems too loose for us to use as the basis for deciding whether the four items considered before come under the same or different logical types. So the claim that critical thinking varies from field to field is not very discriminating.

Interfield commonalities. A second problem is that there are many interfield commonalities in critical thinking, such as agreement that conflict of interest counts against the credibility of a source, and agreement on the importance of the distinction between necessary and sufficient conditions. Fields differ, but, as Govier (1983, p. 172), Resnick (1987, p. 45), and Weddle (1984, p. 24) have noted, there is also a common core of basic principles that apply in most fields (though not every principle applies in every field). Even Toulmin's book on logic devotes about half its space to general interfield principles (Toulmin, Reike, & Janik, 1979). The three epistemological principles do not exclude such interfield commonalities. Thus the limitation to the immersion approach (or even to the infusion approach) does not follow from the given principles of epistemological subject specificity, which do not imply nor state that there are no general overarching principles that bridge fields.

This is not to say that there is complete agreement about and clarity of these general overarching principles. There are discrepancies in vocabulary (including different meanings for such words as "connotation," "theory," and "assumption"), which cause coordination problems. But more seriously there are some disagreements about the principles themselves, such as the role of the distinction between induction and deduction in argument reconstruction, the fact-opinion distinction, and the meaning of "if." Weddle (1985), who has provided a helpful untangling of the fact-opinion distinction, exemplifies the sort of work that needs to be done in this area.

Transfer. A third problem is that of transfer. Will the learning in the individual fields transfer to daily life? If the transfer principle of domain specificity is correct, then immersion will not result in transfer to daily life (the content of which is not much taught in schools), because teaching for transfer does not occur in the immersion approach.

Thus the insights of the epistemological view do not imply that we should limit ourselves to the immersion approach. These insights incorporate the vagueness problem of domain specificity and do not rule out interfield commonalities. Furthermore, the transfer principle of domain specificity is inconsistent with the immersion approach, a reason to be leery of the immersion approach.

Research. The extent of interfield commonalities is a topic requiring extensive research. Arguments offered by specialists in a number of different disciplines need to be examined and compared to see how much they have in common. This has never been done thoroughly, so far as I know. In an informal interview study of Fellows at the Center for Advanced Study in the Behavioral Sciences in 1984, I found that the behavioral and other social scientists interviewed expressed the view that there are more differences in logical type of data, arguments, and conclusions within individual social science disciplines than between them. But this study dealt only with the social sciences (including history) and was impressionistic. Careful comparative analysis of articles and arguments in these and many other disciplines is needed.

CONCEPTUAL SUBJECT SPECIFICITY

According to a third version of subject specificity, conceptual subject specificity, it does not even make sense to speak of critical thinking or critical thinking instruction outside of a subject-matter area; and the idea, *general critical thinking ability,* is meaningless. Hence general instruction in critical thinking is inconceivable.

As offered by the view's most influential proponent, McPeck (1981), the argument for the conceptual view starts with the true premise, "Thinking is always thinking *about* something" (p. 3). Adler (1986) has made a similar statement, though it is not clear that he would take the argument as far as McPeck. McPeck then draws the conclusion that there is nothing general to teach and so we cannot teach thinking in general. He puts the argument as follows:

> It is a matter of conceptual truth that thinking is always *thinking about X,* and that X can never be 'everything in general' but must always be something in particular. Thus the claim 'I teach students to think' is at worst

false and at best misleading…In isolation from a particular subject, the phrase 'critical thinking' neither refers to nor denotes any particular skill. It follows from this that it makes no sense to talk about critical thinking as a distinct subject and that it therefore cannot profitably be taught as such. To the extent that critical thinking is not about a specific subject *X*, it is both conceptually and practically empty. The statement 'I teach critical thinking,' *simpliciter,* is vacuous because there is no generalized skill properly called critical thinking. (pp. 4–5)

This argument assumes that the fact that there can be no examples of critical thinking about nothing (or about everything in general) implies that there can be no general critical thinking skills. But this assumption is not defended anywhere. As Paul (1985, p. 36) has suggested, this is like assuming that since, when we write and speak, we are writing or speaking about something, there can be no teaching of general writing or speaking skills. Siegel (1985) and Groarke and Tindale (1986) have made a similar point. McPeck (1985, p. 49) replied that writing and speaking are different from critical thinking. So Paul, he urges, has not shown that what holds for writing and speaking also holds for critical thinking.

But the argument needs more than this. Since it makes the inference— from the proposition that critical thinking is about something, to the conclusion that general critical thinking instruction is impossible—it needs to make explicit and defend the connection between the two propositions. Why should the fact that critical thinking is always about something imply that we cannot have general critical thinking dispositions and abilities (and instruction of them) that can be applied to particular cases?

In his writing, McPeck provides us with an example of what he says is inconceivable. In his treatment of the work of de Bono, McPeck explicitly employs the general principle taught in logic courses that affirming the consequent is a fallacy. He uses the phrase "affirming the consequent" and employs standard general symbols for explaining the meaning of it: "$P \supset Q, Q \therefore P$" (1981, p. 101). To the extent that he learned the principle well and is able to apply it in a number of circumstances, McPeck has acquired a general critical thinking ability—the ability to identify the fallacy of affirming the consequent. Not only is someone's having the ability not inconceivable; we have evidence that someone has acquired this general ability. We could not have such evidence if it were inconceivable that he could have the ability.

Finally, the conceptual subject-specificity concept, *subject,* like the concepts, *domain* and *field,* is too vague. Suppose that within a physics course students study about bending rods, stretching springs, and rolling spheres down inclined planes. Are these in different subjects or the same subject? If they are in different subjects, then no critical thinking ability that can be developed in one of these subjects can conceivably be applied in the other (because that would be evidence for the existence of a general critical thinking ability). If they are in the same subject, then critical thinking instruction in one of these contexts would presumably help in the other. Which is it? Conceptual subject specificity needs a definition of "subject," but does not provide one.

In summary, conceptual subject specificity appears to have no basis for its basic assumption, is in conflict with the facts, and is too vague.

SUMMARY AND COMMENT

The purposes of this chapter are to clarify the confusing topic of subject specificity and to sketch out some needed research. Crucial distinctions include those among the general, infusion, immersion, and mixed approaches to teaching critical thinking; among the empirical, epistemological, and conceptual versions of subject specificity; between the topic and school-subject senses of "subject"; between content as a necessary condition and as a sufficient condition for critical thinking; between deep and shallow knowledge of a subject; between fields, having no critical thinking principles in common and having some principles in common; between thinking about a particular subject and having a general ability to do that sort of thing in several subjects; between thinking critically without content (not possible) and teaching content-free principles of critical thinking (possible); and between limiting teaching of critical thinking to subject-matter areas (as is recommended by the infusion and immersion approaches) and limiting testing to subject-specific critical thinking tests (a mistake if we want to test for transfer to daily life). These distinctions, though conceptually clear, often reduce to continuums, and have borderline cases in practice.

The three versions of subject specificity differ in their strengths and weaknesses. Conceptual subject specificity has no basis and is too vague, but the other two versions incorporate valuable insights: They share an emphasis on the importance of background knowledge. Epistemological subject specificity notes that there are significant interfield differences in what constitutes a good reason (though its concept, *field,* is vague). Domain specificity sees the importance of deliberate teaching for transfer combined with frequent application of principles in many different areas, and warns us that a critical thinking aspect demonstrated in one situation will not necessarily be applied in another. But its concept *domain,* like its related concepts, *subject* and *field,* is too vague for the prediction-generating job it has been assigned.

Needed research includes the following:

(a) extensive specific studies of the degree of successful application to a topic of a critical-thinking aspect developed in one or more topics, with attention to the variables that affect this degree of success—one result will be to give more meaning to the concept domain as used in the transfer principle;

(b) the study and development of new approaches and instruments for evaluating critical thinking;

(c) the broad long-term study in realistic situations of the effectiveness of the four approaches to critical thinking instruction—with attention to the economic, political, and practical articulation problems impinging on their use; and

(d) the examination of the degree of commonality of the critical thinking aspects found in the standard, existing disciplines and school subjects.

In order to focus on concepts and interpretations, this discussion of subject specificity leaned on thoughtful research reviews done by others. It assumed a broad conception of critical thinking, but applies to more restricted conceptions as well as to broader conceptions of thinking, like higher order thinking, problem solving, and metacognition.

Subject specificity is a crucial, frequently confusing aspect of attempts to improve critical thinking and other thinking instruction and assessment. Let us hope that the distinctions and clarification presented in this essay will better enable us to proceed with the needed research and dissemination.

ACKNOWLEDGMENT

I deeply appreciate the suggestions and encouragement of Sean Ennis, whose frequent, careful reading and insights have been specially helpful, and Nicholas Burbules, Michelle Commeyras, Delores Gallo, Jana Holt, Bruce Lane, Robert McKim, Stephen Norris, Edys Quellmalz, William J. Russell, Robert Swartz, Marc Weinstein, Mary Anne Wolff, the anonymous reviewers of Educational Researcher, and members of my 1989 class in philosophy of educational research; and the support of the Spencer Foundation, the Center for Advanced Study in the Behavioral Sciences, and the Critical and Creative Thinking Program of the University of Massachusetts in Boston.

REFERENCES

Adler, M. (1986). Why critical thinking programs won't work. *Education Week, 6*(2), 28.

Arter, J. A., & Salmon, J. R. (1987). *Assessing higher order thinking skills.* Portland, OR: Northwest Regional Educational Laboratory.

Carey, S. (1985). Are children fundamentally different kinds of thinkers and learners than adults? In S. F. Chipman, J. W. Segal, & R. Glaser (Eds.), *Thinking and learning skills* (Vol. 2, pp. 485–517). Hillsdale, NJ: Erlbaum.

Ennis, R. H. (1962). A concept of critical thinking. *Harvard Educational Review, 32*(1), 81–111.

Ennis, R. H. (1984). Problems in testing informal logic/critical thinking/reasoning ability. *Informal Logic, 6*(1), 3–9.

Ennis, R. H. (1985). Critical thinking and the curriculum. *National Forum, 65*(1), 28–31.

Ennis, R. H. (1987). A taxonomy of critical thinking dispositions and abilities. In J. B. Baron & R. J. Sternberg (Eds.), *Teaching for thinking* (pp. 9-26). New York: W. H. Freeman.

Ennis, R. H., & Norris, S. P. (1990). Critical thinking assessment: Status, issues, needs. In S. Legg & J. Algina (Eds.), *Cognitive assessment of language and math outcomes* (pp. 1–42). Norwood, NJ: Ablex.

Glaser, R. (1984). Education and thinking: The role of knowledge. *American Psychologist, 39,* 93–104.

Glaser, R. (1985). Learning and instruction: A letter for a time capsule. In S. F. Chipman, J. W. Segal, & R. Glaser (Eds.), *Thinking and learning skills* (pp. 609–618). Hillsdale, NJ: Erlbaum.

Govier, T. (1983). Review of *Critical thinking and education. Dialogue, 22,* 170–175.

Groarke, L., & Tindale, C. (1986). Critical thinking: How to teach good reasoning. *Teaching Philosophy, 9,* 301–318.

Hirsch, E. D., Jr. (1987). *Cultural literacy: What every American needs to know.* Boston: Houghton-Mifflin.

Holland, J. H., Holyoak, K. J., Nisbett, R. E., & Thagard, P. R. (1986). *Induction: Processes of inference, learning, and discovery.* Cambridge, MA: The MIT Press.

Kruse, J., & Presseisen, B. Z. (1987). *A catalogue of programs for teaching thinking.* Philadelphia: Research for Better Schools.

Langley, P., Simon, H. A., Bradshaw, G. L., & Zytkow, J. M. (1987). *Scientific discovery: Computational explorations of the creative process.* Cambridge, MA: The MIT Press.

Linn, M. C., Pulus, S., & Gans, A. (1981). Correlates of formal reasoning: Content and problem effects. *Journal of Research in Science Teaching, 18,* 435–447.

McPeck, J. (1981). *Critical thinking and education.* New York: St. Martin's Press.

McPeck, J. (1985). Paul's critique of *Critical thinking and education. Informal Logic, 7*(1), 26–36.

Nickerson, R. S. (1984). Kinds of thinking taught in current programs. *Educational Leadership, 42*(1), 26–36.

Nickerson, R. S. (1988). On improving thinking through instruction. In E. Z. Rothkopf (Ed.), *Review of research in education* (pp. 3–57). Washington, DC: American Educational Research Association.

Nickerson, R. S., Perkins, D. N., & Smith, E. (1985). *The teaching of thinking.* Hillsdale, NJ: Erlbaum.

Nisbett, R. E., Fong, G. T., Lehman, D. R., & Cheng, P. W. (1987). Teaching reasoning. *Science, 238,* 625–631.

Norris, S. P. (1985). The choice of standard conditions in defining critical thinking competence. *Educational Theory, 35,* 97–107.

Norris, S. P., & Ennis, R. H. (1989). *Evaluating critical thinking.* Pacific Grove, CA: Midwest Publications.

Paul, R. W. (1985). McPeck's mistakes. *Informal Logic, 7*(1), 35–43.

Perkins, D. N. (1985). General cognitive skills: Why not? In S. F. Chipman, J. W. Segal, & R. Glaser (Eds.), *Thinking and learning skills* (pp. 339–363). Hillsdale, NJ: Erlbaum.

Perkins, D. N., & Salomon, G. (1989). Are cognitive skills context bound? *Educational Researcher, 18*(1), 16–25.

Resnick, L. B. (1987). *Education and learning to think*. Washington, DC: National Academy Press.

The Review Committee of the National Academy of Education, R. Glaser, Chairman (1987). Commentary by the National Academy of Education. In P. A. Graham (Coordinator), *The nation's report card: Improving the assessment of student achievement* (Part 2, pp. 45–61). Washington, DC: National Academy of Education.

Siegel, H. (1985). Educating reason: critical thinking, informal logic, and the philosophy of education. *APA Newsletter on Teaching Philosophy, Spring-Summer*, 11.

Sternberg, R. J. (1984). How can we teach intelligence? *Educational Leadership, 42*(1), 38–48.

Sternberg, R. J. (1985). Critical thinking: Its nature, measurement, and improvement. In F. R. Link (Ed.), *Essays on the intellect* (pp. 45–65). Alexandria, VA: Association for Supervision and Curriculum Development.

Sternberg, R. J. (1987). Questions and answers about the nature and teaching of thinking skills. In J. B. Baron & R. J. Sternberg (Eds.), *Teaching thinking skills: Theory and practice* (pp. 251–259). New York: W. H. Freeman.

Sternberg, R. J., & Kastoor, B. (1986). Synthesis of research on the effectiveness of intellectual skills programs: Snake oil remedies or miracle cures? *Educational Leadership, 44*(2), 60–67.

Study Group, Lamar Alexander, Chairman (1987). In P. A. Graham (Coordinator), *The nation's report card: Improving the assessment of student achievement* (pp. 3–41). Washington, DC: National Academy of Education.

Swartz, R. J. (1984). Critical thinking, the curriculum, and the problem of transfer. In D. N. Perkins, J. Lochhead, & J. Bishop (Eds.), *Thinking: Progress in research and teaching* (pp. 261–284). Hillsdale, NJ: Erlbaum.

Swartz, R. J. (1987). Teaching for thinking: A developmental model for the infusion of thinking skills into mainstream instruction. In J. B. Baron & R. J. Sternberg (Eds.), *Teaching thinking skills: Theory and practice* (pp. 106–126). New York: W. H. Freeman.

Toulmin, S. E. (1964). *The uses of argument*. Cambridge: Cambridge University Press.

Toulmin, S. E., Reike, R., & Janik, A. (1979). *An introduction to reasoning*. New York: Macmillan.

Weddle, P. (1984). *Critical thinking and education* by John McPeck. *Informal Logic, 6*(2), 23–25.

Weddle, P. (1985). Fact from opinion. *Informal Logic, 7*(1), 9–26.

3 The Problem of Defining Critical Thinking

Ralph H. Johnson
University of Windsor

In this chapter, I begin with some remarks about the theme—the generalizability of critical thinking. It turns out, not unexpectedly, that the concept of critical thinking is the more problematic one of the pair. In the rest of the chapter I shall be concerned primarily with the task of defining critical thinking. I shall review the various definitions and point out some problems, using this critique as the basis for introducing my own account of critical thinking.

PRELIMINARY REMARKS ABOUT THE TOPIC

The theme of this volume is the generalizability of critical thinking. The question motivating it might be phrased in the first instance this way: Is critical thinking generalizable?

This is a complicated question to which the only satisfactory answer at the moment is "It depends." For. as I shall argue, there is at present no substantive consensus about the nature of critical thinking. Although there are patches of agreement among primary investigators, significant areas of disagreement remain—and this very question of generalizability, as we shall see, can be used to highlight some of those areas.

About Generalizability

Let me begin by observing that there is some danger of confusing the question of whether critical thinking is *general* with the question of whether critical thinking is *generalizable*. These are different claims. It is one thing to hold that the critical spirit—or anything else—is general, which would mean

38

that it applies generally, across the board. It is something else again to hold that it is generalizable, that is, if learned in one area, it can and will successfully be applied in (many) other areas. Thus, people seem to have a general capacity to learn language but that capacity is not generalizable. Having learned one language does not allow us to generalize to others: having learned English does not empower us thereby to speak French. Likewise we need to distinguish between *generalizability* and *transferability*. A skill may be transferable from one area to another without being generalizable, that is, transferable from one to all (or most). Finally, we need to note that *generality* is not the same as *universality*. It might be the case that there are general critical thinking principles which apply in many domains, yet that would not make them universal. McPeck (1981) seems opposed to both generality and universality of critical thinking in the following passage: "Just as the rules of a particular game do not necessarily apply to other games, so certain principles of reason apply within some spheres of human experience but not in others. A principle of reason in business or law, for example, might be fallacious in science or ethics" (p. 72).

In effect, McPeck is questioning the idea of general or universal principles of reason. Since McPeck is a well-known defender of the view that critical thinking is subject-specific, we need to ask also about the meaning of "specificity": Is critical thinking general or subject-specific?

Ennis (1989, this volume) makes a much-needed and valuable contribution to the discussion of this issue by distinguishing three kinds of specificity: domain specificity, conceptual subject specificity, and epistemological subject specificity. Later we shall see the impact this distinction has for the question under discussion.

These preliminary observations indicate that the question of generalizability posed at the start is really many questions. What I hope to show now is that further disambiguation of the question, and progress in resolving it, will need intervention from the theory of reasoning. This need will become clearer as I return now to consider the other term in the theme.

About Critical Thinking

It is my impression that, after lying untouched for many years, the issue of defining critical thinking has suddenly become such a hot topic that almost no one can keep clear of it. In recent years, Ennis (1985, 1987, 1989), Lipman (1988), Siegel (1988), and Paul (1989) have all proposed new and apparently distinct accounts of critical thinking. This flurry of activity is a good sign, for it indicates heightened awareness of the problem. In my view, the time has come to purchase some much-needed dialectical clarity regarding the problem of defining critical thinking, and this essay is meant as a contribution to that end.

Let us start by acknowledging the obvious: there are myriad definitions of critical thinking. Each textbook author has a definition, and one is implicit in every test of critical thinking. Educational directives such as EO #338 (which requires a course in critical thinking for matriculation from the California State University College System) also contain at least the elements of a definition. However, I shall not consider those. For strategic reasons, I have limited my review to those accounts of critical thinking that are theoretically funded. What I mean is that these definitions are not free-standing definitions, but rather are imbedded in a fuller, if not entirely developed, theory of critical thinking. There are five such definitions:

   a. Ennis's definition of critical thinking as "reasonable reflective thinking that is focused on deciding what to believe or do" (1987, p. 10);
   b. McPeck's definition of critical thinking as "the skill and propensity to engage in an activity with reflective skepticism" (1981, p. 81);
   c. Richard Paul's notion of strong sense critical thinking as essentially dialogical and distinguished from weak sense (1982); more recently, Paul has offered a definition of critical thinking in terms of a list of perfections and traits of thought: "critical thinking is disciplined, self-directed thinking which exemplifies the perfection of thinking appropriate to a particular mode or domain of thinking" (1989, p. 214);
   d. Lipman's account of critical thinking as "skillful, responsible thinking that facilitates good judgment because it (1) relies upon criteria, (2) is self-correcting and (3) is sensitive to context" (1988, p. 39);
   e. Siegel's definition of the critical thinker as the individual who is appropriately moved by reasons (1988).

For ease of reference I shall refer to this collectivity as The Group of Five. Not only is each a distinguished voice within the critical thinking movement, but each may be said to possess a theory of critical thinking of which the definition is an outgrowth. By a "theory of critical thinking," I mean not only a definition but also the concepts, principles, arguments, and assumptions which support that definition, as well as the interests which fuel the theory and the broader agenda. Thus, differences in definitions may be viewed as indications of deeper differences at the level of the theory of critical thinking.

The next step then is to reflect on the definitions offered by The Group of Five, because perhaps the differences between them are more apparent and more verbal than real. Only if it is determined that there are significant, precisely defined differences would we be in a position to say how these differences might be resolved.

DEFINING CRITICAL THINKING:
A REVIEW OF THE GROUP OF FIVE

In 1988, Siegel reviewed the accounts given by Ennis, McPeck, and Paul. I agree with most of his comments, and rather than repeat them, I simply refer the reader to that work. Thus, my own review will spend proportionately more time focusing on Siegel and Lipman.

Ennis's Definition

Ennis has done extensive work itemizing the skills and the dispositions involved in critical thinking. Perhaps that list can be improved, but there is no denying its importance, not to mention his prodigious efforts to develop better tests of critical thinking. Further, though it is not part of his definition and the supporting theory, the distinction Ennis (1989, this volume) has drawn between three types of subject specificity is an important contribution to clarification of the issues.

However, there are problems. First, Ennis's definition virtually equates critical thinking with rational thinking, and indeed makes a very tight connection between critical thinking, creative thinking, and problem solving. He writes: "Note that this definition does not exclude creative thinking" (1987, p. 10) and that critical thinking is related to problem solving (1987, p. 23). Thus does his definition bring to the fore what I shall call *the network problem*. Let me explain.

"Critical thinking" belongs to a network of terms including: problem solving, decision making, metacognition, rationality, rational thinking, reasoning, knowledge, and intelligence. Sorting out the relationships among the members of this network is, in my view, one of the principal tasks that must be dispatched before we can expect an adequate theory of critical thinking.

Second, in extending critical thinking to the sphere of action in addition to belief, Ennis takes his stand on what I call *the scope problem:* What is the scope of critical thinking? Does it extend to the realm of action no less than belief? Reflective thinking about what one is to do sounds very like a description of problem solving, decision making, or of moral thinking. Does critical thinking contain moral thinking and morality as a proper subset? This question will come to the fore once again when we consider Paul's views.

Third, we need to ask where Ennis's list of proficiencies and tendencies come from. Does his list cover all the needed proficiencies and skills? How does one get from his definition of critical thinking to this list? Unless we are prepared to maintain the view that a critical thinker must have proficiency in all cognitive operations, which seems much too stringent, then we need to know how we index some and not others. These are but a few of the problems raised by Ennis's definition of critical thinking.

Paul's Definition

The great strength of Paul's (1989) account is that it forces us to think about the extent to which critical thinking depends on the capacity of the individual to become aware of egocentric and ethnocentric thinking, the tendency to self-deception, and hence the moral character required for critical thinking. Paul's theory has a strongly Platonic character: critical thinking is dialogical and heavily dependent on moral character. In a different way, the scope problem arises here as well: What is the relationship between critical thinking and character? In order to think critically, must one have a certain moral character or set of traits? If so, which ones? If so, where are the borderlines between critical thinking and morality, and between critical thinking and moral theory?

In building into his definition the idea of being self-directed, Paul is liable to encounter the following sort of objection: Your account places too much emphasis on the capacities of the *individual* thinker, and does not give sufficient attention to the intersubjective character of critical thought. This tendency is not found in Paul alone. Many theorists call for self-criticism as part of the profile of the critical thinker, without making it sufficiently clear just what this means and to what degree it is possible for an individual thinker to satisfy this demand. This criticism will reemerge when we consider Lipman's account.

McPeck's Definition

McPeck's contribution is, first of all, to remind us that we must not, in our enthusiasm for critical thinking, overlook the importance of the disciplinary knowledge and information which can only be gotten through immersion in the disciplines. Further, McPeck's definition might be seen as proceeding from the perspective of someone interested in the shape of the overall curriculum rather than (as with Paul) the teaching of particular courses. Put another way, though there are admittedly differences between Paul and McPeck, it is not clear that their views are irreconcilable. McPeck writes from the perspective of the philosophy of education and has his own agenda for curricular reform—the broader view; Paul writes as a philosopher concerned with how to teach critical thinking to students in a classroom. Clearly, they disagree about some basic issues: for example, whether there should be a freestanding critical thinking course. However, presumably we could get Paul to agree with McPeck's summons to teachers within the various disciplines to do a better job of instilling in students a sense of the epistemology of those disciplines. Presumably, McPeck would agree with Paul's view about the importance of devising strategies to ward off sophistry.

What are the problems with McPeck's definition? First, like Ennis, McPeck includes actions as well as beliefs in the scope of critical thinking. Let me raise the following line of objection. Suppose that Robert Parker is very knowledgeable about wine and brings that knowledge and the appropriate standards to bear when tasting a particular wine. I agree that this activity makes him a connoisseur, but why call him a critical thinker? A thinker (critical or no) is, in my view, someone essentially engaged in thinking. A wine-taster, no doubt, must use wits and judgment in addition to taste buds, but is not for all that a thinker, hence not a critical thinker. The term "connoisseur" says it all. Extending the scope of the term "critical thinking" to include such activity seems gratuitous and confusing.

A second problem with McPeck's definition concerns reflective skepticism. Why not reflective enthusiasm? It seems to me that this definition is unnecessarily negative and contributes to the connotation currently surrounding the term "critical" (a person who is always picking away at the faults of others, never praising, etc.). This connotation, I submit, can only interfere with the advancement of critical thinking as an educational and pedagogical ideal.

Third, for McPeck, the connection between critical thinking and problem solving appears to be very tight: "Similarly, logic texts often 'play at critical thinking' by avoiding the main work, which is solving problems in the context of discovery" (McPeck, 1981, pp. 16–17). For McPeck, rational thinking is the broader category:

> While critical thinking is perfectly compatible with rationality and with reasoning generally, we should not regard the terms as equivalent....All of this does not make critical thinking distinct from, much less incompatible with, rationality; rather, rationality includes critical thinking as a particular aspect (or subset) of itself. (1981, p. 12)

This passage suggests where McPeck stands on the network problem. His stand contrasts significantly with Siegel's theory according to which critical thinking is coextensive with rationality. Let us look at Siegel's view next.

Siegel's Definition

Siegel's definition emerges out of a lengthy and detailed critical commentary on the definitions given by Ennis, McPeck, and Paul, which are too lengthy to review in detail here. The core of the matter is reached where Siegel comments on McPeck: "This is the defining characteristic of critical thinking: the focus on reasons and the power of reasons to warrant or justify beliefs, claims and actions" (Siegel, 1988, p. 23). Thus, Siegel, too, includes actions within the scope of critical thinking. He continues: "A critical thinker is one who is appropriately moved by reasons: she has a propensity and disposition to believe and act in accordance with reasons; she has the ability properly to assess the force of reasons in the many contexts in which reasons play a role" (1988, p. 23).

No doubt, Siegel's succinct definition captures much of the essential thrust of critical thinking (though not the full force of the term "critical"). But I would argue that there are two weaknesses. First, there is no mention of articulation—the critical thinker's ability properly to assess is characteristically revealed in an articulation. A critic is someone who criticizes, that is, produces critical commentary. We know that someone is thinking critically just to the degree that the person's articulation of judgment displays appreciation of and respect for reasons. And I would argue that we, the community—at least as much as Siegel—are the ones who decide whether or not the person is a critical thinker. No individual can certify himself or herself as a critical thinker. In this sense, critical thinking is more like authority than it is like knowledge. I return to this theme later.

Second, on Siegel's account there is no distinction between critical thinking and rationality. Critical thinking is coextensive with rationality; critical thinking is "the educational cognate of rationality." It is not clear to me just what this means, nor what it entails. Siegel denies, and I believe him, that it entails that critical thinking is restricted to educational contexts. Furthermore, for Siegel there is no essential difference between critical thinking and problem solving. Commenting on McPeck, Siegel notes:

> On McPeck's construal of critical thinking as a subset of rational thinking, a person who properly utilized available evidence in order to solve some problem or come to some belief, e.g. one who planned a trip route by carefully examining maps, noting terrain, balancing time demands against the goals of the trip—in short one who planned the trip rationally—would not count as having engaged in critical thinking while planning it. This not only seems absurd on its face, it is incompatible with McPeck's epistemological approach. (1988, pp. 29–30)

My intuitions are closer to McPeck's than to Siegel's. I see nothing absurd in the claim that the individual in question did not engage in critical thinking. That individual did engage in problem solving, and that is a kind of rational thinking. However, I would argue that there is more to rational thinking than critical thinking: for example, devising a hypothesis to explain a phenomenon or fleshing out the plot line of a novel would both be instances of rational thinking but would not necessarily be critical thinking. I admit that I am operating here on my intuitive sense of what comprises critical thinking. My intuitions conflict with Siegel's. What must happen is that we must see where each of these positions leads and assess their pluses and minuses—in other words, subject them to critical scrutiny. In sum, respective theories of critical thinking must themselves be evaluated. That leads to the inquiry which I call "the theory of reasoning," but I cannot here take this line of inquiry further.

Siegel's theory forges a tight connection between critical thinking, rationality, and problem solving. The tightness of this connection is a function of his conception of rationality, which some would criticize as based on a sexist account of rationality and knowledge (Martin, this volume). In his defense, it must be noted that Siegel does have a theory of rationality, and so of all the accounts given by The Group of Five, Siegel's is the most theoretically developed. But his position on the network problem and the scope problem remain problematic.

Lipman's Definition

Because of his emphasis on criteria, Lipman's account comes perhaps the closest to bringing out the sense in which critical thinking is "critical." However, even if we grant that Lipman has specified three properties of critical thinking, it is not clear that they define it. A thinker might be engaged in self-corrective thinking, be sensitive to context, and be guided by criteria, and still fail to be critical, as Paul (1989) also points out. Suppose a scientist is engaged in the process of testing a hypothesis. We may suppose that the scientist is sensitive to context and guided by criteria. But does this mean that the scientist is a critical thinker? Suppose the scientist is absolutely intolerant of any objections or criticisms? In my view, that would disqualify him or her as a critical thinker, at least in this instance. But the scientist seems to satisfy Lipman's criteria.

I now want to argue that the idea of critical thinking as self-corrective is problematic in two ways. First, it runs the risk of placing too much emphasis on the individual and not enough on the community within which that individual practices reflection. Another way to put the same point is this: the concept of thinking that lies beneath this ideal seems Cartesian, and subject to all the difficulties inherent in that conception. What is needed, in my view, is a more pragmatic conception of thinking that accords proper emphasis to the social and communitarian nature of thinking. I return to this theme again shortly.

A second problem arises because it is evident that the model for critical thinking in Lipman's view is scientific and logical thinking:

What has come to be known as scientific method is a distillation of exploratory and self-corrective procedures employed by ordinary persons in everyday life. These same self-corrective procedures are responsible for the emergence of logic. In turn, science and logic provide us with models we can attempt to emulate and internalize in our thinking. (1988, p. 5)

What does it mean to say that science is self-corrective inquiry? It does not mean that science is free from error, but rather that features are built into the scientific method that will allow for the detection and the correction of error. Lipman says very little about these self-corrective procedures, but we may read between the lines and infer that they consist of the submission of one's results to the scientific community for validation and corroboration; that we must be ready today to live by what truth we can find and be ready tomorrow to declare it an error (as William James put the matter so well).

Let me now connect these two problems I have been discussing. I would argue that the property of being self-corrective is possessed essentially by the scientific community in its totality, rather than by individual scientists (Johnson, 1972, Chapter 2). Although clearly people can to some degree monitor their own processes and occasionally discover error, in the final analysis it seems they are led to a recognition of their errors by the challenges and criticisms coming from other minds. Something like this must have been what Robert Burns had in mind when he wrote: "Oh, would some power the gift would give us to see ourselves as others see us." But it is just such a gift that we lack, and just such lack makes us finally dependent on others for insights into our own cognitive shortfall. In short, if we take seriously the pragmatic insights concerning the intersubjective character of human thinking, the ideal of being self-corrective must be played out very carefully.

Lipman claims that only a small portion of our everyday thought is subjected to scrupulous self-criticism. (Lipman seems to be vacillating between critical thinking as self-corrective and critical thinking as self-critical.) The requirement that the critical thinker must be self-critical not only runs into some of the same problems as the notion of being self-corrective, but also does not shed much light on the nature of critical thinking, as it comes close to being circular.

To be sure, much depends on what is built into the notion of self-criticism. But suppose self-criticism refers to that process whereby one looks critically at one's own products: beliefs, theories, and so forth. This is not, however, enough, since it might be that an individual is quite good at this and yet would be highly resistant to criticism from others. If the capacity to take criticism from others is an essential feature of the critical thinker, then being self-critical may not be enough. It is equally important to be able to take criticism and learn from it. Indeed, the truly critical thinker will solicit criticism of his or her ideas from others, realizing that good criticism is invaluable to the growth and development of any intellectual product.

A further problem occurs with Lipman's second feature—critical thinking as thinking with criteria. Lipman provides a detailed account of criteria, which we cannot outline in detail, in which he distinguishes between criteria and standards, and then adds levels of criteria: meta-criteria and mega-criteria. He writes:

> It is generally agreed that critical thinking entails the development and orchestration of cognitive skills and dispositions. Now a skill is a performance that is measured against a standard or criterion. Thus reasoners are adjudged skillful or not by assessing their performances by means of principles of logical validity. To measure, we need standards of measurement; to classify we need classificatory criteria; to be judicious we need standards of judgment. (1988, p. 5)

The point Lipman makes is crucial: if critical thinking does involve—as I would argue it does—evaluation of an intellectual product, then reference to criteria will necessarily be involved. I do not share Lipman's view that the skills of a critical thinker necessarily must be gauged by reference to the principles of logical validity, as this criterion is much too restrictive.

There is one final problem which surfaces most clearly in a chart that Lipman provides (1988); the inference is that for Lipman, critical thinking is, necessarily, good thinking. For Siegel and Paul, it seems evident that critical thinking is by definition a good thing. However, for McPeck, critical thinking is a task and an achievement concept (1981, p. 9), and so it appears that there could be such a thing as bad critical thinking. Is critical thinking by definition something good? Can there be bad critical thinking? Is critical thinking like virtue (necessarily good), or rather like luck (possibly good, possibly bad)?

Summary

Our review of the definitions of The Group of Five has revealed some important differences, particularly as this involves not merely the definition of critical thinking but broader issues within the theory of critical thinking; namely, the network problem. In the course of this review, several questions have arisen. Let me restate them here:

1. What is the scope of critical thinking? Does it extend to the realm of action no less than belief? (The Scope Problem)
2. What is the relationship between critical thinking and character? In

order to think critically must one have a certain moral character or set of traits? If so, which ones? If so, where is the borderline between critical thinking and morality, and between critical thinking and moral theory?

3. What is the best account of the relationship between critical thinking, problem solving, rationality, rational thinking, and metacognition? (The Network Problem)

4. Is critical thinking by definition something good? Or, can there be bad critical thinking? Is critical thinking like virtue (necessarily good) or rather like luck (possibly good, possibly bad)?

An adequate theory of critical thinking will have to contain answers to these, and other, questions.

DEFINING CRITICAL THINKING: A SECOND LOOK

Assume that we have the elements necessary to generate a satisfactory definition of critical thinking. These remarks are intended as a further contribution to that development by reflecting further on the definitions and implicit theories presented by The Group of Five in light of the previous section. In the first section, I deal with omissions, similarities, and differences. In the second section, I return to the theme: the generalizability of critical thinking.

Omissions, Similarities and Differences

Omissions. In my critique of the accounts given by The Group of Five, I have signaled points at which I have difficulties. I want to collect those individual points together now under two main criticisms. First, none of these definitions adequately captures the force of the term "critical"; none makes it sufficiently clear why critical thinking is critical and not just plain thinking, or some other form of thinking like rational thinking or higher-order thinking. (Indeed, as we have seen, both Ennis and Siegel seem prepared to equate critical and rational thinking.) Second, none of them give adequate emphasis to what I take to be a defining characteristic of a critical person— the ability to take criticism.

As to the first point, the term "critical" has historically a number of connotations. Suggested synonyms are indicative of the first and most popular understanding of the word—faultfinding, captious, caviling, carping, and censorious. The Oxford English Dictionary traces the changing nuances from the first use, notably by Shakespeare's Othello, "I am nothing if not critical," meaning "given to judging in an especially adverse or unfavorable way"; to Sir Thomas Browne's use in the seventeenth century, meaning "involving or exercising careful judgment or observation on the basis of which right decisions might be made"; to the use by Thomas Jefferson as "a turning point of decisive importance in relation to an issue." I assume that The Group of Five would identify Browne's use as the appropriate one.

My own account of critical thinking works under four constraints. First, I want to capture most, though not all, of what is encompassed in the current use of the term. Second, for reasons I will make clear, I favor an extension of the term in line with what I take to be present practice in evaluating arguments, because that too must be reflected in the definition. Third, I want my account to honor the etymology of "critical." Fourth, I want my account to allow for differentiation between the critical thinker and the creative thinker, on the one hand; and the critical thinker and the uncritical (or dogmatic) thinker, on the other.

Begin with etymology: the word *krinein,* from which we get our words "critic" and "critical," means to estimate the value of something. A critic is a person who judges, appreciates, and estimates the value of something. Similarly, I propose that a critical thinker is a critic of thought in much the way that a film critic is a critic of film.

To develop this point, consider the role of a good critic. He or she must have certain skills (know what to look for in a film), must have the appropriate background (knowledge of the history of the genre and the appropriate standards and criteria to invoke), and must have traits like fair-mindedness, honesty, and so forth. He or she applies certain standards or criteria (herein Lipman), and insights to the particular product—a film—in order to estimate its worth, taking into account both its strength and its weakness, and coming thereby to an overall appreciation of the film.

In my view, the focus of the critical thinker's scrutiny is *thought,* and I take the word "thought" here in its widest sense of being an intellectual/rational product of some sort, including such items as beliefs, theories, hypotheses, new stories, and arguments, whether they are someone else's or one's own. The task of the critical thinker is to apply the appropriate norms and standards to that product and judge its value—and to articulate that judgment. (Here I part company with those who wish to take actions also to be the focus of critical thought.)

If this is true, then critical thinking may be characterized as *thought evaluating thought.* More specifically, critical thinking is the articulated judgment of an intellectual product arrived at on the basis of plus-minus considerations of the product in terms of appropriate standards (or criteria). With this gloss on "critical" in mind, we can look back to the definitions from The Group of Five and see that none of them gives adequate emphasis to this feature. (Parenthetically, in his criticisms of Paul's account, Siegel models *the very practice of critical thinking* in the expanded sense; that is, not only has he been appropriately moved by reasons—Siegel's own definition—but in addition, he has applied appropriate standards to intellectual products—the proposed definitions by Ennis, McPeck, and Paul—weighed strengths and weaknesses, and articulated that judgment based on an overall plus-minus assessment.)

Take the heart of Siegel's definition: the critical thinker as someone who is appropriately moved by reasons. One can be appropriately moved by reasons in myriad ways. A would-be mugger sticks a gun in your back and asks for your wallet. You would be appropriately moved by reasons if—thinking that your life is worth more than your wallet—you give the mugger your wallet. But that movement of thought does not make you a critical thinker. In this situation, there simply is no time for plus-minus reckoning in terms of principles and criteria. The individual in question has certainly engaged in rational thinking, however; and that indicates to me the difference between rational thinking and critical thinking.

Siegel might counter that the need for consideration of the merits in plus-minus reasoning (or in strengths and weaknesses) is implicit in his AMR conception. Perhaps it is, but this feature of critical thinking is too central and too important to be left implicit. Why? To answer this question, I shall refer to current practice. In his treatment of argument analysis, Scriven (1976) includes the need for discrimination, for assessing both the strengths and the weaknesses in an argument and arriving at a judgment that reflects that. In this movement, critical thinkers display their differences from uncritical thinkers who are dogmatists able to see only the strengths in the products they like, only the weaknesses in those they do not approve.

But I am arguing that we must broaden our account of what is essential to the critical thinker so as to include not only the moment of discrimination, but the moment of articulation as well. A critical thinker is not only one appropriately moved by reasons, but one also able to evidence that movement, including the movement of discrimination, in articulated judgment. One defect in extant accounts is that they mislocate the geography of the term "critical thinking," mapping it much too closely to "knowledge" when it should rather be located closer to "authority."

A second omission—following closely on the one just identified—is that extant accounts do not give sufficient prominence to what is either an important property or defining characteristic of the critical thinker: the capacity to take criticism. The author of the popular *The Road Less Travelled,* M. Scott Peck (1978, p. 53), writes: "The tendency to avoid challenge is so omnipresent in human beings that it can properly be considered a characteristic of human nature." The critical thinker must be wary of this tendency and have to some degree mastered it. Whether we take this tendency to be a property or defining feature, it should be mentioned prominently.

Granted, both Paul and Siegel refer in their accounts to the necessity of considering alternative views and being able to criticize one's own fundamental beliefs. In Paul's case, the basis of this realization is found in commentary on the limitations of egocentric thinking and the need for reciprocity. Likewise, implicit in Siegel's reference to the critical spirit is that the critical thinker will certainly be prepared to take criticisms of his or her own views, and will sometimes be persuaded by such criticisms.

Still, these capacities are not identical with the capacity to take real (not imagined) criticism from other directions; that is, to take hostile, not just friendly, fire. It is one thing to imagine a criticism of your theory and to respond to it; something else again to have to confront real and forceful (and sometimes pungent) criticism. That is an acid test for a critical thinker. (And I might add, any critical thinking theorists who cannot and will not concede any criticism of their own theories of critical thinking are at loggerheads with the very ideal they seek to elucidate. Indeed, any critical thinking theorist must be prepared to face the falsifiability challenge: What would count against your theory of critical thinking?)

Similarities and differences. Substantial agreement exists on three points. All of The Group of Five agree that critical thinking requires many cognitive skills. Second, all agree that critical thinking requires information and knowledge. Third, all include a dispositional or affective dimension, though they describe and weigh it differently. Thus, we can say that critical thinking is a form of reasoning that requires a combination of skills, attitudes, and information/knowledge.

The most apparent differences among our theorists converge around the issue of whether the skills involved in critical thinking are general/generalizable. All seem to grant that the attitudinal factor is general/generalizable. None deny the importance of information/knowledge, though they accord it different amounts of emphasis. Let us return to the theme.

Critical Thinking and Generalizability

The question as originally formulated seemed simple: Is critical thinking generalizable? What we have learned transforms this one question into many. For we have distinguished between generality and generalizability, and within the branch of generality, we have seen that there are three different types of specificity. Moreover, we have learned that critical thinking involves three separate but related components: cognitive skills, dispositions, and information/knowledge. Hence, the original question branches still further:

Q.: Is critical thinking general or specific?
    Q. 1 Are critical thinking skills general or specific?
        Q. 1.1 Are they domain-specific?
        Q. 1.2 Are they conceptually subject-specific?
        Q. 1.3 Are they epistemologically subject-specific?

Q. 2 Are critical thinking dispositions general or specific?
    Q. 2.1 Are they domain-specific?
    Q. 2.2 Are they conceptually subject-specific?
    Q. 2.3 Are they epistemologically subject-specific?
Q. 3 Is critical thinking knowledge and belief general or specific?
    Q. 3.1 Is it domain-specific?
    Q. 3.2 Is it conceptually subject-specific?
    Q. 3.3 Is it epistemologically subject-specific?

CONCLUSION

Throughout this chapter, I have been concerned to point out the problems that we face in attempting to reach consensus on a definition of critical thinking.

1. As we have seen, there are essential areas of disagreement among principal definers. Therefore,
    1.1 All current definitions are stipulative; there cannot be an essential, real, or lexical definition in the midst of such cognitive dissonance; and
    1.2 Each current definition is imbedded in a more or less well-developed theory of critical thinking, which means that evaluating the definitions will require us to evaluate as well the theory in which each is contained.
2. These areas of disagreement are amendable to rational intervention.

For rational intervention to occur, I have argued elsewhere that we need to develop a higher-order theory of reasoning within which to situate and adjudicate the various theories of critical thinking. But, pending that development, we need at the very least some criteria for evaluating various definitions of critical thinking.

3. The following are criteria for evaluating a stipulative definition of critical thinking:
    3.1 The definition should satisfy conventional criteria for stipulative definition;
        3.1.1 It should be broadly reflective of current practice;
        3.1.2 It should not be idiosyncratic.

Any good definition of critical thinking must be able to display its connection with educational objectives and with the history of the term "critical thinking." But a completely idiosyncratic and ahistorical account of critical thinking, no matter how enlightened in other respects, would not be acceptable.

3.2 The definition should be imbedded in a theory of critical thinking. No definition can really hope to stand entirely on its own; and criticisms of definitions are often best seen as criticisms of the broader theory.

3.3 The definition should make plain why critical thinking is "critical" thinking.

3.4 The definition should yield assessment tools. One of the major reasons we define critical thinking is to be able to test for it, or to assess our students' capacities.

3.5 The definition should not assume an a priori identity between critical thinking and problem solving, or any other cognitive operation.

Finally, I propose a moratorium: Given that the field is already dialectically crowded, any further attempts must deal with the issue of burden of proof. No new conception of critical thinking should be tabled without its proponent having shown important defects in the extant definitions.

REFERENCES

Ennis, R. H. (1985). Critical thinking and the curriculum. *National Forum, 65,* 28–31.

Ennis, R. H. (1987). A taxonomy of critical thinking dispositions and abilities. In J. B. Baron & R. J. Sternberg (Eds.), *Teaching thinking skills: Theory and practice* (pp. 9–26). New York: Freeman.

Ennis, R. H. (1989). Critical thinking and subject specificity: Clarification and needed research. *Educational Researcher, 18*(3), 4–10.

Johnson, R. (1972). *The concept of existence in the concluding unscientific postscript.* The Hague: Martinus-Nijhoff.

Lipman, M. (1988). Critical thinking: What can it be? *Analytic Teaching, 8,* 5–12.

McPeck, J. (1981). *Critical thinking and education.* New York: St. Martin's.

Paul, R. W. (1982). Teaching critical thinking in the strong sense: A focus on self-deception, world views, and a dialectical mode of analysis. *Informal Logic Newsletter, 4*(2), 2–7.

Paul, R. W. (1989). Critical thinking in North America: A new theory of knowledge, learning and literacy. *Argumentation, 3,* 197–235.

Peck, M.S. (1978). *The road less travelled.* New York: Simon and Schuster.

Scriven, M. (1976). *Reasoning.* New York: McGraw-Hill.

Siegel, H. (1988). *Educating reason: Rationality, critical thinking and education.* New York: Routledge.

4 The Role of Conceptual Access in the Transfer of Thinking Skills

Robert S. Lockhart
University of Toronto

As with most important matters in philosophy, education, or psychology, the question of whether critical thinking can be taught as a generalizable skill is one that affords no simple answer. In unraveling the complex network of issues involved, it is instructive to consider this same question applied to a simpler case, that of memory, because remembering is an aspect of cognition that raises many of the same questions but, unlike critical thinking, remembering provides some clear answers.

REMEMBERING AS A TRANSFERABLE SKILL

In what sense is remembering a transferable skill and in what sense is it content bound? If we ask whether practice at remembering improves memory generally, the only possible answer is that it "all depends," a sure sign that the question is badly phrased. It was once thought that the memorizing involved in learning Latin would improve memory ability in general in much the same way that exercising a muscle increases its strength. This muscle metaphor is quite misleading: learning Latin is likely to improve memory for little else besides Latin. There are many other examples suggesting that skilled remembering is highly content bound, one of the best documented of these being the highly skilled memory for digit strings. Chase and Ericsson (1981, 1982) trained one subject (S. F.) to a point where he could repeat up to 80 digits immediately after presentation. It took some 250 days of practice to achieve this impressive level. The technique was not complicated. Over the course of his practice session, S. F. learned to exploit his extensive knowledge of track times, grouping the digits into sets of three or four digits each, and then coding them as running times for various races. For example, 3492 might be coded 3:49.2, close to the world record time for running the mile. Needless to say this prodigious feat of memory is highly content specific; it works only for digit strings. When S. F.'s memory for letter strings was tested, it was found to be no better than it had been before.

Should these examples be taken to mean that memory cannot be taught as a generalizable skill? Obviously not. It has been known since earlier times (see Yates, 1966) that remembering can indeed by taught as a generalizable skill. Consider mnemonic techniques such as the method of loci that were once taught in highly respectable courses in rhetoric, and which are still to be found in books on how to improve your memory. It is interesting that these techniques are now less frequently taught despite the ample experimental evidence that they do work. They work because they embody and exploit certain general principles of memory processes, the most basic of which was stated succinctly by William James: "The art of remembering is the art of thinking...our conscious effort should not be so much to *impress* or *retain* (knowledge) as to *connect* it with something already there" (James, 1983, p. 87).

James's statement might be thought of as a principle for generating particular mnemonic techniques—a meta-mnemonic strategy—in that virtually all mnemonic techniques work by using the properties of the rememberer's existing knowledge to structure and pattern the material that is to be remembered. In the method of loci, for example, the items to be remembered are associated with locations in some familiar space and the structure of this known space then becomes the basis of a subsequent retrieval plan; one simply "visits" each location and retrieves its associated item. It is a mnemonic technique well-suited to situations in which order is important, such as the points of a speech.

So the answer to the question of whether practicing memory improves memory in general is both yes and no. Although techniques such as the method of loci have wide application, other forms of skilled remembering are quite content bound, because the knowledge that structures the novel material requiring memorization is content specific and highly specialized. A laboriously acquired digit span of eighty would leave you with a letter span no better than before. On the other hand, knowing the general principle contained in the above quotation from William James and applying it in the form of general mnemonic strategies can improve memory over a wide range of content. The important differences among these various mnemonic techniques is the specificity of the knowledge being used to structure the material to be remembered. But in all applications, the skill of effective remembering hinges on the cognitive system being trained in such a way that the data of experience are able rapidly to trigger knowledge structures that in turn have the capacity to organize incoming information in ways that facilitate remembering.

The general lesson to be learned from the memory example is this: the fact that a high level of cognitive performance in a given content area fails to generalize does not warrant the conclusion that the process cannot be taught as a generalizable skill. Conversely, if a cognitive process can, in fact, be taught as a generalizable skill, it does not follow that any one particular form of practice will produce that generalization.

Are there more specific lessons to be drawn? Can we make a direct analogy between remembering and critical thinking? We might argue that, as with mnemonic strategies, the teachable skills underlying critical thinking vary in their generality. Certain basic rules such as those of propositional logic have wide generality; whereas other skills necessary for critical thinking are more content bound and are designed for more specialized purposes, analogous to mnemonic techniques used in memorizing digit strings. For example, evaluating evidence supporting the claim that Napoleon lost 22,000 men crossing the Berizina River in his retreat from Moscow in 1812, clearly calls on different skills from those needed to evaluate the claim that oatbran lowers blood cholesterol levels. But, so the argument continues, despite these obvious differences, the critically thinking historian and scientist both share a great deal. They both possess a common disposition of reflective scepticism (McPeck, 1981) and, obviously, they both exploit the same basic rules of syllogistic or propositional reasoning. Moreover, given the general conclusion in the preceding paragraph, the fact that no amount of practice at evaluating historical claims such as those about Napoleon's army will lead to an improvement in the ability to evaluate nutritional claims such as those for the health benefits of oatbran is irrelevant to the basic issue at hand. And so it might be concluded that in teaching critical thinking, one should first teach those basic aspects of critical thinking with wide generality and, once they have been mastered and a disposition of reflective scepticism has been acquired, then add additional content-specific skills as needed.

This analysis is seductively straightforward but seriously incomplete. It ignores at least one important problem, and it is this problem that I will explore in the remainder of this paper. I will label it the problem of abductive access or abductive memory. In outline, my argument will be that generalizability depends not only on the generality of the rules for rational thought, but hinges much more critically on factors that control access to those rules. That is, whereas certain schema for critical thinking may have wide application, they may in fact be content bound in their application by virtue of the fact that access to these schema is content bound. It is this access relation between content and schema that I will label abductive remembering.

ABDUCTIVE REMEMBERING

I have taken the term "abductive" from C. S. Peirce in order to capture the idea that this particular form of memory is a transition from data to theory, from the "givens" or thematic content of a problematic situation to those abstract cognitive structures (such as concepts, inference schema, scripts, and so forth) needed to structure the data in such a way as to resolve the problem. My intent is simply to distinguish abductive remembering from the more usual content- or thematically based remembering, although, of course, in any particular problem-solving situation a specific act of remembering might be both.

Perhaps the simplest example of abductive remembering occurs when simple riddles are solved. For example, most people find puzzling the statement "John threw the rock out into the lake. It landed on the surface and rested there for several weeks before sinking to the bottom five meters below" until they receive a hint such as "ice" or "winter" or think of it themselves. The initial failure to make sense of statements such as these is a failure of abductive remembering—the puzzling sentence fails to access the concept that is essential to its comprehension. On the other hand, being reminded of other stories of throwing rocks into lakes would be an example of content- or thematically based remembering. Many problems (serious ones as well as the trivial examples given here) constitute riddles precisely because the data, for reasons to be discussed below, function as effective content-based cues, but fail to cue abductively (that is, to cue the retrieval of relevant concepts or schema) if there is a change of content. Similarly, many apparent errors in problems involving critical thinking can be traced to the way in which content and context, rather than the problem's formal underlying structure, control and bias abductive memory.

The class of phenomena known as mental set or mental blocks (Adams, 1976) constitutes a good example of the manipulation of abductive memory. A very dramatic example is that of Levine (1971). Subjects were shown a sequence of cards, each containing two side-by-side circles, one large and one small, with the large circle sometimes to the left of the small one, sometimes to the right. They were required to learn a simple discrimination rule (for example, large) applied to these pairs of circles. Under normal conditions, subjects learned such a rule in an average of about three trials. If, however, this same problem is preceded by a set of other problems for which the rules to be learned consist of position sequences, and size is irrelevant (for example, left, right, left, right...), then an average of 62 trials was required; indeed 28 of 60 subjects had not solved the simple discrimination problem after 115 trials.

This breakdown in thinking skill is a consequence of the contextual biasing of abductive memory: a previously strong data-to-concept association is undermined or "overwritten" by the repeated association of that same class of data to an inappropriate concept or hypothesis space. Conversely, a strong abductive association between data and an inadequate concept can block retrieval of a weaker association required to solve the problem. Scientific discovery is full of such examples but the best known is probably Kepler's replacement of the circle with the ellipse. Kepler's insight was also Peirce's favorite example of abduction. In experimental psychology, the best example of a problem made difficult by a strong a priori abductive association is probably Wason's notorious "2 4 6" problem (Wason & Johnson-Laird, 1968). In this problem, subjects are instructed that their task is to discover a number-series rule by generating data and asking whether or not such data conform to the rule. They are given an initial instance of the rule, the series 2 4 6. This initial instance is, of course, strongly associated with the rule "ascending even numbers" which, in fact, is not the rule the experimenter has in mind. It is not uncommon for intelligent subjects to take over thirty minutes to discover the rule "any set of ascending numbers," or, indeed, not to discover it at all and give up the task.

Abductive Memory and Tulving's Encoding Specificity Principle

Many of the observed failures to obtain generalization or transfer from the solving of one problem to the solving of novel, isomorphic problems can be thought of as a failure of abductive memory, and understood in terms of what we know about memory access. Perhaps the best example of failure to obtain transfer is the work on analogical transfer. Gick and Holyoak (1983) studied analogical transfer using Duncker's classic radiation problem: how can a patient with an inoperable tumor receive radiation strong enough to destroy the tumor but not harm surrounding tissue? This problem requires for its normal solution the application of a "convergence schema" in which a series of low-powered rays are simultaneously focused on the tumor from many directions. Efforts to increase solution rates to this problem by prior presentation and solving of an analogous problem—one with quite different content but also requiring application of the convergence schema—have consistently failed. One of the reasons for this failure is not difficult to see, but it illustrates an important principle. Solving the radiation problem requires that its specific content (the "givens") abductively access the convergence schema. There is no reason to suppose that prior training that establishes some other content as an effective cue to that schema should enhance the cue-effectiveness of a quite different content. Indeed, the data that Tulving (1983) has amassed in support of his encoding specificity principle should lead us not to expect such transfer. To assume otherwise is to make the common mistake of supposing that memory is a matter of stamping in the response (in this case the schema) without regard to the fact that all remembering is dependent on the building in of effective retrieval cues.

One subsidiary result from Gick and Holyoak's work helps illustrate this point. Whereas most of their experiments were concerned with the effects on problem solving of solving prior analogous problems, one (Experiment 2) was an attempt to teach subjects the convergence schema explicitly, with the help of a diagram and without any accompanying story. They found that this attempt to teach the schema directly had very little beneficial effect. A parallel result was obtained some forty years earlier by Clark Hull in his famous study of concept learning. Hull (1920) used Chinese ideographs as stimuli, with a conceptual class being defined by the presence of an invariant component fig-ure hidden within the ideograph. In Experiment E, Hull presented subjects with the defining common element without any context at all. That is, they were essentially given the answer. Granted that under normal conditions the identification of the defining component within the context of the entire ideo-graph is a major aspect of the task's difficulty, it might be expected that such a "give-away" condition would yield a substantial improvement in the rate of learning. Hull found that it produced no improvement at all. Again, the con-clusion is that exposure to a solution-giving concept will be ineffective if that exposure does not incorporate elements that will function in the context of the novel problem as effective retrieval cues to access that concept.

More recent experimental work has repeatedly shown that giving subjects "practice" by having them use a concept or schema in one context does little to increase the likelihood that they will use that concept or schema when it is needed to solve a subsequently presented problem, unless the conditions are such that the initial context lays down concept-related retrieval cues that will be activated by the subsequent problem. Of course one condition that achieves this cuing is similarity of surface or thematic content but this result is no more interesting than it is surprising, since our concern is with transfer of conceptual access across changes in surface content.

Let me illustrate this point by describing the results from a simple demonstration experiment. The task is one inspired by Werner and Kaplan (1963) in which subjects are required to discover the meaning of a nonsense word, given its use in a set of English sentences. Subjects are told that it is a word in a foreign language and that they are to work out its English transla-tion. For example, the pseudo-foreign word might be "julvert" and the sen-tences might be:

Most people have many julverts;
If a julvert runs into too many difficulties it may cease to exist;
A julvert may form gradually over a long period of time, or may form very
    quickly;
We may use some of our julverts more than others;
A person cannot have a julvert completely on their own;
Close julverts can be rare and difficult to come by.

Before attempting to solve a number of these problems, subjects are given a set of single sentences. Each of the English words that will be the solutions for the subsequent translation problems occurs in one of these sentences. Various techniques are used to ensure that subjects attend to these critical words. For example, the word might be underlined and subjects asked to judge the appropriateness of the word's meaning for that sentence. In one condition, this practice sentence reappears as one of the set of five sentences in the translation task, except that the English word is replaced with the pseudo-foreign word. In a second condition, there is no such repetition of the prior sentence. Compared to a control measure (in which there is no prior presentation of the solution at all), subjects in the sentence repetition condition show substantial facilitation measured in terms of either speed or accuracy. Subjects who were exposed to the solution, but within the context of a sentence not repeated in the test set, show no facilitation whatsoever, despite the strenuous efforts to highlight the word in the initial phase, and despite the fact that under these conditions subjects can free-recall most of the solution words if asked to do so. That is, the solutions are readily available under one set of retrieval conditions, but not under the conditions of the translation task.

The lesson to be drawn from this and similar results is that whereas problem solving (and effective thinking generally) depends on effective abductive remembering (content-cuing of conceptual structure), normal memory processes operate on a content-to-content basis. That is, under normal conditions transfer is governed by similarity of thematic content, not by similarity of the conceptual structure. The problem of generalizability is not therefore solved by simply "stamping in" the conceptual structure, but rather by increasing the abductive cue-effectiveness of different forms of content.

Content Specificity in a Propositional Reasoning Task

This same kind of analysis can be seen more clearly by examining empirical studies of the role of thematic content in simple reasoning problems. The literature contains many examples of reasoning problems that are formally equivalent (isomorphic) but which vary in their difficulty depending on their content. Probably the best known example of such a problem, and certainly the one experimentally most studied, is Wason's (1966) four-card selection task. In its original form it consisted of showing subjects four cards each with a letter on one side and a single digit on the other. Subjects in the experiment are informed about the cards, but are shown only one side of each card. What they might see is "A," "D," "4," and "7" on cards one through four respectively. Subjects are given a rule: "If a card has a vowel on one side, then it has an even number on the other side." They are then instructed, "Your task is to say which of the four cards you need to turn over in order to find out whether the rule is true or false." The answers most frequently given are "only A" and "A and 4," both of which are wrong; all but a small minority of subjects fail to appreciate the falsifying potential of the "7" card.

For a short period of time, it was thought that this apparent failure of rationality could be attributed to the abstract nature of the materials used in the task since several subsequent experiments showed a considerable improvement in subjects' performance when digits and letters were replaced with content that was more realistic and concrete. The most dramatic of these early demonstrations was that of Johnson-Laird, Legrenzi, and Legrenzi (1972) who instructed subjects to imagine that they were postal workers whose job it was to sort letters and to determine whether the following rule had been violated: "If a letter is sealed, then it has a 5d [d = penny] stamp on it." Subjects were shown four envelopes: the fronts of two envelopes, with a 5d and 4d stamp respectively, and the backs of two envelopes, sealed and unsealed respectively. This version is, of course, isomorphic with the original version, but unlike that version which yielded 15 percent correct answers, the percentage of correct responses for the realistic version was 81.

Subsequent findings have made it apparent that such a difference cannot be attributed in any simple way to the contrast between abstract and realistic materials. The literature contains many examples of failed replications; realistic content seems to help for some types of content and not in others, for some subject populations and not in others. For example, the envelope version of the problem, so effective with British subjects in 1972, produced no facilitation for American subjects used by Griggs and Cox (1982), the latter subjects having had no experience with this former regulation of the British post office. Such a conclusion is further supported by a result reported by Golding (1981) that the facilitation is not obtained with younger British subjects who have had no experience with the since discontinued regulation, and by the result of Cheng and Holyoak (1985) who found that facilitation is obtained with subjects from Hong Kong where the rule is familiar.

These kinds of results (and there are many others; see Evans, 1982 for a review) seem to argue strongly for a highly content-dependent view of logical reasoning, and this is exactly the conclusion drawn by a number of psychologists (for example, Griggs & Cox, 1982; Manktelow & Evans, 1979). These writers claimed that rather than use general rules of inference, subjects draw upon domain-specific experience. It now seems clear, however, that such a conclusion is overly pessimistic. In supporting this claim I will draw on the work of Cheng and Holyoak (1985) who, as noted above, also used the envelope problem as one of their tasks. Cheng and Holyoak's experiments show that it is not the specific experience (for example, with rules governing the stamp value required with sealed and unsealed letters) that is critical, but rather whether or not the content of the task activates more general schema that embody appropriate rules of inference. They term such schema *pragmatic reasoning schema,* and what they show experimentally is that correct reasoning ceases to be narrowly content bound, provided the novel content accesses the appropriate schema. Let me offer two examples, one from Cheng and Holyoak (1985) and one from a quite different source.

Cheng and Holyoak argue that the pragmatic reasoning schema relevant to the envelope problem is one that they term a "permission schema," in which performing a particular action requires that a certain precondition be satisfied. They formalize the schema in terms of a simple production system. If one examines the particular realistic problems (ones that are isomorphic to the four-card selection task) that have yielded high levels of correct performance, they do seem to fit a permission schema. For example, the rule "if he is drinking beer then he is over eighteen years of age" or the rule "if a purchase exceeds thirty dollars, then the receipt must have the signature of the manager on the back," both yield high levels of performance. Cheng and Holyoak show that American subjects who normally perform poorly on the envelope task will perform much better if they are given a rationale for the task that serves as an effective cue to activate the permission schema. Thus it is not the familiarity of the literal content that is critical but rather whether or not the particulars of the problem access an appropriate schema.

The second example concerns the activation of causal schema, and another well-worn problem, the taxicab problem first introduced by Kahneman and Tversky (1972). The standard version of the problem is as follows:

A cab was involved in a hit-and-run accident at night. Two cab companies, the Green and the Blue, operate in the city. You are given the following data:

1. Eighty-five percent of the cabs in the city are Green and 15 percent are Blue.
2. A witness identified the cab as Blue. The court tested the reliability of the witness under the same circumstances that existed on the night of the accident and concluded that the witness correctly identified each one of the two colors 80 percent of the time and failed 20 percent of the time.

What is the probability that the cab involved in the accident was Blue rather than Green?

Application of Bayes's theorem gives the answer as 0.41; the model response is 0.80. The usual interpretation of this result is that subjects ignore the differential base-rates (a priori probabilities) of the two cabs and equate the answer with the reliability of the witness. However, a slight modification of the problem yields a sharp change in subjects' responses, even though the two versions are formally equivalent. The modified version involves replacing the incidental base rate of cabs with a causal base rate of accidents: "Although the two companies are roughly equal in size, 85 percent of cab accidents in the city involve Green cabs and 15 percent involve Blue cabs." With this form of the problem base rate is no longer ignored.

A further example involving causal schema is the frequent ambiguity between causal and diagnostic schema and the dominance of the former over the latter. The confusion is captured in joking statements such as, "the likelihood of death is greater among those who have made a recent visit to their doctor than those who have not," which is a joke precisely because it evokes a causal schema which after a moment's reflection is replaced with the more appropriate diagnostic schema. Tversky and Kahneman (1982) provide a detailed analysis of this ambiguity.

The point of these examples is that reasoning is governed neither by general abstract rules on the one hand, nor by the particularities of experience on the other, but by conceptual structures or schema of intermediate levels of generality. Subjects were able to reason correctly about the envelope problem, not by being made familiar with that particular situation, but by ensuring that abductive memory accesses an appropriate reasoning schema.

Expertise

There have been many recent studies contrasting the problem-solving strategies of experts and novices. Abductive memory provides a way of thinking about certain aspects of these results. One general finding is that experts have specialized reasoning schemas, especially in well-structured domains such as physics. But expertise in physics does not consist merely in "possessing" such schemas, since real physics problems do not come with a label indicating which schema to use. Expertise also includes the ability to discern from the surface features of a problem the schema appropriate to its solution. Thus in a study comparing experts and novices in the area of physics, Chi, Feltovich, and Glaser (1981) had subjects sort problems into classes on the basis of "similarity." Novices tended to form categories on the basis of relatively surface features of the problems, whereas experts sorted the problems with respect to those underlying physical laws relevant to the problem's solution. Thus a novice might group problems on the grounds that they all dealt with blocks on an inclined plane; the expert was more likely to form groups based on criteria such as that they all involve the principle of conservation of energy. Physics experts have well-trained abductive memories, at least for the domain of physics.

THE GENERALITY OF MNEMONIC STRATEGIES
AND OF THINKING SKILLS

The above analysis makes clear one of the reasons why the teaching of generalizable memory skills is so much more straightforward than the corresponding teaching of thinking skills. Once a mnemonic technique has been taught and mastered, there is little confusion as to which technique to use and when to apply it. The situation with reasoning is quite different: practice with an abstract rule, no matter how general its application, does not guarantee that it will be accessed in the context of the content of a particular problem. Practice at reasoning modus tollens (reasoning that if p implies q, then *not q* implies *not p)*, for example, does not in itself guarantee success in the Wason four-card selection task.

There is, however, a common principle. The skill of effective remembering and of effective thinking both hinge on the cognitive system being trained in such a way that the data of experience are able rapidly to trigger the cognitive structures appropriate to the task at hand. In the case of memory, extensive practice enabled Chase's and Ericsson's subject S. F. to achieve a digit span of eighty digits because the digits triggered knowledge that served to restructure a "randomly" ordered sequence into something more meaningful. Once this process is understood, the feat is not more mysterious than most people's ability to remember a sequence of eighty letters—provided the letters are ordered so as to form English words that in turn form a sentence. To the person who reads only Swahili, however, such a letter string may well appear as random as strings of digits appeared to S. F. before he developed his "digit vocabulary." More importantly, this same understanding makes the question of transfer quite transparent. Although both ordinary reading and S. F.'s memory for digits are clearly teachable skills, and although they both embody a common set of laws of memory, there is no need to hold a workshop to establish that there will be no direct transfer from one domain to the other.

Corresponding arguments can be applied to thinking skills. Although there may be a set of common principles underlying sound reasoning, training is not just a matter of "knowing" these principles. Rather the skill to be taught is that of correctly "reading" a specific content as an instance embodying that principle. From this point of view, training thinking skills is not dissimilar from teaching diagnostic skills to a trainee physician. The skill involved is being able to "read" specific content as clues to an underlying process that is not directly observable but which holds the key to making correct inferences. In both cases the problem of transfer is that the same underlying principle may manifest itself in a bewildering array of symptoms. Skill will generalize only with adequate exposure to this range of symptoms; no amount of practice with the principles themselves will do the job. As Margolis (1987) has argued, there is much to be gained from adopting the view that thinking is a form of pattern recognition.

ACKNOWLEDGMENT

Preparation of this manuscript was supported by an operating grant from The Natural Sciences and Engineering Research Council of Canada.

REFERENCES

Adams, J. L. (1976). *Conceptual blockbusting.* New York: Norton.

Chase, W. G., & Ericsson, K. A. (1981). Skilled memory. In J. R. Anderson (Ed.), *Cognitive skills and their acquisition* (pp. 141–189). Hillsdale, NJ.: Erlbaum.

Chase, W. G., & Ericsson, K. A. (1982). Skill and working memory. In G. H. Bower (Ed.), *The psychology of learning and motivation* (Vol. 16, pp. 1–58). New York: Academic Press.

Cheng, P. W., & Holyoak, K. J. (1985). Pragmatic reasoning schemas. *Cognitive Psychology, 17,* 391–416.

Chi, M. T. H., Feltovitch, P. J., & Glaser, R. (1981). Categorization and representation of physics problems by experts and novices. *Cognitive Science, 5,* 121–152.

Evans, J. St. B. T. (1982). *The psychology of deductive reasoning.* London: Routledge and Kegan Paul.

Gick, M. L., & Holyoak, K. J. (1983). Schema induction and analogical transfer. *Cognitive Psychology, 15,* 1–38.

Golding, E. (1981). The effect of past experience on problem solving. Paper presented at the Annual Conference of the British Psychological Society, Surrey University.

Griggs, R. A., & Cox, J. R. (1982). The elusive thematic-materials effect in Wason's selection task. *British Journal of Psychology, 73,* 407–420.

Hull, C. L. (1920). Quantitative aspects of the evolution of concepts. *Psychological Monographs, 28,* (Entire Issue).

James, W. (1983). *Talks to teachers on psychology and to students on some of life's ideals.* Cambridge, MA: Harvard University Press.

Johnson-Laird, P. N., Legrenzi, P., & Legrenzi, S. M. (1972). Reasoning and a sense of reality. *British Journal of Psychology, 63,* 395–400.

Kahneman, D., & Tversky, A. (1972). Subjective probability: A judgment of representativeness. *Cognitive Psychology, 3,* 430–454.

Levine, M. (1971). Hypothesis theory and nonlearning despite ideal S-R reinforcement contingencies. *Psychological Review, 78,* 130–140.

Manktelow, K. I., & Evans, J. St. B. T. (1979). Facilitation of reasoning by realism: Effect or non-effect. *British Journal of Psychology, 70,* 477–488.

Margolis, H. (1987). *Patterns, thinking, and cognition.* Chicago: The University of Chicago Press.

McPeck, J. (1981). *Critical thinking and education.* New York: St. Martin's Press.

Tulving, E. (1983). *Elements of episodic memory.* Oxford: Oxford University Press.

Tversky, A., & Kahneman, D. (1982). Causal schemas in judgment under uncertainty. In D. Kahneman, P. Slovic, & A. Tversky (Eds.), *Judgment under uncertainty: Heuristics and biases* (pp. 117–128). New York: Cambridge University Press.

Wason, P. C. (1966). Reasoning. In B. Foss (Ed.), *New horizons in psychology* (pp. 135–151). Harmondsworth, Middlesex: Penguin.

Wason, P. C., & Johnson-Laird, P. N. (Eds.) (1968). *Thinking and reasoning.* Harmondsworth, Middlesex: Penguin.

Werner, H., & Kaplan, B. (1963). *Symbol formation.* New York: Wiley.

Yates, F. A. (1966). *The art of memory.* London: Routledge & Kegan Paul.

5 Finding Generalizable Strategies in Scientific Theory Debates

James Ryan
Memorial University of Newfoundland

At the center of the generalizability of critical thinking issue are the questions of whether there is interfield variation of reasoning skills, abilities, and dispositions, and whether transfer of these skills is possible. Ennis (this volume; 1989, p. 8) suggests that, although the notion of field is vague, there is some plausibility and usefulness to the proposition that in different fields different things count as good reasons for beliefs. In order to test this proposition, "arguments offered by specialists in a number of different disciplines need to be examined and compared to see how much they have in common" (Ennis, 1989, p. 8). Likewise, the question of transfer might be answered best by first turning "the transfer principle around by using empirically determined nontransfer as one criterion for separate domains" (Ennis, 1989, p. 7), and then investigating the extent to which skills or dispositions taught in the context of certain subject matter are likely to transfer to other subject matter.

McPeck (1981, pp. 5–13) claims that different fields, or different subjects of thought, have different criteria for forming beliefs. However, he concurs with Ennis that further research is required on these matters. Some of his comments, such as those regarding the relationships between skills and domains (McPeck, this volume), suggest that for him this research could well be directed toward an account of the different kinds of arguments considered effective in different disciplines.

For Siegel, criteria of assessment "do not vary in any systematic way with 'fields,' however that latter notion is construed" (Siegel, this volume). Instead, the variation in criteria of assessment indicate that "different sorts of claims require different sorts of evidence for their establishment." Siegel concurs with Ennis that empirical research is needed to determine which skills and criteria of assessment are specific to, or best taught in the context of, school subjects.

So, empirical results are deemed necessary to advance the generalizability issue. As yet, though, there is no framework in critical thinking to guide empirical research. Also, there seems to be a variety of questions to be answered. Some of these are: (a) What unit of knowledge has to be studied: school subjects, disciplines as found in colleges and universities, broad fields of knowledge, research domains? (b) What is being looked for in the research: skills, strategies, criteria of assessment, dispositions? (c) What can the results show: similar strategies used in different fields, strategies that are learned the same way, strategies that can be learned in the field and applied in another, strategies that can be taught as general skills?

Some small set from this large number of questions will have to be chosen to start any empirical research. Some of the research can be done by psychologists, educators, and other social scientists within frameworks already in place.

In this chapter, I will first outline a framework for research into scientific reasoning. The framework should be able to serve similar efforts in many fields of knowledge such as history, law, and political debate. Next, I will attempt to characterize and analyze the reasoning found in one area of science—the study of continental drift. The focus will be three lines of reasoning in the debate over the acceptability of that theory wherein three different sets of strategies are used. Then, I will argue that both the lines of reasoning and the strategies are not unique to geology, but can be found in other fields, disciplines, and areas of general knowledge. Lines of reasoning as defined and exemplified here seem the appropriate unit of analysis for research on the generalizability issue in debates in other fields, disciplines, and areas of general knowledge. The kinds of midsized strategies found also seem the most appropriate to critical thinking instruction.

How do we go about characterizing the reasoning used in a particular discipline? One might try to identify a characteristic methodology, for example, and isolate the standard reasoning procedures therein. Consider the natural sciences. Frequently, inductive methods or hypothetico-deductive methods are said to be characteristic of them. Hypothetico-deductive or inductive procedures could be used as standards to construct examples by means of which a general skill for identifying and applying the standards could be learned. It is a commonplace, however, that critical thinking is concerned with a broader range of items than can be captured under this rubric of hypothetico-deductive and inductive procedures. Is this fuller concept of critical thinking necessary for comprehension of and instruction in the reasoning of the natural sciences?

I would like to argue that there is a more fruitful way to characterize the reasoning in the natural sciences, which can both exploit and enrich the now common conception of critical thinking. The argument rests on a recent example from the history of geology explored with the help of Kuhn's (1970) conception of the nature and development of science. The result is the identification of the characteristic reasoning from a fairly well-defined field that can be compared and contrasted with proposals from the field of critical thinking.

A MODEL FOR APPLICATION TO GEOLOGICAL REASONING

If we study a geology textbook, follow an academic program in geology, and become a practicing researcher in geology, much of what we read, study, and practice may seem to correspond well to what Kuhn has labeled "normal science." We learn to do cross sections; then we select a piece of terrane or ocean floor that we survey to produce an acceptable cross section that may be used to explore for oil, or to construct a history of the area for some early period. Principles such as that of superposition and techniques such as carbon dating may be used. Application of the principles and techniques is guided by a hypothesis about why the area may be of interest—a hypothesis that is tested by the final result. So, the characterization of geology as methodologically inductive or hypothetico-deductive might seem justified after all.

But the principles and techniques applied in this activity come to be accepted for some reason; the hypothesis was derived from a theory or a paradigm accepted in the discipline. Can the methodology practiced in normal scientific activity furnish the reasoning for the acceptance of the theory or paradigm? The historical record on instances of theory acceptance indicates, Kuhn pointed out, that the methodological rules and practices operative when research is conducted under an accepted theory do not apply to the acceptance itself. In normal science, hypotheses are tested and theories expanded according to well-established procedures, which indicate that a formal methodology is at work. But for revolutionary science, where the previously accepted theory is in question and alternatives are being proposed, no such formal methodology is operative. When there is discussion of what theory to accept or what principles are acceptable, the ensuing decision is based, according to Kuhn, on good reasons but not on a formal method.

Whereas formal rules could be followed to *determine* choice, good reasons, functioning as values, serve only to *influence* choice. Good reasons find expression in the arguments and counterarguments used to persuade members of a scientific community to favor one theory or another. The role of good reasons thus is predominant in the early phase of a theory's development, because then there are no well-established and accepted methodological rules available.

Within any community of scientists there is, according to Kuhn, a standard accepted set of values. The members of the set correspond to what traditionally have been considered criteria for a good theory, and include simplicity, accuracy, internal and external coherence, broad scope, and fruitfulness.

As with values elsewhere, there can be disagreements over the interpretation and appropriate application of any one of them; as well, there can be disagreement over how to weigh and balance the members of the set when theories vying for acceptance each meet a number of the standards. The various interpretations and weightings of factors are the result of personal, subjective features of individual scientists. These alone, however, cannot dictate a choice, because no one argument can convince a community, and because the final decision is due to the community reaching a consensus on which subset of the shared values are most appropriate for the circumstances.

A number of important questions remain unanswered in Kuhn's good reasons model. Can we say, for example, that the final decision of what theory to accept can be a result of agreement on subjective factors? Is it acceptable to ask for no other final arbiter than the scientific community involved in the decision? Is there a way of distinguishing, even if we accept the scientific community as final arbiter, between good reasons and poor reasons as expressed in the arguments and counterarguments?

Despite the difficulties posed by these unanswered questions, the model as outlined has attractive features for our present purposes. The model includes a significant portion of scientific activity that is neither formalistic nor an unsubstantiated form of expression. Thus, it would seem that the reasoning strategies of interest to critical thinking would be deployed in that portion of scientific activity. Consequently, that portion of scientific activity should provide a fruitful source in the search for generalizable features of critical thinking. Also, the set of values shared by scientists both identifies a discipline and permits the kind of investigation that we seek here across theories within the discipline.

It would be helpful for our purposes to further define the model we have so far been discussing. We have said that good reasons are expressed in the arguments and counterarguments over a theory's acceptance. However, good reasons are found in wider contexts of science. A more appropriate unit of appraisal is the debate; this unit proves both faithful to scientific practice and fruitful for philosophical scrutiny. For example, good reasons play a crucial role in the early stages of a theory's development, and it is legitimate to say that the theory is being debated at this stage and that the debate is about the acceptability or nonacceptability of any number of alternative theories. Also, we could identify an ongoing debate about some theory that has been on the scene for an extended period of time, perhaps being modified, serving to generate other theories, or even being used as a kind of counterfactual that reinforces the alternative dominant paradigm. We can speak further of the proposers or supporters of a theory debating it with their potential audience, and of the respondents entering into the debate with their substantiations or criticisms. The participants in the debate, we can say, are giving lines of reasoning either in favor of or against the worthiness of the theory. The specific strategies providing data for the question of interfield variation and generalizability would be displayed in these lines of reasoning.

The theory debates that culminated with the acceptance of the theory of plate tectonics in the earth sciences in the 1960s and 1970s reveal, by an application of the model just outlined, instances of reasoning that are relevant to the generalizability of critical thinking issue. Historians of science, and most of the geologists who write historically on their subject, claim that the acceptance of plate tectonics was an archetypal Kuhnian revolution. The theory postulates that the earth's surface is composed of a number of plates, some containing continents, others oceans, others both. The plates move horizontally, and their movement causes a large portion of the earth's surface features such as mountain chains, volcanoes, earthquakes, and displaced terranes. The theory is said to be revolutionary for a number of reasons: (a) by itself, it accounts for a variety of phenomena that previously had separate explanations, or none at all that were considered acceptable; (b) it was rapidly accepted by a large majority of the earth science community, and, once accepted, served as a paradigm for much of its research; (c) it was treated as at least the best if not the definitive theory in textbooks; and (d) no serious effort was made subsequently to search for an alternative. In other words, the revolution resulted in a period of normal science which is still continuing.

Some forty years before plate tectonics was proposed, another theory suggesting horizontal movement with a nearly identical time frame and series of reconstructions was proposed. This was Alfred Wegener's (1924) theory of continental drift, or displacement, as he called it. Wegener's theory was rejected by the earth science community of the day. The relationship between this early theory of drift and the recent theory of plate tectonics is still being discussed; there is a spectrum of claims from those saying that there is little relation between the theories to those saying that they are practically identical. Most agree, though, that there is at least sufficient relationship between the two to warrant comparisons.

Both Wegener's theory and the theory of plate tectonics have received extensive analysis from philosophers of science proposing or testing different models of scientific theory development. A few views seem to dominate: (a) plate tectonics was able to make novel predictions that subsequently were confirmed and this led to its acceptance, (b) plate tectonics was accepted because of its ability to unify and explain a large body of previously disparate evidence, and (c) Wegener's theory was rejected because it left a larger amount of data unexplained or problematic than it explained.

However, a careful reading of the historical record fails to substantiate any decision of rejection or acceptance being made on the basis of any of these reasons. A problem, I would argue, is that philosophers of science start with some preconceived general criteria for theory acceptance, and their reading of the history of the development of that theory selects the events that validate their preconception. However, the historical record indicates that it is questionable whether any one criterion or small set of criteria can account for the acceptance or rejection of a theory. The ongoing debate over continental drift theories usefully illustrates this point, and is also relevant to the generalizability question.

EXAMPLES OF REASONING
IN THE DRIFT DEBATE
AND THE RELATION TO CRITICAL THINKING

If we can see theory change as the product of a debate where lines of reasoning are employed, then I think we have a felicitous opportunity to consider the relation of critical thinking to scientific thinking. We can identify the strategies used in arguing for and against a theory, see how there might be a match between these strategies and critical thinking, and determine what implications might arise for the generalizability of critical thinking.

Let us start with the debate over the early version of drift. Wegener presented and argued for his theory in a book entitled *Die Entstehung der Continente und Ozeane,* the third edition of which was translated into English as *The Origin of Continents and Oceans* (1924). He begins with a summary of his proposed model, and follows with a comparison of other relevant theories. He then indicates how the geophysical nature of the earth allowed for horizontal movement of the continental land masses. There are separate chapters on the geological, paleontological, and paleoclimatic evidence for the theory, the latter of which contains most of the reasoning which was central in the debate over the acceptability of the theory. A few longer chapters follow on some consequences of the theory and speculations on the nature of the interior of the earth.

Wegener states that he came to the idea of drift by noticing how the coastal outlines of Africa and South America matched. He also was aware of the inadequacies in proposed explanations for paleontological findings, and saw his own theory as offering a better alternative. In accord with the model outlined in the previous section, I will isolate three lines of reasoning in the debate over Wegener's theory and comment on how they can provide something of interest for the generalizability of critical thinking question. I will first describe portions of each line of reasoning, and after all three are described, turn to implications for the generalizability question.

The Reasoning About Graphics

The first line of reasoning concerns the match of the continental blocks across present oceans. A large part of the line of reasoning for the matching is contained in Wegener's chapters on the geological, paleontological, and paleo-climatic evidence. But an important part of the debate took place, not over Wegener's verbal arguments, but over his maps. Perhaps the most important use of maps by Wegener was to represent the reconstruction of the continents, first for the Permo-Carboniferous period, then for the Eocene, and finally for the Quaternary. He presents two maps from two different projections for each of these three periods. On the maps for the Permo-Carboniferous, the continents are adjoined into one large mass, except for a few small sections where deep seas are indicated. If we consider the continental masses now separated by the Atlantic Ocean, they are all adjoined on Wegener's Permo-Carboniferous map with the exception of an area which, in the west, would stretch from the southern United States to Central America. The response of Wegener's critics to this graphic portrayal of the Atlantic continents in the Permo-Carboniferous period was one of the significant reasons for the rejection of the displacement theory.

Two papers by Philip Lake (1922, 1923), which both exemplified the style and substance of the case against drift and seem to have played an important role in the outcome of the debate, propose an alternative to Wegener's graphic reconstruction. Lake reasoned as follows:

> On Wegener's map, Ireland and Newfoundland appear contiguous at the same time as Brazil and Southern Africa. Take a globe of the present earth and stretch a thread from the Gulf of Guinea in Africa to Ireland; then, if the Gulf of Guinea end is placed at Cape St. Roque in Brazil, the Ireland end will be in the Atlantic west of Spain, hundreds of miles from touching Newfoundland. On the other hand, if the ends of the thread are placed first at St. John's, Newfoundland, and Valentia, Ireland, then Africa and Brazil fail to join.

Lake's thread technique is assumed reliable, and it produces an arrangement of continents that does not look like Wegener's arrangement; it does not bring the coastlines adjacent as needed to construct the displacement model.

Using an analogous argument, Charles Schuchert, an influential American paleontologist, demonstrated a model globe where a plasteline replica had been placed over the Americas and then shifted onto the European and African continents (Schuchert, 1928). Again, when Newfoundland and Ireland adjoined, parts of Africa and South America, which adjoin on Wegener's map, were close to 2000 kilometers apart. Schuchert's argument is as follows:

Wegener's map does not represent a possible arrangement of continents; using a technique that is assumed reliable, and reproducing
one part of the fit from Wegener's map, prevents another part of that
fit; thus the coastlines do not fit together as represented by Wegener's
map; so that map is no reason to accept the theory, given that the
graphic story the map tells is an essential feature of the theory.

Schuchert's plasteline method produced a result similar to Lake's thread
technique. In both cases, the rule of construction is to adjoin the land masses
now separated by the Atlantic using a reliable method. The result in each case
is failure to make the adjoinment.

Lake proposed another operation on a globe. The Australian mass can be
placed in the Arabian sea and made to fit with no more adjustments than
Wegener allows to get his matchings. Chester Longwell (1928) elaborated on
this suggestion by drawing a map with the Australian mass traced into the
Arabian Sea and the adjustments needed to make the fit outlined. Longwell's
map represents a fitting of coastlines that is not on Wegener's map. It says
that the arrangement on Wegener's map is not the only possible one. It takes
the following as a rule of construction: adjoin those coastlines whose outlines
fit together. Using this technique a fit is found that is not permitted by
Wegener's displacement theory.

Reasoning About Effects and Causes

The second line of reasoning to be considered concerns scientists' epistemic attitude to causal forces. A number of authors comment that the early
drift theory was not accepted because there was no known mechanism for
moving continental masses. Wegener cites possible mechanisms suggested by
other authors, such as the effect on the earth's axis of rotation due to the
attraction of the sun and moon, and movements due to elevations of the
earth's surface above its equilibrium level. But his conclusion is that details of
the causal forces of the movement are not well enough known to be stated satisfactorily. What he does assert is that the movement of the continents, the
folding of mountains, the occurrence of volcanoes, transgressions of the sea,
and the wandering of the poles "stand in one great causal connection with one
another" (Wegener, 1924, p. 205), and their interrelations and alternating
relations seem to be quite complex.

So he accepts the movement (the effect) as fact, without knowing its
cause. The reasons in favor of the effect are strong enough in his view to warrant waiting for continental drift's equivalent to Sir Isaac Newton. The cause is
not ignored by him, or claimed unnecessary, but reckoned to be only one element in a complex interaction of events.

A large number of the authors who reject drift do treat the question of cause, mainly by demonstrations of the inadequacy of the forces suggested. Lake, however, treats the issue directly with the remark that Wegener's "contention is that whether the cause is known or not the movements have actually taken place" (Lake, 1922, p. 430). The context of this remark and the other authors' statements regarding the inadequacies of the proposed mechanism suggest that another of the important influencing reasons for not accepting the theory is that effects are assumed whose causes are not known. But the same geologists who rejected the theory on these grounds described plenty of phenomena whose cause was unknown. For example, at the time, a textbook in geology would have an extensive chapter on volcanoes, describing the different types, the material produced, the life span, and so on. It would be admitted that not enough was known about the interior of the earth to state satisfactorily their origin or cause. Likewise, no cause was known for mountain folds and fractures in the earth's surface. Yet, the earth was assumed to have folded and fractured. Authors sometimes suggested causes, but would stress that doing so was speculation, and they were careful to distinguish clearly such speculation from the factual descriptions and the more immediately observable causes. Phenomena such as dykes, sills, and other igneous intrusions, for example, were known to have as their immediate cause the solidification of magma beneath the surface, and it was known that the coarse-grain of the intrusive igneous rocks was caused by the slow cooling of the magma from which they were formed (Pirsson, 1920).

We can distinguish, then, three positions geologists would take on the cause and effect relation of events. Some events have known causes; some events have unknown causes, but their occurrence was considered unproblematic, and it was assumed that knowledge of the cause would be forthcoming with normal progress in the understanding of, for example, the earth's interior; some events called for a cause, but their cause was unknown, and therefore the events would not be accepted as having occurred until their causes were known. Drifting continents were seen as either of the second or third type depending upon the scientist's persuasion. However, some scientists implied that any phenomenon that could not be classified, mapped, or described according to the accepted principles operative in the discipline should be considered of the third type (Pirsson, 1920; Schuchert, 1928).

Different lines of reasoning and different strategies were needed when events from these different categories were included in some model of the earth's history or structure. Where the causes were known, maybe accumulated instances would be cited in support; where the causes were unknown, but expected to become known, connections to other phenomena which seemed promising for uncovering these causes would be sought in the model; where the causes were unknown, and the phenomena themselves not accessible by accepted principles (as with drifting continents), alternative models would probably be sought.

Reasoning About Simplicity

The final example is of reasoning about simplicity, one of the values Kuhn claims is shared by any community of scientists. In the debate over drift, Wegener and his critics frequently have recourse to it as a reason for one or another of their positions. I shall consider three contexts in which reasoning about simplicity occurs.

Most of the paleoclimatic arguments for drift centered on its ability to account for the climatic conditions in the Permo-Carboniferous period, conditions very different from those of the present day. For example, parts of tropical Africa were ice-covered while areas around Greenland had tropical vegetation. Now, by means of the northwestward drift of the continental masses as postulated by the drift model, and the additional complementary hypothesis tracing the movement of the earth's poles for that period, Wegener claimed to be able to give an account of Permo-Carboniferous climatic conditions. In his account, today's polar to tropical climatic zones are exactly paralleled for the Permo-Carboniferous period when the indicators of climatic conditions such as coal beds, salt and gypsum deposits, and polar vegetation are positioned consistent with the drift hypothesis. The result is an elegant and logically consistent sequencing of the climatic belts. Wegener claims it is a simplification compared to other attempts to account for the data on climates of the period. It is the elegance and logical consistency that make it simpler.

Elsewhere, Wegener considers the paleontological arguments for drift. A major paleontological problem was posed by the affinities of species on now widely separated land masses. Wegener claims that drift provides a simpler solution than does the more popular land-bridge hypothesis, which postulated the temporary existence of narrow strips of land adjoining the continents. Both hypotheses provide land connections for species transfer, in contrast to some other proposed solutions that relied mostly on transfer by ocean currents or wind. But consider the island of Juan Fernandez which, while adjacent to the coast of Chile at present, has its botanical affinities with the more distant Tierra del Fuego, Antarctica, New Zealand, and Pacific Islands. In the drift model, South America, including Chili, would have been far from Juan Fernandez until recent times, while Tierra del Fuego and the other land masses would have been closer historically, allowing the species now common on each to have spread to each piece of land. Wegener suggested that the land-bridge hypothesis would need at least four or five bridges and an additional explanation as to why the bridges were not, as was usual, between more closely associated lands. Here, simplicity is a function of both the number of entities and the number of hypotheses needed to account for some phenomenon. Thus, extending the boundaries of the domain of entities or hypotheses might change our opinion on which model was simpler. For example, in order to account for species transfer, would either model have to invoke additional geophysical processes or principles, such as those of displacement or viscosity of solid masses of certain sizes, either to have the bridges rising from and sinking into the ocean, or to have the continents move laterally? The number of geophysical processes and principles invoked could affect the decision on which hypothesis is simpler.

So it would seem that simplicity is a function of those factors one wants to circumscribe as relevant for a particular line of reasoning. We might note that one of Lake's reasons for rejecting Wegener's theory was that it did not provide a simpler explanation of the distribution of one particular floral species, the Glossopteris—its fossils were found in regions far from the region to which drift seemed to restrict them. So, in this case, explanatory comprehensiveness seems to define simplicity. The line of reasoning is different enough between the Juan Fernandez and Glossopteris examples to illustrate that appeal to the standard of simplicity is made in a broad scope of contexts.

RELATION TO CRITICAL THINKING

What are the implications of these examples for the generalizability question? We have looked at a debate in a discipline (science), and in a field within the discipline (geology), over the choice of a specific theory in that field. Three important lines of reasoning in the debate reveal the use of three different sets of strategies. Now, one way of claiming that critical thinking strategies are not generalizable is to claim that the lines of reasoning and their strategies are unique to fields or disciplines. Thus, if the antigeneralizability view were true, it should be the case that the strategies and the lines of reasoning we have identified are unique to geology, or at least to science. But is there reason to believe that is the case? Rather, would not the strategies and lines of reasoning likely be found in debates in various fields, disciplines, and areas of common knowledge?

Consider first the three lines of reasoning from geology. The first was about a number of nontextual devices and their credibility as evidence in support of a hypothesis. The second was about the concept of a causal force and what epistemic status it should have. The third was about the concept of a commonly accepted value and its concrete interpretation. A cursory observation indicates that these three lines of reasoning define debates in a variety of fields, disciplines, and areas of knowledge.

For example, in all of the sciences there is extensive use of graphs, illustrations, and diagrams as evidence. In advertising, images are probably the preferred means of attempting to convince an audience that a particular choice is well-founded. The status of the causal agent is often in dispute in medicine, in cases where the direction of treatment is determined according to etiology. In criminal investigation, the decision to identify an act as criminal or not is a result of a debate over the cause of the act; some debates in criminal cases, for example, center on whether an uncontrolled emotional impulse is sufficiently recognized as the cause of an act, and thus that the act is not criminal. Debates focusing on commonly held values also are found in various areas. In any community endeavor where there is debate, the issue of how to interpret a commonly held value is usually at the forefront—our modern democracies supposedly value justice, freedom, and equality, but different groups and individuals claim to have better interpretations of these values. More specifically, in news reporting, amongst other fields, accuracy is a recognized value. Not uncommon, though, are calls for retraction, rebuttals taking issue with the accuracy of some report, and differing interpretations of accuracy (evident when one looks at both sides). Again, in education, literacy is a foundational value, but different pedagogical approaches are recommended based upon differing interpretations of literacy.

But, it may be claimed, the strategies used for these lines of reasoning are limited by the fields or disciplines in which they occur. Again a review of the strategies show the implausibility of that claim. What strategies did we find in the line of reasoning over maps? They could be summarized as follows: making an assumption about the technique used; using an implicit rule of construction; applying the rule to existing phenomena, data, or parts of the world; checking for coherence with some proposed or accepted position or theory; and judging the proposed or accepted position or theory. In the causal-force example, the strategies could be summarized as follows: making an assumption that the data or information has been reliably assessed or understood; accumulating instances; seeking connections to other phenomena; and seeking an alternative model. The strategies in the simplicity argument are: deciding on the factors relevant to the line of reasoning; invoking the standard value in a way appropriate to the case; and concluding that a case is better because it displays this value.

According to the claim that critical thinking strategies are limited to a field or discipline, the strategies just listed should be unique to debates in geology or in science. There is, however, no empirical evidence to support the claim. Support through conceptual analysis would have to show that the strategies listed display content or concepts that identify them as uniquely geological or at least uniquely scientific. The strategies here, to the contrary, listed without the context of the geological debates, could not be identified as unique to those debates. No specialized terminology is needed to state them, and they can be conceptualized as operating within debates outside of geology.

Another premise of some antigeneralizability positions is that any strategy not unique to a field or discipline comes under the rubric of formal logic or inductive logic. Again, the listed strategies at most come under the rubric of informal logic or perhaps rhetoric.

If we have correctly characterized these lines of reasoning in geology and the strategies within them, then two important consequences seem to follow. One is that the burden of proof shifts to the antigeneralizability position to argue convincingly that the strategies are reducible to formal logic or are context dependent. The other is that a framework for empirical research in locating lines of reasoning with their attendant strategies has been established. Critical thinking generalizability becomes empirically well-founded if investigations of lines of reasoning from other fields, disciplines, and areas of common knowledge reveal use of the same strategies that we saw used in geological debates.

CONCLUSION

A modified Kuhnian model has been used to characterize and analyze the reasoning employed in a scientific theory debate. The model provided a framework for finding aspects of the debate that yielded data on generalizable reasoning strategies of the kind appropriate to critical thinking. This framework should prove applicable for finding similar data in debates in other fields of science and in other disciplines and areas of general knowledge. In the debate over continental drift, three lines of reasoning were identified which revealed use of three different sets of strategies. There is good reason to believe that these lines of reasoning and the accompanying sets of strategies are duplicated elsewhere. Also, they seem to be the appropriate units for the empirical investigation which would substantiate the conceptual analysis made here, claiming that at least one kind of reasoning strategies is generalizable.

Though not described in this paper, the continental drift debate also contained expressions of ridicule, chauvinism, and disregard of relevant information, items recognized as impediments to the development of the debate. These items are also recognized as impediments to good thinking in other fields. Thus, there is some reason to believe that the reasoning in different fields could benefit from the same infusion of critical thinking skills. Use of theory debates in critical thinking instruction might, then, help to provide the needed skills to improve these debates. Also, their use would demand a degree of focus on subject content that some claim necessary to isolate critical thinking skills worth getting excited about.

REFERENCES

Ennis, R. H. (1989). Critical thinking and subject specificity: Clarification and needed research. *Educational Researcher, 18*(3), 4–10.

Kuhn, T. S. (1970). *The structure of scientific revolutions* (2nd ed.). Chicago: The University of Chicago Press.

Lake, P. (1922). Wegener's displacement theory. *Geological Magazine, 59,* 338–346.

Lake, P. (1923). Wegener's hypothesis of continental drift. *The Geophysical Journal, 61,* 179–194.

Longwell, C. (1928). Some physical tests of the displacement hypothesis. In W. A. J. M. van Waterschoot van der Gracht (Ed.), *Theory of continental drift* (pp. 145–157). Tulsa, OK: The American Association of Petroleum Geologists.

McPeck, J. (1981). *Critical thinking and education.* New York: St. Martins.

Pirsson, L. V. (1920). *A text-book of geology.* New York: Wiley.

Schuchert, C. (1928). The hypothesis of continental drift. In W. A. J. M. van Waterschoot van der Gracht (Ed.), *Theory of continental drift* (pp. 104–144). Tulsa, OK: The American Association of Petroleum Geologists.

Wegener, A. (1924). *The origin of continents and oceans.* New York: Methuen.

II Defenses of Generalizability

In her defense of generalizability in Chapter 6, Sharon Bailin challenges McPeck's thesis that logic is relevant to the context of justification of hypotheses but is useless in the context of their discovery. The link between this issue and critical thinking is that justification and discovery correspond, at least roughly, to the evaluative and generative sides of critical thinking. For McPeck, logic is largely irrelevant to an important part of critical thinking, the generative part. Furthermore, McPeck argues that logic is not even very efficacious in the evaluative part of critical thinking, since logic neither provides definitive criteria for evaluation nor provides all the tools that are needed.

Taking a stance on the epistemological dimension of critical thinking generalizability, Bailin contends that both of McPeck's theses are incorrect; they founder on the assumption that critical thinking can be divided neatly into two distinct phases: a generative and nonevaluative phase, and an evaluative and nongenerative phase. If generated ideas are to be worth checking out, as McPeck claims they must be, then the generation of the ideas must be constrained by some evaluative criteria. Bailin agrees with McPeck that subject-specific knowledge and criteria play a crucial role in this evaluation, but she maintains that general logical principles also have a role. Bailin also agrees with McPeck that evaluation is not algorithmic but requires judgment and creativity. However, she disagrees that, merely because judgment and creativity are required, logic is thereby ruled out. Judgment must be used, but one is not free to violate the norms of logic, she claims. Thus, while logical principles do not determine evaluation, they do provide guidance and constraint.

Bailin goes on to argue that McPeck's error is to misinterpret the distinction between the contexts of discovery and justification as originally formulated by Reichenbach. McPeck, Bailin maintains, interprets the distinction as one between the mental processes involved in discovery and those involved in justification. Actually, the distinction is between the psychological processes of discovery and the epistemology of justification. The psychological processes are not relevant to justification's epistemology, because the psychological origin of an idea is not relevant to its justification. Thus, to uphold the distinction as Reichenbach intended is to locate rationality in epistemology and outside psychology (and sociology). The epistemology of justification is fully generalizable to all subjects, according to Bailin. So, therefore, is the evaluative aspect of critical thinking.

Harvey Siegel acknowledges from the outset of Chapter 7 that whether or not critical thinking is generalizable depends upon what critical thinking is. This position is in accord with Norris's position in Chapter 1 and Johnson's in Chapter 3. Siegel posits that, minimally, critical thinking has reason assessment and critical spirit components. Under this assumption, he asks two subquestions: (a) is the reason assessment component generalizable? and (b) is the critical spirit component generalizable?

First, Siegel argues that the skills and criteria that comprise a portion of the reason assessment component of critical thinking are partly generalizable. Whether the notion of field is construed broadly or narrowly, the principles of reason assessment are likely to differ as much within fields as among them, and hence they are not field specific. That is, what counts as a good reason from field to field is basically the same. The nuance that is often overlooked according to Siegel is that criteria for reason assessment are complex and varied, and do not line up neatly with fields. Regardless of this complexity and variety, however, Siegel maintains that the criteria of reason assessment are united under a common epistemology which sanctions them all.

Second, Siegel argues that the portion of the reason assessment component comprised by the epistemology underlying critical thinking is fully generalizable. This epistemology presupposes a radically nonepistemic notion of truth that requires rational justification and truth to be distinguished; an absolutism regarding reasons and justification such that they are not relative to persons, times, cultures, and so on; and a fallibilism regarding justification as an indicator of truth.

Finally, Siegel argues that the critical spirit is fully generalizable. The critical spirit refers to a complex set of dispositions, attitudes, habits of mind, and character traits that are not restricted in application. As I interpret his work, this critical spirit is what Siegel takes to be the trait that underlies the natural kind, *critical thinker.*

Focusing more narrowly than Siegel, David Hitchcock argues in Chapter 8 that the criteria for good analogical inference, although disjunctive and more specific than a general theory of good inference, nevertheless straddle fields. In arguing by analogy, we project a queried property from source cases, which share certain features, to a target case, which also has those features. Analogical arguments for the existence of God belong to a different field than analogical arguments about the stopping distance of a car or the province in which a certain address is located. But all these arguments are best appraised by the same criteria. Naturally the specific content of the criteria will vary from one argument to another, and working out whether the criteria are satisfied will require knowledge of the field of inquiry to which the subject matter of the argument belongs. But the general strategy of identifying the variables to which the predictor properties belong, and thinking about whether those variables determine the variable to which the queried property belongs, is common. Thus, Hitchcock argues, epistemological subject specificity fails for the critical thinking skill of evaluating analogical inference; the criteria for good analogical inference are not entirely field specific.

In Chapter 9, J. Anthony Blair adopts the tactic of focusing on an aspect of critical thinking that he believes belongs paradigmatically and uncontroversially to critical thinking—the evaluation of information sources. This approach avoids the problem of formulating a widely acceptable definition of critical thinking (which, however, Blair feels is needed), and enables attention to be turned to the generalizability of the uncontroversial aspect.

According to Blair, evaluating sources of information is just one aspect of overall belief maintenance, the ultimate aim of which is a set of well-managed beliefs. As examples, he focuses on a set of principles that have been proposed for evaluating reports of observations—for instance, that there be sufficient time for making an observation for it to be believable. Noting that the principles are stated in general form, Blair addresses condition (d) of critical thinking generalizability listed in Chapter 1 by asking the empirical question whether becoming familiar and self-conscious of the principles will make it more likely that people will evaluate observations correctly. Since initial learning of principles can impede activity, Blair contends that a proper test of this question cannot be conducted unless there is sufficient time for internalization of the learned principles.

Adding a new twist, Blair then argues that the principles of observation appraisal are inherently general, but that their application is inherently specific to different contexts. For instance, the generalizability of the disposition to deploy the principles when appropriate depends upon the relationship between ability and disposition: in some cases, ability and disposition are quite distinct; in other cases, ability and disposition are logically distinct, but causally related; and in some cases, ability and disposition are logically inseparable.

In the case of assessing the credibility of observation reports, Blair argues that the ability and disposition are logically distinct. Hence, there are two things to be taught. Given this, the extent to which the disposition will generalize will depend on the extent to which the motivation to do so has been instilled, the thinker is familiar with the skill's application in the context in question, the principles were taught as general, and teaching for transfer occurred.

Blair maintains that the same conclusions should apply to the evaluation of sources of information other than observation. Furthermore, to the extent that the evaluation of sources is paradigmatically critical thinking, then many of the conclusions about this aspect should apply to critical thinking generally.

Linda M. Phillips argues in Chapter 10 that, at the level of self-regulatory thinking, there are strategies that generalize across a variety of boundaries. She assumes generalizability along the epistemological dimension and explores it along the psychological one. In particular, she produces evidence showing that certain strategies generalize from youngsters to adults reading narrative text, from the reading of narrative text to problem solving in mathematics, and from the reading of narrative text to the reading of expository science text. In addition, she suggests that the strategies might also generalize to texts of other genres, such as documents and poetry.

Since the primary focus of her analysis of self-regulatory strategies is in the area of reading, she begins with a critical analysis of the concepts of reading prior to the last decade. For over 2000 years, theories of reading were primarily look-say based, she claims, in that they postulated that good reading consisted in getting correct the correspondence between letters and sounds or between written and spoken words.

Around the turn of this century, several theorists offered views that placed more emphasis on the derivation of meaning from text, and cast reading as a process of thinking. However, this view was not well-articulated at first. In the hands of some theorists, even though thinking was seen as part of reading, it was seen as something that was done after comprehension, as if comprehension could occur without thinking. Phillips indicates that current theory sees reading well as a species of thinking well—there can be no principled distinction between the two.

Then, she reviews some empirical research into the self-regulatory thinking strategies used by adults and young readers reading narrative text. The conclusion is that both groups employ similar strategies, although some of the adult strategies appear to be composites of those used by the young readers. In the case of the young readers, she reports that their prior knowledge of the topic they were reading inter- acted with their measured reading proficiency in determining their use of productive reading strategies. Specifically, higher prior knowledge led to greater use of productive strategies only in the presence of read- ing proficiency; but reading proficiency led to greater use of productive strategies regardless of prior knowledge. This evidence suggests that prior knowledge is not a sufficient condition for thinking well while reading.

Phillips draws parallels between her findings with young readers and some of the findings of students solving mathematics problems. She concludes that the parallels are striking. In addition, she presents evidence to show that one of the primary impediments to learning sci- ence is students' lack of the same set of self-regulatory strategies. As such, this chapter represents the sort of empirical study of critical thinking generalizability that Ennis and others have sought.

6 Discovery, Justification, and the Generalizability Question

Sharon Bailin
Simon Fraser University

John McPeck's *Critical Thinking and Education* (1981), in which he argues that critical thinking is not generalizable, has spawned considerable discussion and debate. His principal arguments in defense of this view have been treated extensively by a number of philosophers, for example, Ennis (1989), Govier (1983), Norris (1985), Paul (1985), Siegel (1988), and Weddle (1984), and it is not my intention here to add to the debate regarding these particular arguments. There are, however, two arguments that McPeck offers which have not been examined in any detail. Both arguments attempt to lend support to the nongeneralizability thesis by pointing out the creative, imaginative dimension to critical thinking. I shall argue that there are problems with both these arguments, and, further, that these arguments do not constitute support for the nongeneralizability thesis. I do, however, think that these arguments are important because they point out some common but problematic assumptions about the relationship between critical thinking and creativity. An examination of the problems with these assumptions can help to shed some light on one aspect of the generalizability issue.

MCPECK'S ARGUMENTS

Both of the arguments in question center on approaches to critical thinking that focus on logic. The first concerns the importance of logic for generating hypotheses, theories, or arguments in a problem-solving situation. McPeck argues that critical thinking involves both the generation and the evaluation of theories and arguments, but that logic is of use only for the latter. In support of this claim, he makes reference to the distinction made in philosophy of science between the context of discovery and the context of justification. He describes the distinction thus: "Very briefly, the context of discovery concerns those thought processes that are involved in forming (or generating) a hypothesis, whereas the context of justification is concerned with the acceptability of proofs of hypotheses once they have been put forward" (1981, pp. 14–15). McPeck agrees with the view of the logical positivists that logic is relevant only to the context of justification and is "virtually useless" in the context of discovery. Logic deals with the assessment and justification of hypotheses and theories but not with their generation. Critical thinking is concerned, however, with the generation of theses or arguments as well as with their assessment, and McPeck even suggests that generation is the more important part of the process. Thus, according to McPeck, logic is largely irrelevant to an important aspect of critical thinking. He summarizes his position thus:

> The most serious deficiency of teaching logic as a surrogate for critical thinking, then, is its virtual impotency in helping one to construct alternatives and possible solutions for oneself....One might object that logic is useful in helping us to solve problems because it enables us to eliminate incorrect hypotheses or poor solutions, thus bringing us closer to a solution. I would not deny this. But logic cannot initiate or propose hypotheses (or putative solutions); the problem-solver must construct them for himself. (1981, p. 16)

The second of the arguments which is of interest here concerns the inefficacy of logic even for the justificatory enterprise. McPeck criticizes the methods of logical analysis proposed by informal logicians because they do not and, indeed, cannot provide a definitive method for the evaluation of arguments. He notes, for example, "the absence of definitive criteria for distinguishing fallacious from non-fallacious propositions" (1981, p. 73), and points to the role of judgment and subject-specific knowledge in the evaluation of arguments. Of particular interest is his discussion of Scriven on finding unstated assumptions. Scriven (1976) acknowledges that assumption-hunting is not a mechanical process but requires imagination and creativity on the part of the analyst, and McPeck takes this to show that there is really no clear-cut and definitive method involved in the analysis of arguments. According to McPeck, such an admission acknowledges "that at the heart of argument analysis there is no method and at bottom one is left to one's own devices" (1981, p. 91). He goes on to state: "While Scriven's suggestions rule out some strategies as unreasonable, ineffective or unfair, they cannot be said to have provided a positive method for argument analysis, as promised. Creativity and imagination are the antithesis of method" (1981, p. 91).

CRITIQUE OF THE ARGUMENTS

Let us turn now to an examination of the two arguments described above. The first argument is that logic functions only in the assessment of arguments or theories but is virtually useless in generating ideas, and is thus irrelevant to the context of discovery. This argument is based on the idea that critical thinking is characterized by distinct generative and evaluative phases, and thus that the generation of ideas is nonevaluative and that the evaluative phase has no generative component. This view is highly problematic, however. If the ideas that are generated are valuable, sound, or in McPeck's words, "worth checking or trying out," then it seems plausible to believe that the generation of these ideas is itself constrained in some way by the same criteria and principles that constrain evaluation. If this were not the case, then it would seem more likely that the result would be random generation unconnected with the problem situation rather than thinking that solves a problem. This point seems, in fact, to be emphasized in a statement by Bakan quoted by McPeck. Bakan claims that by the time the investigatory enterprise has reached the state of testing hypotheses, most of the important work has already been done (McPeck, 1981, p. 16). Yet this would seem to make sense only if the initial phase of the investigatory enterprise itself involves some element of evaluation. Otherwise, there would seem no reason to think that what is generated would, in fact, be important. There would be no reason to think that the ideas generated would be related to the problem situation or provide potentially viable solutions.

This idea that the very generation of ideas is itself constrained by criteria of evaluation has been supported by studies of cognitive processes. Perkins (1981), for example, has studied individuals engaged in creative activities and his results indicate that there is a considerable degree of evaluation which takes place in the very generation of successful ideas. As one example, in his study of poets composing poetry, the best poets did not generate large numbers of possible words and then choose among them. Rather, they were able immediately to come up with the words that were aesthetically appropriate in the particular context. Perkins explains this in terms of the way we perform mental searches, citing our ability to search simultaneously according to multiple criteria. It might be objected here that this is not an example of evaluation involved in the process of generation but rather of the generative and evaluative phases taking place so quickly that they are virtually indistinguishable. But if this were the case, then there would seem to be very little ground for claiming that there are really two distinct phases going on in the actual process.

Given the implausibility of the view that the generation of successful ideas is unconstrained by critical criteria, the question arises as to why such a view is widely held. I think that the answer rests on another belief about the generation of ideas and about the nature of creativity more generally, namely that created products exhibit a radical discontinuity with the traditions out of which they develop. According to this sort of view, logic and the principles and procedures of specific disciplines keep one locked into the prevailing mode of operating. On the other hand, the generation of new ideas requires the defying of logic and the ignoring of disciplinary knowledge and method. This is the type of view that grounds de Bono's distinction between vertical and lateral thinking (1970), a distinction to which McPeck makes reference. Vertical thinking is traditional, sequential, logical thinking, whereas lateral thinking is "low-probability, sideways thinking," which violates logic in order to generate new ideas.

Such a view of the nature of creativity is, as I have argued elsewhere (Bailin, 1991), completely untenable. An analysis of creative achievement in all fields demonstrates considerable continuity between created products and their antecedents. Created products have their roots in the problems and paradigms of existing traditions, and conform to a considerable degree to their principles, procedures, and rules. Indeed, this must be the case in order for domains to retain some coherence and in order for departures to have some significance. If creative achievement does exhibit this type of continuity, then there do not seem to be any grounds for believing that the rules, methods, and indeed logic, of the previous framework must be violated in order to innovate. Moreover, the principles and procedures of the disciplines include procedures for the criticism of existing disciplinary beliefs and practices, and so the generation of new ideas does not require defying logic or ignoring disciplinary knowledge and method.

I have been arguing, then, that the generation of successful ideas is itself constrained by critical criteria. What is the nature of these constraints? McPeck at times appears to acknowledge that there are constraints that govern the generation of ideas, but he maintains that these constraints are discipline-specific and content-dependent, rather than general and logical. This is clear in the following claim: "The ingredient that renders any putative solution plausible in the first place is not logic but knowledge and information from within the field or problem area" (1981, p. 16). Such an acknowledgement is evident, as well, in the following criticism which he levels at de Bono's notion of lateral thinking: "Without some kind of content-dependent guidelines, lateral thinking could produce an infinitely large collection of literal nonsense" (1981, p. 21). If one views the generation of ideas as entirely unconstrained and nonevaluative, then it would seem to follow that logic would be inefficacious in generating ideas. But if one acknowledges that generation is itself constrained by evaluative criteria, then it is difficult to see on what basis one would rule out logic as a constraint. Indeed, one could add a companion statement to McPeck's statement above to the effect that without some kind of general, logical guidelines, lateral thinking could produce an infinitely large collection of literal nonsense.

If the constraints operating in the generation of ideas are those that govern assessment, then the question at issue reduces to whether logic constrains the assessment of ideas, theories, and hypotheses. This is an issue which has been debated extensively by others and so I shall simply register my agreement with those, such as Govier (1983) and Siegel (1988), who have argued that logic clearly does constrain the assessment of theories to some extent, and that even McPeck admits this at times. The crucial issue concerns the relative roles of these general logical principles, and subject-specific knowledge and criteria in actual critical thinking. I am inclined to believe, with McPeck, that the latter play an extremely important role. I would maintain, however, that this particular argument of McPeck's does not give us any reason for ruling out logic from the process of generating ideas, and thus does not provide support for the nongeneralizability thesis.

I would argue, then, that both general logical principles and subject-specific criteria constrain the generation of successful ideas and so are relevant to discovery. But a further problem which McPeck seems to be pointing to centers on the fact that logic by itself cannot generate hypotheses or theories. The problem solver has to do this himself or herself. There is no logic of discovery, and this seems to strike McPeck as a shortcoming of logic. This is not, however, an attribute of logic that is peculiar to the generation of ideas, for there is an exactly parallel argument which can be made with respect to evaluation—namely that logic by itself cannot evaluate arguments and that the argument assessor has to do this himself or herself. This is, in fact, the central point of the second argument under consideration, an argument to which I shall now turn.

The second argument concerns the inefficacy of logic because it cannot provide a definitive method for assessing arguments. McPeck demonstrates the variability which is possible in the evaluation of arguments, pointing out, for example, that there are no definitive criteria for determining whether a fallacy has been committed, that there is judgment involved in determining what is going to count as an assumption, and that background knowledge will play a role in how an argument is assessed. He agrees with Scriven that critical thinking involves creativity and imagination, but asserts that these are the antithesis of method.

In claiming that argument criticism is not algorithmic but requires judgment and creativity, I believe that McPeck is absolutely correct, and this is a point which I have argued in detail elsewhere (Bailin, 1990). The first task in assessing an argument is to understand what the argument says, but this is often far from simple and straightforward. Texts are always and necessarily incomplete and the assessor must construct an interpretation guided by textual information and background knowledge (see, for example, Phillips, this volume). McPeck has duly outlined the problems and possible variations involved in supplying missing premises and unstated assumptions. The actual process of evaluation also requires judgment and exhibits this imaginative dimension. And this is not surprising given that the types of arguments that are of interest are generally not deductive, but rather exhibit a structure in which, to quote Blair and Johnson, the fit between premises and conclusion is not so tight as to rule out other conclusions (1987, p. 42). Thus it would be impossible to totally formalize the procedures for evaluating arguments, to create algorithms for assessment. This can be seen with respect to detecting fallacies, as McPeck points out. It is fallacious to appeal to a premise that is irrelevant to the conclusions of an argument, yet relevance is not always easily determined. Although there are guides to appropriate considerations, they cannot lead infallibly to judgments regarding relevance. The situation is similar with respect to sufficiency, there being no reliable method for determining how much evidence is sufficient in any particular case. Determining the acceptability of premises is likewise an imprecise enterprise, a judgment with respect to acceptability requiring consideration of the audience as well as the purposes of the argument (Johnson & Blair, 1983).

It can be seen, then, that logic cannot provide algorithms for the assessment of arguments and that there is judgment and creative imagination involved in this process, just as McPeck claims. This is, however, a point that is acknowledged by many Informal Logic theorists (for example, Scriven, 1976; Johnson & Blair, 1983). The important question here is what can be concluded from this point. One can conclude that general, logical principles do not, except in the case of formal deductive arguments, uniquely and unambiguously determine outcomes. Thus Informal Logic should not be seen as a quasi-mathematical enterprise that involves algorithmic procedures for the correct assessment of arguments. One cannot conclude, however, that there are no general logical principles nor that such principles are useless in assessing arguments. Although logical principles cannot automatically determine assessments, they do provide guidance for assessing. Thus it seems quite misleading to state that because there is no infallible method of argument analysis, one is ultimately left to one's own devices. Certainly one must use one's judgment, but one is not free to assess an argument in any way one chooses. One's assessment is constrained by logical principles. Creativity and imagination are the antithesis of method only if method is seen as consisting in an algorithmic procedure for automatically calculating outcomes. Creativity and imagination are not the antithesis of logic, principles, guidelines, or constraints.

Another point which needs to be made here is that McPeck's argument with respect to the inefficacy of logic could be applied just as well to subject-specific principles and criteria. The latter cannot, by themselves, evaluate arguments; the argument assessor has to do this himself or herself. Such principles and criteria do not, in general, uniquely and unambiguously determine outcomes nor provide infallible methods for assessing claims and arguments in their area. If they did, there would be no debate or disagreement within disciplines, but these certainly exist. Recent work in philosophy of science has revealed many examples in the scientific realm (Kuhn, 1970). The same type of variability, judgment, and imagination that are evident with respect to general logical principles are evident with respect to discipline-specific knowledge and criteria as well. Argument criticism can best be seen, then, as having a generative, imaginative component but constrained by critical criteria, both of a general logical and a subject-specific nature.

CONTEXTS OF DISCOVERY AND JUSTIFICATION

I have argued thus far that there is good reason to think that the generation of successful ideas, hypotheses, and theories is constrained by the criteria and principles that govern the assessment of them and, moreover, that this assessment itself has a generative dimension. If this is the case, then it would seem to call into question the distinction between the context of discovery and the context of justification, at least as characterized by McPeck and others. If this distinction is taken to mean that there is a generative phase of discovery in which logic and evaluation are irrelevant, and a distinct, evaluative phase that involves an algorithmic method of assessment, then the distinction is ill-founded. I would argue, however, that this is not how the distinction ought to be interpreted. The point of the distinction, at least as originally formulated by Reichenbach (1938), is a conceptual one—namely that the mode of origin of an idea or theory is not relevant to its validity. Whether an idea occurs to an individual in a dream, stems from infantile fantasies, or is a result of painstaking analysis is irrelevant to the justification of the idea. The psychological processes of discovery, which make up the context of discovery, are not relevant to the epistemological justification of a theory, which is what is referred to by the context of justification.

It is a mistake, however, to take the distinction as being descriptive of the actual process of creation or discovery. The distinction is not intended to give psychological accounts of discovery and assessment, but rather to distinguish between psychology and epistemology. The distinction does not mark a symmetrical relationship. Reichenbach is not distinguishing between the thought processes involved in generating hypotheses and the thought processes involved in evaluating proofs. Rather, he is distinguishing between thought processes and epistemological criteria. The intention is to locate rationality in principles of justification and to rule out psychological and sociological factors from consideration in the assessment of theories. The intention is not to give a psychological account of discovery that excludes logic (Scheffler, 1982). Siegel (1980) makes the point thus:

> Reichenbach is not concerned to demonstrate anything like a "logical gulf" between the two contexts; nor is he concerned to demonstrate any irrelevance of principles of justification to discovery. For example, it is perfectly compatible with Reichenbach's position that a scientist who keeps certain principles of justification in mind will be aided, by doing so, in the attempt at discovery. In this sense, justification *is* relevant to discovery. It is only the converse—that discovery can be relevant to justification—that Reichenbach is concerned to deny. (p. 300)

The discovery-justification distinction is, then, a conceptual one that points out that how an idea comes to be is of no philosophical interest with respect to the justification of that idea. Thus, it is logically possible that a successful unified field theory could suddenly arrive, full blown, in the mind of someone who had no knowledge of physics. But for those of us interested in critical thinking, how an idea comes to be, particularly a good idea, is of great interest. And the preceding scenario, although logically possible, is highly improbable (Bailin & Siegel, 1987). I have been arguing throughout that the most plausible way to view critical thinking is not in terms of a nonevaluative phase involving the generation of ideas and an evaluative phase that is mechanical and definitive, but rather in terms of a process that involves an intimate interplay of generation and evaluation.

One reason for the hold of the distinct phase picture might be that acts of critical thinking or discovery are often viewed in isolation. Once removed from the intellectual context in which they developed, the origin of ideas may appear mysterious or inexplicable. But once viewed in the context of the history of thought and the development of the views of the individual, such ideas can be seen to be part of an ongoing problem-solving enterprise in which views develop and are modified over time, and solutions to some problems give rise to new problems. Hattiangadi (1980) argues, in fact, that pure contexts of discovery are almost impossible to find and that what is evident, instead, are nested contexts of justification.

IMPLICATIONS FOR GENERALIZABILITY

Thus far, I have concentrated on two specific arguments presented by McPeck. I believe, however, that the assumptions that underpin these arguments are implicit in many theoretical accounts, and in addition are often held explicitly by students. In the latter case, they can give rise to beliefs that can present barriers to critical thinking. One such belief is that the generation of ideas is totally unconstrained, and that, consequently, in order to have innovative ideas or to be creative, one has to abandon logic and disciplinary standards. Creativity, according to this belief, has nothing to do with critical thinking. A second belief is that critical thinking involves methods for arriving at correct assessments. Such a belief can have the effect of reinforcing the type of traditional authority-oriented and right-answer-oriented education, which critical thinking instruction expressly aims at countering, and may also reinforce the desire for certainty, which is the antithesis of the open-mindedness characteristic of critical thinking. Moreover, if students discover that this type of certainty is not possible, then this may reinforce a relativistic attitude, a belief that assessment really is just a matter of opinion after all.

These mistakes are complementary and rest on faulty epistemological understanding. They demonstrate a lack of appreciation of the nature of knowledge development and a consequent failure to appreciate the nature of the critical enterprise. It is important, then, that students recognize that critical thinking involves a joint and integrated process of generation and evaluation, the generation constrained by critical standards and the evaluation involving a generative dimension. Some activities may emphasize more the one or the other, for example, critiquing an argument emphasizes evaluation whereas coming up with a new theory emphasizes generation. Nonetheless, evaluating an argument involves generation in all the ways previously described, as well as the assessment of alternative arguments and ultimately the generation of one's own view based on one's assessments. And coming up with a new theory involves an assessment of the arguments for prevailing and alternative theories.

Most current conceptions of critical thinking focus on skills, abilities, dispositions, and techniques. While I am not here disputing the importance of any of these elements, what I do want to argue is that they are insufficient. The additional element that is needed, in whatever context critical thinking occurs, is the type of epistemological understanding which has been described above. Students need to understand the process by which knowledge is developed and assessed. It is crucial for them to understand the structure of inquiry that operates through a dynamic interplay of generation and constraint, and to understand that this type of inquiry is characteristic of critical thinking in all disciplines. This type of understanding is not an adjunct to learning a discipline but is central to what it means to learn a discipline and is central to the development of critical thinking.

REFERENCES

Bailin, S. (1991). *Achieving extraordinary ends: An essay on creativity.* Norwood, NJ: Ablex.

Bailin, S. (1990). Argument criticism as creative. In R. Trapp & J. Schuetz (Eds.), *Per-

spectives on argumentation: Essays in honor of Wayne Brockriede (pp. 232–240). Waveland Press.

Bailin, S., & Siegel, H. (1987). Discovery, creativity and methodological rule-breaking. Paper presented at VIII International Congress of Logic, Methodology and Philosophy of Science, Moscow.

Blair, J. A., & Johnson, R. (1987). Argumentation as dialectical. *Argumentation, 1*(1), 41–56.

de Bono, E. (1970). *Lateral thinking.* London: Ward Lock Educational.

Ennis, R. H. (1989). Critical thinking and subject specificity: Clarification and needed research. *Educational Researcher, 18*(3), 4–10.

Govier, T. (1983). Review of *Critical thinking and education. Dialogue, 22,* 170–175.

Hattiangadi, J. (1980). The vanishing context of discovery. In T. Nickels (Ed.), *Scientific discovery, logic and rationality,* (pp. 257–265). Dordrecht: Reidel.

Johnson, R., & Blair, J. A. (1983). *Logical self-defense.* Toronto: McGraw-Hill Ryerson.

Kuhn, T. (1970). *The structure of scientific revolutions.* Chicago: University of Chicago Press.

McPeck, J. (1981). *Critical thinking and education.* Oxford: Martin Robertson.

Norris, S. P. (1985). The choice of standard conditions in defining critical thinking competence. *Educational Theory, 35*(1), 97–107.

Paul, R. (1985). McPeck's mistakes. *Informal Logic, 7*(1), 35–43.

Perkins, D. (1981). *The mind's best work.* Cambridge, MA: Harvard University Press.

Reichenbach, H. (1938). *Experience and prediction.* Chicago: University of Chicago Press.

Scheffler, I. (1982). *Science and subjectivity.* Indianapolis: Hackett.

Scriven, M. (1976). *Reasoning.* New York: McGraw-Hill.

Siegel, H. (1980). Justification, discovery and the naturalizing of epistemology. *Philosophy of Science, 47,* 297–321.

Siegel, H. (1988). *Educating reason: Rationality, critical thinking and education.* New York: Routledge.

Weddle, P. (1984). *Critical thinking and education* by John McPeck. *Informal Logic, 6*(2), 23–25.

7 The Generalizability of Critical Thinking Skills, Dispositions, and Epistemology

Harvey Siegel
University of Miami

Whether or not critical thinking is generalizable depends, of course, on what critical thinking is. There are many extant accounts of critical thinking that differ from one another in a variety of ways. However, most of the main accounts, including those of Ennis, Paul, McPeck, and Lipman, agree at least to this extent: critical thinking has (at least) two central components: a *reason assessment* component, which involves abilities and skills relevant to the proper understanding and assessment of reasons, claims, and arguments; and a *critical spirit* component, which is understood as a complex of dispositions, attitudes, habits of mind, and character traits (Lipman, 1988; Siegel, 1988a). Assuming that these two are indeed central components of critical thinking, the question concerning the generalizability of critical thinking can be usefully broken down into two separate and more manageable questions concerning the generalizability of each of the two components. Most discussion of the generalizability of critical thinking has concerned the reason assessment component; advocates and opponents of generalizability have debated whether the skills and criteria that constitute part of the reason assessment component are subject specific, or, rather, are subject neutral and capable of application across specific subjects or domains. There has been very little discussion of the generalizability of other dimensions of the reason assessment component. There has also been very little discussion of the generalizability of the critical spirit component. Both of these last two issues deserve more attention than they have received.

In what follows, I hope to do three things. First, I will address the much discussed question concerning the generalizability of the skills and criteria that constitute an important part of the reason assessment component of critical thinking. Second, I will address the infrequently discussed question concerning the generalizability of other aspects of the reason assessment component. Third, I will address the infrequently discussed question concerning the generalizability of the critical spirit component of critical thinking. I will argue that all three questions should be answered in ways that provide comfort to the "generalists": those who hold that critical thinking is at least in some important respects generalizable. In the first section, I will argue that the skills and criteria that constitute a portion of the reason assessment component are partly generalizable. On this question I think that the generalists and the "specifists" are both importantly right. In the second section, I will argue that another aspect of the reason assessment component—the *epistemology underlying critical thinking*—is fully generalizable. In the third section, I will argue that the critical spirit is also fully generalizable. In so arguing, I hope both to clarify further the extant debate concerning the generalizability of the skills of reason assessment, and also to point to two other important aspects of critical thinking that are generalizable. In so doing, I hope to broaden the focus of the initial question concerning the generalizability of critical thinking.

Before beginning the substantive discussion, I wish first to note an ambiguity which plagues much of the extant discussion concerning the generalizability of critical thinking. Principles and criteria of reason assessment may or may not be generalizable in the theoretical sense that they are *applicable* across a wide range of cases or domains. Alternatively, they may or may not be generalizable in the practical sense that it is *pedagogically useful* to teach them, or expect them to transfer, across a wide portion of the curriculum. These issues are obviously distinct: the practical question concerning how we best teach for critical thinking is different from the abstract, theoretical question concerning the nature and applicability of the skills and criteria of reason assessment. McPeck and other specifists deny generalizability in both senses; Ennis and other generalists endorse generalizability in both senses. But McPeck's arguments against generalizability are typically addressed to the theoretical issue, while Ennis's arguments are typically addressed to the practical, pedagogical one. Ennis's advocacy of the "mixed" approach (Ennis, 1989) clearly is addressed to the practical, pedagogical question of how best to teach for critical thinking. This accounts, I think, for some of the cross-purposes, speaking-past-one-another character of the generalizability debate. In what follows, my arguments for generalizability are aimed at the theoretical issue of applicability; I do not here address the pedagogical issue, though I agree with Ennis about it in the main. But it is important to realize that even if principles of critical thinking are *general* in the sense that they are, theoretically, broadly applicable, it does not follow that they enjoy a high degree of transfer or are, pedagogically, usefully *generalizable* (see Johnson, this volume).

THE GENERALIZABILITY OF THE SKILLS
AND CRITERIA OF REASON ASSESSMENT

Rather than rehash old discussions, I will concentrate in this section on Robert Ennis's (Ennis, 1989, this volume) recent discussion of this issue. Ennis's paper is enormously helpful, and, as advertised, it provides important clarification of several matters central to the generalizability issue. Since I agree with most of Ennis's discussion, I will describe only briefly his clarificatory achievements. Where we disagree, I will argue that the situation is even more rosy for the generalists than Ennis supposes.

Ennis points out that "subject" is ambiguous in that it can mean either "topic" or "school subject"; while it is true that critical thinking is always thinking about some topic, it is false that it is always about some school subject. Noting this ambiguity helps to block the erroneous inference: critical thinking always concerns some subject (topic); therefore teaching for critical thinking must take place in the context of teaching some (school) subject. Ennis also points to the vagueness of the terms "domain," "field," and "subject," and notes that arguments for the subject specificity of critical thinking often founder on this vagueness. Epistemological subject specificity—the idea that different fields utilize different, incompatible criteria for the determination of the goodness of reasons, so that what counts as a good reason in one field does not so count in another, and therefore that principles and skills of reason assessment must differ from field to field and so be taught in the context of the subject matter of each field—fails because of the vagueness of "field." If "field" is construed broadly—for example, if science is a field—then it turns out that the field does not have principles of reason assessment unique to itself, since what counts as a good reason in science (for example, that the putative reason in question provides the best explanation of the phenomenon under consideration; or that it significantly increases the probability of the hypothesis being considered) often counts as a good reason both in other fields and in countless ordinary, everyday life contexts. Moreover, if "field" is construed broadly in this way, principles of reason assessment will differ across various subregions of the field. For example, a causal explanation may constitute a good reason in biology, but not in quantum mechanics. In these cases, reasons and principles of reason assessment are not field specific, and the thesis of epistemological subject specificity is false.

On the other hand, if "field" is construed narrowly, such that virtually every topic of inquiry is a field unto itself (for example, the field of radio design, or radio tuning, or radio turning off/on, or radio turning off, or radio turning off for a single sort of radio), then the thesis of epistemological subject specificity is only trivially true, since a reason in one field—for example, turning off my Zenith portable radio because leaving it on might wake the baby—fails to be an equally powerful reason in the alternative field in which it is your Radio Shack tabletop model radio that needs to be turned off, only because of a willful neglect of common circumstances which make for the existence of good reasons across these artificially disparate fields. Either way we interpret "field," then, the thesis of epistemological subject specificity—the claim that "within different fields, different sorts of reasons can (and do) count as good reasons" (McPeck, 1981, p. 28)—does not survive critical scrutiny.

Ennis (1989, p. 8) agrees with McPeck that reasons and principles of reason assessment vary from field to field, although, unlike McPeck, he does not infer from this variation that critical thinking instruction should be of the "immersion" approach only. In addition, Ennis (1989, p. 8) notes the existence and importance of "interfield commonalities," and rightly calls for research concerning the extent of such critical thinking commonalities. It is on the point of interfield variation, however, that Ennis and I disagree. He regards this principle of interfield variation as plausible on the following grounds:

> (a) Mathematics has different criteria for good reasons from most other fields, because mathematics accepts only deductive proof, whereas most fields do not even seek it for the establishment of a final conclusion; (b) in the social sciences, statistical significance is an important consideration, whereas in many branches of physics it is largely ignored; (c) in the arts, some subjectivity is usually acceptable, whereas in the sciences, it is usually shunned. (Ennis 1989, p. 8)

Here Ennis fails to pay sufficient heed to his own earlier arguments concerning the vagueness of "field." For example, a growing portion of mathematics accepts nondeductive proof in the form of brute-force computer programs that establish theorems by systematically examining enormous numbers of possible cases. In such cases we rely on inductive evidence that the computer functioned as planned, because the deductive validity of the program results is not verifiable by human scrutiny—we rely, in effect, on inductive evidence concerning one computer-generated result proffered by another. Mathematicians have come to rely more and more on nondeductive reasons for accepting theorems as "proved." The famous computer proof of the Four Color Map Theorem is only one of many examples of such nondeductive proof (Tymoczko, 1979). Contrary to Ennis's suggestion, reasons do not have to meet a single criterion—namely, that of deductively guaranteeing that for which they are reasons—in order to count as good reasons in mathematics. Mathematics is not a unitary field across which the same principles of reason assessment hold.[1]

Similarly, statistical significance is an important consideration in some but not all branches of the social sciences. It is relatively unimportant, for example, in archaeology, in some branches of economics, and in some branches of sociology. The social sciences, too, fail to constitute a field across which specific principles of reason assessment univocally hold. Similar remarks could be made concerning the arts.

The point is not that these three areas are too large and varied to be properly considered as fields; for, even across such large fields as these, certain criteria for the constitution of good reasons are shared. For example, both in branches of mathematics (number theory, logic, proof theory, and so forth) and in branches of the social sciences (for example, economics and portions of sociology) good reasons must deductively establish their conclusions; in some social sciences and areas of physics and engineering—and even in some approaches to literary analysis—some specific level of statistical significance is an important criterion which putative reasons must meet to be good. Moreover, in ordinary life contexts, both of these criteria of reason assessment might be applied appropriately. The point, rather, is that criteria of reason assessment are complex and varied, and do not line up in any neat way with "fields," however the latter are individuated. The thesis of "interfield" variation—that is, the thesis that certain criteria of reason assessment apply only within or across certain well-defined "fields," but that such criteria necessarily differ across fields—is false. Criteria of reason assessment are much more complicated than the thesis of interfield variation suggests. Some such criteria are very narrow in application; others are very broad and apply in virtually any context or field.

This point deserves additional comment. Ennis holds that "[e]pistemological subject specificity notes that there are significant interfield differences in what constitutes a good reason" (Ennis, 1989, p. 9). Even if this were true— that is, even if it were true that differences in criteria of reason assessment varied systematically across fields—it would be a mistake to regard such a fact as establishing, as specifists such as McPeck (1981) and Toulmin (1958) do, that different fields have *their own epistemologies*. It should rather be taken as a sign that different sorts of claims require different sorts of evidence for their establishment, but that these differences do not vary systematically across fields. To promote such differences into the status of alternative epistemologies is to suggest systematic variation where there is none, to ignore the crucial point that what varies is what it takes to establish claims of various sorts, and to ignore the obvious self-reflexive difficulty of specifying by what criteria this claim can be established and to what field such criteria would belong.

Let us grant the undeniable: it takes *this* sort of evidence to establish *this* sort of claim, and *that* sort of evidence to establish *that* sort of claim.[2] Nevertheless, to say that we therefore have *two different epistemologies* at work in such situations is to fail to distinguish between different epistemologies and different criteria of reason assessment. When we have two different criteria of reason assessment, which we utilize to establish two different sorts of claims, we nevertheless have only one epistemology. In both cases, a good reason is that which warrants a conclusion. The *epistemology* across these alternative and varied criteria of reason assessment is the same.

Consider cases. My fuel gauge reading "E" (for empty) provides good reason for thinking that I am out of gas; the illuminated "idiot light" on my dashboard provides good reason for thinking that my door is ajar or my battery dead. This doesn't mean that fuel tanks and batteries have different epistemologies. The very same sorts of reasons provide warrant in all sorts of different contexts (for example, gauge readings of all sorts); standards of reason assessment stretch beyond fields, whether construed as broadly as science or as narrowly as idiot lights. Moreover, differences in appropriate criteria of reason assessment do not translate into different epistemologies. Across alternative criteria of reason assessment is a unitary epistemology: reasons are good reasons if (and only if) they afford warrant to the claims or propositions for which they are reasons. Alternative criteria come into play according to the sort of claim under consideration, but they do so under the auspices of a common epistemology. Epistemology involves the study of the determination of the goodness of reasons. There are all sorts of good reasons—causal, inductive, explanatory, purposive, deductive, and so forth—but they all share this crucial epistemic feature: they provide warrant for that for which they are reasons.

One might think that the preceding argument amounts to little more than a turf war over the word "epistemology." But it is not. Rather, it underlines two points that are central to the debate concerning the generalizability of critical thinking. First, while there are indeed different criteria of reason assessment by which we evaluate the power, convicting force, and goodness of reasons, those criteria do not vary in any systematic way with fields, however that latter notion is construed. All these alternative criteria—from "does the reason deductively establish the conclusion?" to "does the proposed explanation provide the best explanation of the phenomenon in question?"; from "is this a representative sample?" to "is this the relevant sort of idiot light, such that its being illuminated indicates such-and-so?"—apply across a wide variety of school subject and/or ordinary life contexts. Second, we are entitled to regard these various criteria as appropriate criteria of reason assessment, and to appeal to them in order to establish or determine the goodness of putative reasons, only because they are sanctioned by a common epistemology: a theoretical understanding of the nature of reasons, according to which putative criteria are recognizable as appropriate criteria of reason assessment. To fail to acknowledge that even narrow, field- or context-relative criteria of reason assessment depend upon a common epistemology in order to count as appropriate criteria of reason assessment, is to ignore the possibility that putative reasons may only mistakenly be regarded as warrant-conferring (Siegel, in press). To appeal to epistemological subject specificity in order to argue against the generalizability of critical thinking is to ignore the distinction between putative principles of reason assessment and the overarching epistemology that sanctions those principles as legitimate. It is to grant to fields the power to legislate the goodness of reasons within their own domains which they do not by themselves possess. A field may be the *partial* arbiter of the goodness of reasons within its domain, but it is not, and cannot be, the *sole* arbiter (Siegel, 1988a, pp. 36–37). To regard it as such is to reduce epistemology to a rubber stamp subject (see Siegel, 1984, pp. 668–669) with no critical leverage or normative force of its own; it is to deny the very possibility that a field could be mistaken in regarding a putative criterion as legitimate within its domain.

What are the ramifications of all this for the generalizability of critical thinking? The ramifications are favorable, on balance, for the generalist. The specifist's argument that critical thinking is not generalizable because of epistemological subject specificity fails: neither the skills nor the criteria of reason assessment line up neatly according to fields, however broadly or narrowly these are defined. Moreover, the plethora of criteria of reason assessment— though varied in character, and ranging from very narrow to quite broad—are united by an underlying epistemology, which sanctions these criteria as legitimate. With all this, the generalist should be pleased.

I have not shown, however, that there are no skills or criteria of reason assessment that are narrow, or subject specific. There remains room to acknowledge the specifist's point, and to allow that some skills and criteria of reason assessment are narrow and specific. In this sense, both the generalist and the specifist are right, a point that Moshman (1990) and Lipman (1988, p. 37) have also suggested. Which criteria are specific, or best taught in the context of a school subject, I take to be an open question; I join Ennis in calling for empirical research into these matters. But I think that Ennis grants the specifists too much, in granting plausibility to epistemological subject specificity. I hope to have strengthened Ennis's case against the specifist—I endorse his arguments against conceptual subject specificity, and I hope to have provided reason for being more skeptical of epistemological subject specificity than he apparently is—and to that extent, to have strengthened the case for the generalizability of a significant portion of the reason assessment component of critical thinking.[3]

THE GENERALIZABILITY OF THE EPISTEMOLOGY UNDERLYING CRITICAL THINKING

I have been arguing against epistemological subject specificity, claiming mainly that skills and criteria of reason assessment do not, in general, function only within the context of specific subjects, fields, or domains. In making this argument, I have made reference to the unitary epistemology that I claim underlies and sanctions our regarding criteria of all sorts as appropriate criteria of reason assessment. I wish now to deepen the discussion of this underlying epistemology. I want to claim that this epistemology is an important part of the reason assessment component of critical thinking, and that it is fully generalizable. If I can make good on this claim, I will have strengthened further the generalist's position.

What is the epistemology underlying critical thinking? There is more to be said in answer to this question than I can say here (see Siegel, 1989). Briefly, the answer is this: as long as there is a reason assessment component to critical thinking, so that critical thinking is conceived as thinking that is appropriately guided by reasons, then critical thinking must be understood as requiring an epistemology which does justice to the central notions of reasons and rationality. Such an epistemology must, first, maintain a distinction between rational justification and truth, and hold that the critical thinker might justifiably believe that which is false, and unjustifiably believe that which is true. In other words, the epistemology underlying critical thinking must maintain a *radically nonepistemic* conception of truth, and hold that truth is independent of rational justification. The theory of critical thinking, moreover, must regard critical thinking as aiming at rational justification rather than truth. Second, it must reject relativism, and hold that the goodness of reasons and the rationality/justifiability of particular beliefs is *absolute* in that it does not vary across persons, times, cultures, and so on, but rather depends only on relevant criteria of reason assessment and the evidence for those beliefs at hand. Finally, the epistemology underlying critical thinking must recognize (despite their independence, just noted) the following connection between truth and rational justification: the *upshot* of rational justification is a *prima facie* case for truth; rational justification is a *fallible* indicator of truth.

The epistemology underlying critical thinking thus involves particular, and in some circles contentious, positions regarding reasons, criteria of reason assessment, rationality, rational justification, and truth. This epistemology requires an *absolutism* with respect to reasons and justification, a *radically nonepistemic* conception of truth, and an embrace of *fallibilism*. There is obviously much more to be said concerning all these points. However, I believe I have elsewhere (Siegel, 1988a, 1989) secured the case for my claim that this complex of epistemological theses is required for a coherent conception of critical thinking, at least if critical thinking is to be regarded as a defensible educational ideal.

It should be clear that this epistemology is best seen as constituting part of the reason assessment component of critical thinking, since it underwrites our understanding of the proper assessment of reasons and our conception of reasons, rationality, and rational justification. It is a dimension of the reason assessment component of critical thinking which has nevertheless been neglected in most discussion of the generalizability of critical thinking, for that discussion has centered on the subject specificity of particular skills and principles of reason assessment and has mainly ignored the epistemology underlying those principles. We have before us, then, a portion of the reason assessment component of critical thinking that is distinct from the portion discussed in the first section concerning the putative subject specificity of particular skills, principles, and criteria of reason assessment. We must therefore consider whether or not this newly introduced part of the reason-assessment component, the part I have been calling "the epistemology underlying critical thinking," is generalizable.

Is the epistemology underlying critical thinking generalizable? Yes—it is a fully generalizable part of the reason assessment component of critical thinking. This epistemology provides the theoretical underpinning of our understanding of the principles and criteria of reason assessment to which we appeal when thinking critically. It is shared throughout the domains or fields in which critical thinkers assess reasons; it underlies our best conception of what critical thinking is. Indeed, this epistemology is presupposed by that conception of critical thinking; without it, we can make no coherent sense of critical thinking as an educational ideal concerning the proper assessment of reasons. The epistemology underlying critical thinking constitutes a part of the reason assessment component of critical thinking which is fully generalizable, a view that appears related to Lipman's (1988, pp. 82–83, 150; Siegel, 1988b). This, I take it, is good news for the generalist.

THE GENERALIZABILITY OF THE CRITICAL SPIRIT

There is yet a further component of critical thinking—the critical spirit—which has been by and large ignored in recent discussion of the generalizability of critical thinking. That it has been so ignored is surprising, given the near unanimity of opinion in the theoretical literature concerning the centrality to critical thinking of the critical spirit (Siegel, 1988a, Ch. 1; Lipman, 1988, p. 63).

I take the critical spirit to be a complex of dispositions, attitudes, habits of mind, and character traits. It includes: dispositions, for example the dispositions to seek reasons and evidence in making judgments and to evaluate such reasons carefully in accordance with relevant principles of reason assessment; attitudes, including a respect for the importance of reasoned judgment and for truth, and a rejection of partiality, arbitrariness, special pleading, wishful thinking, and other obstacles to the proper exercise of reason assessment and reasoned judgment; habits of mind consonant with these dispositions and attitudes, such as habits of reason seeking and evaluating, of engaging in due consideration of principles of reason assessment, of subjecting proffered reasons to critical scrutiny, and of engaging in the fairminded and nonself-interested consideration of such reasons; and character traits consonant with all of this. People who possess the critical spirit *value* good reasoning, and are disposed to believe, judge, and act on its basis. It is this genuine valuing, and the dispositions, attitudes, habits of mind, and character traits which go with it, which constitute the core of the critical spirit (Siegel, 1988a, Ch. 2).

Is the critical spirit, so conceived, generalizable? It clearly is. The valuing of good reasoning and the desire and disposition to exercise reasoned judgment is not restricted to any domain or field; nor does it differ in character or substance from field to field. The dispositions, attitudes, and habits of mind constitutive of the critical spirit apply *generally;* the character traits constitutive of the critical spirit, like all character traits properly so called, are general and not restricted in application. It is only the fact that the debate over generalizability has been conceived as concerning skills and principles of reason assessment, rather than critical thinking more generally, that the generalizability of the critical spirit component of critical thinking has not been apparent. Once the question of the generalizability of this component of critical thinking is raised, however, it is answered in the obvious way: The critical spirit is *fully* generalizable.

CONCLUSION

I have argued that much of critical thinking is generalizable. First, I have joined with Ennis in arguing that epistemological subject specificity fails to secure the specifist's position. While it is true that there are many and varied criteria of reason assessment, some of which apply only to particular sorts of claims (which may but need not occur only within some specific field), there is no systematic alignment of those criteria with particular subjects, fields, or domains, however those notions are defined or their referents individuated. What counts as a good reason for some claim depends not on the field in which the claim is made, but on the type of claim it is and the possible sorts of evidence to which one can legitimately appeal in attempting to establish it. The criteria to which we turn in order to evaluate the strength of the reasons and evidence offered for particular claims are neither bound to nor sanctioned by particular fields. They are not bound to such fields except in special, atypical cases in which the sort of claim being made can be made only in some particular field. Far more typical are criteria that extend across both fields and everyday reasoning: criteria of deductive validity, inductive strength, observational adequacy, explanatory power, and so forth. Nor are specialized criteria of reason assessment sanctioned solely by the fields to which they apply. If they were, there would be no possibility of critical scrutiny concerning the appropriateness of such criteria: each field would in such cases declare certain sorts of reasons to be good, and other sorts to be bad, but there would be no possibility of a field's being mistaken about its own understanding of its criteria of reason assessment. But that such a mistake is not only possible, but actual, is manifest—all we need to do in order to see this is to contemplate important, long-standing, difficult-to-resolve controversies concerning any intrafield debate. The field of philosophy provides endless examples; so do fields as diverse as art criticism, sociology, economics, biology, chemistry, and physics.

McPeck and other specifists are right in pointing out that subject-specific content knowledge is frequently necessary for thinking critically within a subject. But this point adds little to the specifist's case: it is independent of epistemological subject specificity, on which the specifist's position depends and which, we have seen, is dubious; moreover, it is compatible with the generalist's position, and indeed is acknowledged by most generalists (for example, Ennis, 1989).

Moreover, the specifist fails to acknowledge the epistemology underlying critical thinking skills and criteria. Even if it were the case that criteria of reason assessment varied systematically by field, it is nevertheless also the case that the appropriateness of such criteria is determined not solely by the field in which the criteria are operative, but rather by (in addition to intrafield considerations) a more general theoretical understanding of the goodness of reasons, and of related issues concerning truth, fallibilism, rationality, and the like. This general theoretical understanding—the epistemology underlying critical thinking—is central to the coherent conceptualization of critical thinking, and is fully generalizable across the varied subjects, domains, and fields to which critical thinking is relevant.

So too is the critical spirit component of critical thinking. The critical spirit is also fully generalizable across the varied landscape of critical thinking.

I hope, then, to have shed some additional light on the extant controversy concerning the generalizability of critical thinking, a controversy prompted by the argument against generalizability put forward on the basis of the thesis of epistemological subject specificity. This thesis is vague, as Ennis suggests, almost certainly false, as I have argued, and the source of much mischief concerning our understanding of critical thinking and its generalizability. I hope, in addition, to have pointed to two aspects of critical thinking which have been wrongly neglected in the debate concerning generalizability. Both aspects—the epistemology underlying critical thinking, and the critical spirit—are integral to our overall conception of critical thinking. Both are fully generalizable.

While it is true, then, both that certain specialized criteria of reason assessment are restricted to particular fields, and that specialized content knowledge is frequently required in order to think critically, it seems nevertheless to be the case that critical thinking is overwhelmingly generalizable.

NOTES

1. For further discussion of alternative criteria of proof in mathematics and the modification of such criteria, see Kitcher (1983).

2. Even here we must be careful, for claims—if understood as propositions—can be variously described, and in ways that make alternative sorts of considerations relevant to their establishment. That is, what evidence is relevant to the establishment of a claim is at least sometimes dependent on how the claim is individuated.

` 3. *Strong* epistemological subject specificity, the view that it is *logically necessary* that different fields have their own criteria for the constitution and evaluation of reasons (which is very close to what Ennis calls *conceptual* subject specificity and which is apparently endorsed by Toulmin and at least in some passages by McPeck), is false. It falls both to Ennis's argument against conceptual subject specificity and to those made above. *Medium* epistemological subject specificity, the view that it is *contingently* true that fields have their own criteria for the constitution and evaluation of reasons, is also false, and falls to the arguments offered above. *Weak* epistemological subject specificity holds that, as a contingent matter, *some* criteria of reason assessment are unique to fields. This version of epistemological subject specificity is true, and is acknowledged above. It is, however, a weak enough version of epistemological subject specificity that is creates no difficulty for the generalist.

REFERENCES

Ennis, R. H. (1989). Critical thinking and subject specificity: Clarification and needed research, *Educational Researcher, 18*(3), 4–10.

Kitcher, P. (1983). *The nature of mathematical knowledge.* New York: Oxford University Press.

Lipman, M. (1988). *Philosophy goes to school.* Philadelphia: Temple University Press.

McPeck, J. (1981). *Critical thinking and education.* New York: St. Martin's.

Moshman, D. (1990). Rationality as a goal of education, *Educational Psychology Review, 2,* 335–364.

Siegel, H. (1984). Empirical psychology, naturalized epistemology, and first philosophy, *Philosophy of Science, 51,* 667–676.

Siegel, H. (1988a). *Educating reason: Rationality, critical thinking, and education.* London: Routledge.

Siegel, H. (1988b). Epistemology and philosophy for children, *Analytic Teaching, 8*(2), 32–42.

Siegel, H. (1989). Epistemology, critical thinking, and critical thinking pedagogy, *Argumentation, 3,* 127–140.

Siegel, H. (in press). Justification by balance, *Philosophy and Phenomenological Research.*

Toulmin, S. E. (1958). *The uses of argument.* Cambridge: Cambridge University Press.

Tymoczko, T. (1979). The Four-color problem and its philosophical significance, *The Journal of Philosophy, 76,* 57–83.

8 Reasoning by Analogy: A General Theory

David Hitchcock
McMaster University

In arguing by analogy we reason from an assumed likeness between a case of interest (the *target*) and one or more other cases (the analog cases or *sources*) to some further resemblance. To think about whether the conclusion of such an argument follows from the premises advanced in its support is to engage in critical thinking.

Is evaluating analogical inference a general critical thinking skill? We might discover that there are people who are generally good at evaluating analogical inferences, who recognize both good analogies and faulty analogies when they see them. The existence of such people would not prove that there is a general skill at work in the strong sense of some single semipermanent mental or neurological structure causally responsible for their consistently good performance. Again, we might abstract from their performance, or derive from theoretical reflection, a general criterion of good analogical inference. But the mere existence of such a criterion would not show that one can make people generally good at evaluating analogical inferences by inculcating the criterion in a general way.

On the other hand, the nonexistence of a field-transcendent criterion for evaluating analogical inferences would show that there was no general skill of evaluating analogical inferences. If their evaluation was field specific, as Toulmin (1958) claims, then we would have to accept the doctrine which Ennis (this volume) calls "epistemological subject specificity" for this aspect of critical thinking.

My concern in this chapter is to develop and defend criteria for good analogical inference. Although the criteria are disjunctive, each criterion in the disjunction straddles fields, in any reasonable sense of that vague term. The same criterion applies, for example, to William Paley's famous argument (1802/1963) for the existence of God from the analogy between the eye and a watch, and to a real estate appraiser's estimation of the market value of a property on the basis of the sale price of recently sold comparable properties. These arguments by analogy obviously belong to different fields. I am therefore arguing against epistemological subject specificity for the critical thinking skill of evaluating analogical inferences. More positively, I am arguing for epistemological generality.

I have chosen this test case for epistemological subject specificity because it is a good test also of a general theory of good inference which I have been developing (Hitchcock, 1985, 1987). The experts differ markedly in their views about what constitutes good analogical inference. Some (Beardsley, 1950; Keynes, 1921; Nagel, 1961; Stebbing, 1939) think there is no such thing: "the suggested conclusion stands just as much in need of testing as though it had never been arrived at by the process of thinking by analogy" (Stebbing, 1939, p. 121). Others (Copi, 1986) give a list of criteria, the most important being the relevance of the assumed similarities to the inferred similarity; this concept of relevance requires clarification. Still others (Govier, 1985b; Levi, 1949; Wisdom, 1957) point to a different kind of analogical inference, but give no evaluative criteria for it.

A general theory of good inference ought to be of some help in sorting out such a confused theoretical situation. If the theory has merit, it will suggest independently acceptable criteria for good analogical inference. My strategy, therefore, will be to motivate and sketch my general theory of good inference, then to use it as a heuristic device for constructing a succession of criteria for good analogical inference, each of which will be considered on its merits. To the extent that the meritorious criteria for good analogical inference cohere with my general theory of good inference, they will not only refute epistemological subject specificity but also confirm my general theory of good inference.

GOOD INFERENCE

From an early age we criticize inferences by constructing a parallel argument with true premises and a false conclusion. We can illustrate the practice with this imaginary but realistic dialogue between a mother and her four-year-old son:

> MOTHER: You can't have any dessert, because you didn't eat
>   your peas.
> SON: But Mary didn't eat her peas, and she got dessert.

Here the child describes a state of affairs in which an argument parallel to his mother's, with "Mary" substituted for "you," has a true premise but a false conclusion. Such a description is an objection that his mother's conclusion does not follow: she is not entitled to conclude from the fact that he did not eat his peas that he can't have any dessert.

In raising such objections, we are selective about which parts of an argument are subject to substitution in constructing a counter-exampling parallel argument. We make substitutions only on what I have elsewhere (Hitchcock, 1985, 1987) called content expressions, whether simple or complex. And we do not make substitutions on all of them. Nobody would object to the argument, "Oak trees are deciduous, so they drop their leaves in the fall," for example, by constructing a counter-exampling parallel argument by substitution on both "oak" and "deciduous": "Spruce trees are coniferous, so they drop their leaves in the fall." In general, we confine substitution to content expressions that are repeated, and we regard as subject to substitution at least one repeated content expression that occurs both in the premises and in the conclusion.

If the existence of a counter-exampling parallel argument is not just a sufficient but also a necessary condition for bad inference, we can (by contraposition) take the nonexistence of such a counter example as a necessary and sufficient condition for good inference. That is, there would be a good inference when (and only when) there was one or more repeated content expressions on which no substitution produced true premises and a false conclusion.

On this conception of good inference, the condition in virtue of which a conclusion follows from certain premises may be a substantive fact about the world or a normative principle. Such an argument does not have a missing premise; its conclusion follows from just its explicit premise(s), only not formally. The argument is, as we might say, materially or enthymematically valid.

As one might expect, the basic account of good inference that I have just motivated and sketched requires elaboration to cope with counter examples. One needs restrictions, for example, on the type of substitution. In the first place, it must be uniform, in the sense that every occurrence of a content expression being replaced is replaced by an occurrence of the same substitute content expression. Secondly, it must be within the same logical or metaphysical category, to avoid spurious refutations like the argument in Plato's *Euthydemus* (298d–e) that, since that dog is yours and is a father, that dog is your father; thus the full elaboration of the theory would require a theory of categories, perhaps a formal grammar in the style of Montague (1974). Thirdly, in some cases it may be within a subcategory; the argument, for example, that marijuana should be made legal, because it is no more dangerous than alcohol, which is already legal, is most plausibly interpreted as resting on a principle specific to mind-altering drugs, so that it would be unkind to object that driving without a seat belt should not be made legal, even though it is no more dangerous than hang gliding, which is already legal.

Again, Bolzano, who seems to have first articulated this theory (1837/1972), perhaps on the basis of medieval precedents, wanted to rule out trivial cases in which there was no counter example because no substitution could make the premises true or no substitution could make the conclusion false; more recently, George (1983) has followed him in this respect. To achieve this end, one adds requirements that at least one substitution on the variable content expressions makes the premises true and at least one substitution makes the conclusion false. A consequence of these added requirements is that an argument with a good inference has a content expression repeated in a premise and the conclusion.

Again, counter examples to arguments with normative or conceptual conclusions may have purely hypothetical premises.

So elaborated, this conception of good inference applies to arguments where we look for truth-preservation between premises and conclusion, that is, what we might call conclusive arguments. It can be extended to arguments where we are prepared to be satisfied with a merely probable or provisional (provided-that-there-are-no-overriding-considerations) transmission of truth from premises to conclusion. For with these arguments too, as Govier (1985a) has pointed out, we use the technique of refutation by logical analogy, a technique which implies that there is a good inference only if there are content expressions on which substitutions which produce true premises also produce a true conclusion—either for the most part, or subject to provisos. The extension of the conception of good inference to these looser arguments would therefore consist in qualifying the requirement that every substitution producing true premises also produces a true conclusion.

These elaborations and qualifications are incorporated in the following complicated conception of good inference:

> The argument contains one or more repeated content expressions on which uniform substitutions within a category or subcategory sometimes make the premises true, sometimes make the conclusion false, and either always, mostly, or provisionally make the conclusion true when they make the premises true.

This is the conception of good inference which I shall apply to arguments by analogy. I shall refer to it as "the general conception of good inference," thus alluding both to its *general* application to all inferences and to its key requirement that there be a true *generalization* of the conditional proposition that, if the premises are true, then the conclusion is true.

REASONING BY ANALOGY

In reasoning by analogy, as I indicated at the beginning of this chapter, we project a property to a case of interest from one or more similar cases.

"Cases" should be understood broadly; a case might be a legal case, an ethical situation, a natural phenomenon (token or type), a concrete object, and so forth. Following a customary terminology (Helman, 1988), I shall refer to the case of interest as the *target* (also called the primary subject), to any of the similar cases as a *source* (also called a base, analog, precedent, or comparable), to postulated similarities as *predictor* properties, and to the inferred further similarity as the *queried* property. The form of an analogical inference is thus as follows:

> The source(s) and the target are alike in having the predictor
>   properties.
> The source(s) has (have) the queried property.
> Therefore, the target has the queried property.

In everyday conversation, and in such strongly persuasive discourse as political speeches and advertising, the shared predictor properties are often not explicitly mentioned; the premise is simply that the target is like the source. In the most elliptical cases even the queried property is unmentioned and the conclusion is left unstated. (President of the Ontario Flue-Cured Tobacco Marketing Board: "This anti-smoking thing is like trying to ban sex.")

Arguments by analogy are common. In court proceedings, lawyers and judges reason about nonstraightforward cases by citing precedents, analogizing the present case to some of them and distinguishing it from others. In moral casuistry, moralists will decide a case with reference to a comparable case, for example, by analogizing the withholding or cessation of artificial feeding of a terminally ill patient to the withholding or cessation of artificial ventilation. Analogies between a currently unexplained phenomenon and one which is well understood will suggest a hypothesis for investigation in scientific research; in all probability, for example, the explanation of solar eclipses started out as an analogical extension of what happens when an opaque object comes between a light source and something it illuminates. Analogies are used in science not only to suggest hypotheses, but also to justify them; a well-known example is Darwin's argument for the theory of natural selection by analogy to the effects on domesticated animals of artificial selection. Students trying to solve mathematical and science problems use strategies based on the similarities they see to previously worked problems; an important difference between good and bad solvers is that the bad ones focus on superficial but misleading similarities, whereas the good ones grasp the deep structural similarities (Perkins & Simmons, 1988). In rhetorically charged contexts, the analogies used are usually suspect. But one everyday use of analogical reasoning which is carefully worked out and commonly accepted is in real estate appraisal, where the market value of a property is sometimes inferred by projecting the selling prices of a group of recently sold comparable properties. And arguments from analogy are used in philosophy, as in standard arguments from design for the existence of God, Hume's critiques of those arguments, arguments for the existence of other minds, and Judith Jarvis Thomson's famous argument (1971) from the outrageousness of an argument deployed in the hypothetical case of an unconscious violinist to the faulty character of what she takes to be the standard argument for the impermissibility of abortion.

SIMILARITY-BASED CRITERIA
FOR GOOD ANALOGICAL INFERENCE

Our general theory of good inference enjoins us to consider for any piece of reasoning by analogy whether it has a covering generalization which is definitely or probably or provisionally true. Since any such argument will repeat the content expressions that refer to the target, the source(s), and the predictor and queried properties, and since any repeated content expression is a candidate for generalization, let us first try to generalize over them all. This gives us the purely formal general statement:

> If a target and some sources are alike in sharing some properties,
> then the target possesses any further property which the sources
> share.

Without some qualification, this generalization is clearly false. A counterfeit twenty dollar bill, for example, may resemble a large number of real twenty dollar bills in a large number of respects, but it is not legal tender, even though they are.

A more difficult question is whether this generalization is probably or provisionally true. At first glance, one would think not. Without any special assumption about a connection between the predictor properties and the queried property, we might suppose that properties are randomly scattered among cases in the universe, and thus the coinstantiation of predictor properties with the queried property in the source(s) will not increase the probability that the target, which possesses the predictor properties, will also possess the queried property.

In fact, however, as various theorists of analogical inference have noticed (Russell, 1988; Shaw & Ashley, 1983), we do not live in this sort of universe. Properties are not randomly distributed, but tend to cluster together. Days that are cloudless tend to be sunny, cases of homicide to be morally culpable, internally repetitive artistic creations to be banal. These clusterings occur for a variety of reasons. Sometimes there are causal connections between the properties (cause to effect, effect to cause, effects of a common cause). In other cases one of the properties is a supervenient property; this is true of deonto-logical, axiological, and classificatory properties. Even if we are completely ignorant of the presence of such connections between the predictor properties and the queried property, the mere similarity of the target case to the source cases can provide a weak probabilistic basis for analogical inference. In the absence of background knowledge, it may be justifiable on pragmatic grounds to make analogical inferences on the basis of such mere similarities; perhaps infants do this. The weakness of such inferences may be illustrated by super-stitious behavior in cases where we have every reason to think that there is only a chance coincidence of two properties; for example, an athlete who wins an important game wearing a certain piece of clothing may wear that piece of clothing in future games because it "brought him good luck."

Several traditional criteria for good analogical inference are best under-stood as amplifications of this weak appeal to mere similarity. Copi (1986, p. 411–414), for example, treats arguments by analogy as a species of inductive argument, by which he means an argument intended merely to support its conclusion as probably true. The more sources appealed to, the more similari-ties between sources and target, the fewer dissimilarities between sources and target, and the more dissimilar the sources are to each other, he claims, the more probable does the conclusion of an analogical argument become. We can see why these claims would be true of any universe in which properties some-times cluster together. A large number of sources increases the probability that the predictor properties and the queried property form a genuine cluster, not just a chance coinstantiation. A large number of similarities and a small number of dissimilarities between sources and target both decrease the proba-bility that some feature that the target does not share is responsible for the sources' possessing the queried property. The dissimilarity of the sources to each other also decreases the probability that some common feature not shared by the target is responsible for the sources' possessing the queried property.

DETERMINATION-BASED CRITERIA
FOR GOOD ANALOGICAL INFERENCE

The standard response to the weakness of mere similarity as a basis for analogical reasoning is to impose an additional requirement of relevance: sim-ilarities must be relevant to the queried property in order to justify projecting it from the sources to the target. Copi (1986), for example, cites such rele-vance as the most important of his six criteria for evaluating analogical inference. Since sources necessarily differ in some respects from the target, the concept of relevance also imposes some constraint on which differences can count against the target's possession of the queried property: they count negatively only if the property possessed by the source(s) but not by the target is relevant to possession of the queried property. A target which is both relevantly similar to and relevantly different from some source(s) can be justifiably concluded to possess the queried property only if the relevant similarities outweigh the relevant dissimilarities. The justification in such cases is taken to be defeasible, such that the conclusion may need to be revised if further evidence comes to light, even though the premises of the analogical reasoning remain warranted.

This account makes a neat package, but it needs explication. What does it mean to say that possession of a given property is relevant to possession of another property? How is the strength of a relevance relation weighed so as to determine whether relevant similarities outweigh relevant dissimilarities?

Copi tells us confidently (1986, p. 413) that "it is doubtful that there is any disagreement about the *meaning* of relevance" (his emphasis; the contrast is to disagreement about what attributes are relevant).

> An analogy is relevant to establishing the presence of a given attribute...provided that it is drawn with respect to *other circumstances affecting it*. One attribute or circumstance is relevant to another, for purposes of analogical argument, if the first affects the second, that is, if it has a *causal* or determining effect on that other. (p. 414)

Copi amplifies this account by allowing that analogical arguments are highly probable also when they go from effect to cause and even when they go from effect to another effect of the same cause.

A difficulty with Copi's position is that it fails to cover cases where the relevance of the predictor properties is not causal but what we might call constitutive: the predictor properties constitute, partly or fully, the queried property, which is supervenient on those properties (and perhaps some others). Such a relationship appears in cases of legal, moral, or philosophical reasoning by analogy where the conclusion is an evaluation, deontic statement, or classification of the target case. It would be odd to say that certain features of a contemplated action caused it to be morally permissible. Certainly it would not be true to say of such connections, as Copi says of the connections which justify causal relevance, that they "are discovered only empirically, by observation and experiment" (1986, p. 414).

If there is to be a single general formula covering both causal relevance and these other sorts of relevance, we might be tempted to express it by saying that the predictor properties are relevant to the possession of the queried property if and only if cases having the predictor properties either always, mostly, or provisionally have the queried property. But such a relevance condition would undermine reasoning by analogy, for it would make appeal to the source cases probatively unnecessary. They could have at best a mnemonic function of reminding the audience of the justifying covering generalization. Keynes (1921), Nagel (1961) and others argued for precisely this reason that arguments by analogy are useless for proving anything, since they are sound only if we have background knowledge that every case with the predictor properties has the queried property, in which case information about the source cases is logically irrelevant.

A second reflection on the construction of a covering generalization for arguments by analogy, however, may point to a type of background knowledge that would not make the appeal to sources in such arguments redundant. As I mentioned above, substitution on a repeated content expression in an argument with a good inference may be restricted to a subcategory within which the expression falls. If the expressions in arguments by analogy that refer to predictor and queried properties are to be treated as subject to substitution, is there some way of restricting substitution on them to a subcategory? We note that the properties signified by such expressions come in sets, each of which we might call a variable; a case has exactly one value of any such variable. Thus, for example, blue is a color, a sixty-five thousand dollar selling price is a selling price, and so on. So, if we restrict substitution to other values of the same variable, we could express a more restricted condition for good analogical inference as follows:

> If a target case has the same values of the predictor properties' variables as the sources, and the sources have the same value of the queried property's variable, then the target has this value of the queried property's variable.

In other words, the values of the variables of the predictor properties determine the value of the variable of the queried property.

This sort of determination relation has been explored in detail in recent work in artificial intelligence (Davies, 1988). Such a relation is sometimes known, renders the argument by analogy for which it is the covering generalization valid, and yet does not make redundant the premise that appeals to the experience of the source cases. A simple example of a determination relation is that in Canada the first letter of a postal code for a given address determines the province in which that address is located. We could express this relation in the form of the above general schema for determination relations as follows:

If a Canadian address has the same first letter in its postal code
as a number of other Canadian addresses, and those other addresses
are in a certain province, then the first address is in the same
province.

Note that this determination relation could be known even if one did not
know the province determined by a specific initial letter, say, S. (Indeed, if one
knew the actual allocation of first letters to provinces in the Canadian postal
code system, one would not resort to analogical inference; operating in the
presence of incomplete background theoretical knowledge is typical of reasoning by analogy.) In order to determine the province in which a target address
whose postal code began with an S was located, it would suffice to know the
province of some source address whose postal code also begins with an S. In
such a context, information about the source would not be redundant.

An interesting feature of this type of argument is that it is, in our terminology, materially or enthymematically valid. That is, given the determination
rule that licenses the inference by analogy, the truth of the premises guarantees the truth of the conclusion. In such cases, reasoning by analogy is not
provisional or probabilistic, as it usually is, but quite tight. Another interesting feature is that none of the similarity-based criteria make a difference to
the goodness of the inference. One source is enough, as is one similarity
between source and target; if there are several sources, it makes no difference
how dissimilar they are in other respects.

A real-life common example of reasoning by analogy based on a somewhat
looser determination relation is real estate appraisal. The task of a real estate
appraiser is to determine the current market value of a piece of real estate, say,
a house. One way to do so, widely accepted as reliable, is to find a number of
comparable houses that have sold recently, and to project the sale price of
those sources onto the target case. An appraiser might regard as relevant factors (that is, variables, in our current terminology) the neighborhood, lot size,
frontage, zoning, square footage of the house, number of bedrooms, number
of bathrooms, condition of the home, date of sale, and so forth. Because it is
recognized that many factors influence the price at which a house sells,
including some that have nothing to do with its intrinsic characteristics or the
time at which it is sold, the sale price of comparable houses can provide only a
rough guide to the market value of the target case. Hence, the more compara-
bles, the better. (Again we see reasoning by analogy operating on the basis of
weak theory; there is no well-substantiated theory of real estate prices
enabling one to infer its market value from its intrinsic characteristics and the
date.) The covering generalization with which real estate appraisers work
would therefore look something like this:

If a number of houses comparable to the target house (in neighborhood, lot size, frontage, zoning, home size, number of rooms, home condition, and so forth) have recently sold on average for a certain price, then the current market value of the target house is (probably) approximately that price.

We could express the general condition for "validity" of arguments by analogy of this type as follows:

If a target resembles a number of sources in having the same values of a specified set of variables, and the sources have roughly the same value as another specified variable, then the target will probably or provisionally have roughly that value of the other variable.

Or, more simply, the values of the predictor properties' variables determine loosely the value of the queried property's variable.

In principle, this theory of determination relations as the warrant for reasoning by analogy could apply equally well to the noninductive arguments by analogy identified by Levi (1949) and Wisdom (1957). In a civil suit in which one corporation sues another for misappropriating trade secrets, whether the information counts for legal purposes as a trade secret may be determined by such factors as whether the plaintiff disclosed it to outsiders, whether the plaintiff imposed restrictions in disclosing it to outsiders, how many outsiders the plaintiff disclosed it to, whether the plaintiff took measures to keep the information secure, and so forth. Ashley (1988) has used such information, gathered from legal treatises and articles, to construct a program which, given the facts of a hypothetical target case expressed in a legal-case-frame language, will go through an adversarial reasoning process with reference to real legal precedent cases and come up with an overall evaluation of the various arguments by analogy that can be deployed concerning the hypothetical case. (Here again, there is only weak theory to go on. The law does not define precisely what counts as a trade secret, and the accumulation of precedents never amounts to a complete determination of such a concept.)

Ashley's program, called HYPO, models well the adversarial process in which attorneys for the two sides analogize the case under consideration to precedents that favor their side and distinguish it from precedents that favor the other side. It provides a partial adjudication procedure in cases where only one side can cite precedents for which there are no counter examples closer to the target case (in terms of the relevant variables). And it models the judgment involved in judicial decision making by coming to no conclusion when both sides (or neither) can cite such "untrumped" precedents. Its weakness, however, is that it works from a knowledge base in which the relevant features of the precedents are antecedently identified. In legal reasoning, as Levi (1949) and others have pointed out, lawyers and judges habitually redescribe precedent cases so as to make them more or less distinct from a target case under discussion.

CRITERIA FOR GOOD A PRIORI
ANALOGICAL INFERENCE

What seems to happen in such appeals to precedent is that the very consideration of the precedents leads to the covering generalization, even when there is only one precedent. Such generalization from single cases occurs also in moral casuistry. Judith Thomson's consideration (1971) of the hypothetical case of the unconscious violinist is a good instance. Imagine, she says, that you wake up one morning back to back in bed with an unconscious violinist. The violinist is suffering from a fatal kidney ailment and the Society of Music Lovers, having discovered that you alone have the right blood type to keep him alive, have kidnapped him and plugged his circulatory system into yours. If unplugged, he will die. The hospital director explains to you that, although you have a right to decide what happens in and to your body, the violinist has a right to life, which outweighs your right, so the violinist must remain plugged into you.

Thomson takes it that her readers will immediately see that the hospital director's argument is outrageous, because it falsely assumes that a right to life always outweighs a right to decide what happens in and to one's body. She can then project to her target—the standard argument for the moral impermissibility of abortion—the generalization that any argument which makes this assumption is flawed.

On an account like Ashley's, Thomson would be taking advantage of an antecedently conceded relationship between whether an argument assumes that a right to life outweighs a right to bodily integrity and the quality of that argument. But she is doing no such thing. She is arguing dialectically against opponents of abortion who, antecedently, concede no such relationship. In fact, she takes them to assert the opposite relationship. So the point of the analog argument about the unconscious violinist is to bring home to the reader the very relationship that licenses the transition from that case to Thomson's target.

What shall we say about the legitimacy of such a move? It is clearly not a valid way of establishing an empirical claim, a prediction. For, in the absence of some antecedently known covering generalization (such as a determination relation) or background theory, a single instance will not justify a generalization from it. But normative and classificatory claims seem to be justifiable in this way. Is the fact that a student does not benefit from a certain action relevant to whether it is an act of academic dishonesty? No, someone might argue, because a student who steals a copy of an exam has still acted dishonestly even if he is found out and the exam changed. Here we recognize in a single case the irrelevance of a certain factor to the classification of an action as one of academic dishonesty.

Wisdom has argued at length (1957) for the legitimacy of a distinctive form of argument by analogy based on such insights. His argument for the sometime legitimacy of proof by parallels or reasoning by a priori analogy seems compelling. From the point of view of our general theory, however, such arguments pose a difficulty. The covering generalization that would license the inference from the source to the target is not known independently of the premise concerning the source. Our conception of what makes an action dishonest, or a piece of information a trade secret, or an act of bringing about one person's death which also saves the lives of several others morally permissible (Thomson, 1985) is not antecedently fixed. In picking a source that has certain affinities with and dissimilarities from the target, we implicitly form a judgment about the features of the source in virtue of which it possesses the queried property and the features that are irrelevant to having the queried property. But this judgment may not be reached, or reachable, independently of consideration of cases that can serve as sources. If so, we may perhaps represent the form of an a priori argument by analogy as follows:

The sources have the queried property by virtue of the predictor
    properties.
The target has the predictor properties.
Therefore, the target has the queried property.

Here the first premise is justified by direct inspection of the individual case(s), a procedure which is fallible and in any case has merit only where the queried property is supervenient. (We cannot get insight into causal connections by direct inspection of one individual case.) Where the queried property is supervenient, conjectures as to the features responsible for its presence in clear-cut cases can be tested by a method of attempting to construct hypothetical cases that have those features but clearly do not have the queried property. (For a good example of this method, see Thomson (1985).)

If we construe a priori arguments by analogy as suggested above, then we can state the condition for their validity in the form of a restricted covering generalization:

If some cases have a queried supervenient property by virtue of certain features, then any case with those features provisionally has that property.

This statement seems to me to be true, and thus to indicate that the conclusions of arguments by a priori analogy can follow provisionally.

SUMMARY AND CONCLUSION

In arguing by analogy, we project a queried property from source cases that share certain features (predictor properties) to a target case that also has those features. Such projections are sometimes legitimate, even where we lack antecedent knowledge that any case with the predictor properties also has the queried property.

The strongest legitimation for such inferences is the existence of a determination relation according to which the variables of which the predictor properties are values determine the variable of which the queried property is a value. If such determination relations are tight and exceptionless, they legitimate conclusive analogical inferences. If they are loose, they legitimate only probable or provisional analogical inferences.

Such determination relations hold mainly for what have been called inductive arguments by analogy (Barker, 1965), where the conclusion is a statement of fact that can in principle be empirically tested independently of the analogical argument. But a moral or legal tradition may be sufficiently worked out in some respects to ground a determination relation between certain variables and a normative, evaluative, or classificatory variable, as in the case law on trade secrets discussed above.

More commonly, sound analogical inferences to a recommendation, evaluation, or classification rest on an insight into the relevance of the predictor properties to the supervenient queried property, an insight which may require only one source case to substantiate. In such inferences the premise is not merely that the source has both the queried property and the predictor properties, but that the source has it by virtue of those predictor properties; in Judith Thomson's memorable example, the hospital director's argument is outrageous because it assumes that a right to life always outweighs a right to decide what happens in and to one's body. Given such a premise, the conclusion follows, usually provisionally.

The weakest form of analogical inference is one where there is no known determination relation and no insight into the supervenience in the source cases of the queried property on the predictor properties. Here the sorts of similarity-based criteria advanced by Copi (1986)—greater numbers of sources, more similarities and fewer dissimilarities between the sources and the target, dissimilarities in other respects among the sources—can raise the inferential connection to one of weak probability. Such similarity-based criteria can also increase the confidence and precision of loose determination and supervenience relations. But, without such a relation, inference by analogy is risky. It would be wise to take it as probative only under extreme circumstances for pragmatic reasons.

The fact that these sorts of good analogical inference fit my general theory of good inference provides some support for that theory. We should now be a little more inclined to accept the suggestion that an argument has a good inference if and only if it contains one or more repeated content expressions on which uniform substitutions within a category or subcategory either always, mostly, or provisionally make the conclusion true when they make the premises true.

The criteria for good analogical inference, although disjunctive and more specific than the general theory, nevertheless straddle fields. Analogical arguments for the existence of God belong to a different field than analogical arguments about the stopping distance of a car or the province in which a certain address is located. But all these arguments are best appraised by determination-based criteria. Naturally, the specific content of the determination relation will vary from one argument to another, and working out whether it holds will require knowledge of the field of inquiry to which the subject matter of the argument belongs. But the general strategy of identifying the variables to which the predictor properties belong, and thinking about whether those variables determine the variable to which the queried property belongs, is common. Likewise supervenience-based criteria for analogical inference straddle at least moral and legal reasoning, and perhaps other fields as well. Thus epistemological subject specificity fails for the critical thinking skill of evaluating analogical inference; the criteria for good analogical inference are not entirely field specific.

ACKNOWLEDGMENT

I would like to thank Lee Brooks, John Burbidge, Robert Ennis, Nick Griffin, Ralph Johnson, John McMurtry, and Harvey Siegel for helpful comments on earlier versions of this chapter.

REFERENCES

Ashley, K. D. (1988). Arguing by analogy in law: A case-based model. In D. H. Helman (Ed.), *Analogical reasoning: Perspectives of artificial intelligence, cognitive science, and philosophy* (pp. 205–224). Dordrecht: Kluwer.
Barker, E. (1965). *Elementary logic.* New York: McGraw-Hill.

Beardsley, M. (1950). *Practical logic.* New York: Prentice-Hall.

Bolzano, B. (1972). *Theory of science* (R. A. George., Trans. & Ed.). Berkeley: University of California Press. (Original work published 1837).

Copi, I. M. (1986). *Introduction to logic* (7th ed.). New York: Macmillan.

Davies, T. R. (1988). Determination, uniformity, and relevance: Normative criteria for generalization and reasoning by analogy. In D. H. Helman (Ed.), *Analogical reasoning: Perspectives of artificial intelligence, cognitive science, and philosophy* (pp. 227–259). Dordrecht: Kluwer.

George, R. (1983). Bolzano's consequence, relevance and enthymemes. *Journal of Philosophical Logic, 12,* 299–318.

Govier, T. (1985a). Logical analogies. *Informal Logic, 7,* 27–33.

Govier, T. (1985b). *A practical study of argument.* Belmont, CA: Wadsworth.

Helman, D. H. (Ed.). (1988). *Analogical reasoning: Perspectives of artificial intelligence, cognitive science, and philosophy.* Dordrecht: Kluwer.

Hitchcock, D. (1985). Enthymematic arguments. *Informal Logic, 7,* 83–97.

Hitchcock, D. (1987). Enthymematic arguments. In F. H. van Eemeren, R. Grootendorst, J. A. Blair, & C. Willard (Eds.), *Argumentation: Across the lines of discipline* (pp. 289–298). Dordrecht: Foris.

Keynes, J. M. (1921). *A treatise on probability.* London: Macmillan.

Levi, E. H. (1949). *An introduction to legal reasoning.* Chicago: University of Chicago Press.

Montague, R. (1974). *Formal philosophy.* New Haven: Yale University Press.

Nagel, E. (1961). *The structure of science.* New York: Harcourt, Brace and World.

Paley, W. (1963). *Natural theology: Selections* (Edited, with an introduction, by F. Ferre). New York: Bobbs-Merrill (Original work published 1802).

Perkins, D. N., & Simmons, R. (1988). Patterns of misunderstanding: An integrative model for science, math, and programming. *Review of Educational Research, 58,* 303–26.

Plato. *Euthydemus.* In E. Hamilton and H. Cairns (Eds.) (1961), *Plato: Collected dialogues* (pp. 385–420). New York: Pantheon Books.

Russell, S. J. (1988). Analogy by similarity. In D. H. Helman (Ed.), *Analogical reasoning: Perspectives of artificial intelligence, cognitive science, and philosophy* (pp. 251–269). Dordrecht: Kluwer.

Shaw, W. H., & Ashley, L. R. (1983). Analogy and inference. *Dialogue, 22,* 415–432.

Stebbing, L. S. (1939). *Thinking to some purpose.* Middlesex: Penguin Books.

Thomson, J. J. (1971). A defense of abortion. *Philosophy and Public Affairs, 1,* 47–66.

Thomson, J. J. (1985). The trolley problem. *The Yale Law Journal, 94,* 1395–1415.

Toulmin, S. E. (1958). *The uses of argument.* Cambridge: Cambridge University Press.

Wisdom, J. (1957). *Proof and explanation: Lectures delivered in the University of Virginia.* Unpublished transcript.

9 The Generalizability of Critical Thinking: The Evaluation of Sources

J. Anthony Blair
University of Windsor

Is critical thinking generalizable? This looks like a single question, but if critical thinking denotes a variety of abilities and dispositions—as many observers hold (Ennis, 1981, 1987; Norris & Ennis, 1989, Ch. 1)—then the question of the generalizability of critical thinking becomes many questions, and the answer may be affirmative in some cases and negative in others. We shall need to consider what "critical thinking" denotes.

There are at least two ways to specify what critical thinking is. One is to provide a general definition (see, for example, Ennis, 1981; Norris & Ennis, 1989, p. 3). Another is to identify particular abilities or dispositions such that, whatever else critical thinking denotes, it uncontroversially denotes them. Rather than offer a general definition and face the accompanying onus of having to defend it against alternatives, I will instead take the route of specifying some of the things for which generalizability is in question if the generalizability of critical thinking is in question.

It also seems advisable to try to form a clear conception of the ability or disposition in question, and of what its generalization would involve, in order to be able to draw any warranted conclusions about whether it is generalizable or even to know how to decide that question. I shall try to set out accurately what is entailed by someone's having one subset of the abilities and dispositions that seem to belong paradigmatically and uncontroversially to critical thinking. Then, I shall consider what conclusions can be drawn about the generalizability of those abilities and dispositions on the basis of those depictions. In particular, the focus in this chapter will be on those abilities and dispositions that are connected with the critical appreciation of the sources of beliefs.

125

ABILITY TO EVALUATE INFORMATION SOURCES

One objective of critical thinking instruction is to make students aware of the importance, for the management of their beliefs, of reliable sources of information, and to develop their critical appreciation of such information sources.

A source of information for a person is any means whereby information from others gets communicated to that person. Someone telling you the time of day, a magazine article that you read, a street name sign that you notice—all are examples of information sources.

The immediate end that gives this objective its value is having well-managed beliefs. Managing our beliefs well includes (but is by no means restricted to) the following activities: (a) believing what we have good reasons to believe and not believing what we have good reasons not to believe (for example, believing that there are biting insects in the Canadian forests in June, not believing that one has a realistic chance of winning a provincial or state lottery); (b) qualifying our beliefs according to the degree of support for them available to us—or holding beliefs with the degree of conviction appropriate to the strength of the support we have for them (for example, based on the meteorological records, it will *probably* snow in Windsor, Ontario in February; given what I have seen of his work, it is *highly doubtful,* though *certainly possible,* that student Slim Chance will succeed in law school); (c) investigating the support for beliefs that are important to us (for example, the solvency of one's pension plan); (d) modifying our beliefs appropriately in the light of new information (for example, based on the events of 1989–90, the Soviet Union is probably not an "evil empire" after all); and (e) assigning to our beliefs or areas of belief their correct epistemic status (for example, "all politicians are dishonest" should be treated as an empirical belief subject to disconfirmation, not regarded as true by definition; "virtue is always rewarded" is probably more defensible as an article of faith than as an empirically confirmed fact). The ultimate rationale for maintaining a well-managed belief system is that it is more likely to produce true beliefs, and to issue in successful action choices, than any alternative method. That rationale will have to remain an undefended presupposition of this chapter.

This critical appreciation of the reliability of sources is of utterly central importance to good doxastic management, for most of our beliefs derive from the affirmations of sources of information. Relatively few of our beliefs originate from our own direct experience (see Code, 1987; Hardwig, 1985), although, as Siegel (1988) has argued persuasively, such dependence does not entail the rejection of our epistemic responsibility for our beliefs. Appreciating our dependence on others for our beliefs means recognizing the roles of various sources, making the appropriate evaluative judgments of their reliability, and continuously adjusting our beliefs accordingly.[1]

That we rely on sources for a large percentage of our beliefs is uncontroversial. That it is perfectly appropriate to do so, as long as we monitor the credibility of the information we get from these sources, is perhaps somewhat less uncontroversial among philosophers, many of whom still suffer from Cartesian epistemology, a disease that deranges philosophical perspective, causing extreme epistemic individualism. Hardwig (1985) and Code (1987) are just two philosophers who have recently presented strong cases in favor of epistemic dependence, and I shall assume that their arguments show decisively that most of our beliefs—beliefs we are entirely *justified* in holding—derive from sources beyond our respective individual sensory observations and theorizing. Those unaffected by an overexposure to Cartesian epistemology, namely most nonphilosophers—which is to say, nearly everyone in the world—will, at least after brief reflection, find this claim uncontroversial. But even those who deny that *most* of our justified beliefs are dependent on sources must concede that at least *some* of them are. From the weaker claim it still follows that monitoring the credibility of the information we get from these sources is one segment of critical thinking, if not the lion's share I take it to be.

The various criteria for evaluating different kinds of sources of information are well known and I will not spell out and defend details. Let me summarize some of the points that a critical thinker will know and be able to apply (Pinto & Blair, 1989):

1. A proposition is credible just in case it is worthy of belief or acceptance. Many, and perhaps most, of our beliefs come from other people. The assertions of these sources are credible to the extent that the sources are reliable and their assertions are plausible, given everything we know. A proposition is credible *to* a person, relative to what that person is justified in accepting. Whether a source has to be an expert to be credible depends on the subject. Reliability and credibility are always matters of degree.
2. Whether a source's claim is credible depends on three things: the opportunity the source had to know what is claimed, the source's ability to understand or interpret the claim, and the trustworthiness of the source. These apply to nonexpert and expert sources alike.
3. The assertions of nonexpert sources are to be evaluated by judging whether: (a) the matters can be known to nonexperts, (b) the sources have the competence to make reliable judgments, (c) they have had the opportunity to do so, and (d) there is no reason not to trust them on

this occasion. When dealing with citation and reportage, we want to know that the sources understand the material well enough to report it accurately, and that the original sources were reliable. When dealing with observation reports, we want to check, among other things, the conditions of the observations—such as the situation and attitude of the observers in relation to what was observed, the observers' perceptual acuity, the quality and condition of their instruments, whether they had any necessary training, and what the conditions of the observations were—as well as on conditions affecting the credibility of their reports.

4. Expertise is extensive specialized knowledge and skill. Nonexperts can identify experts only by their credentials, which indicate an authority bestowed on them by other experts. Nonexperts assess the credibility of an expert's testimony by seeing if: (a) expertise is required, (b) this person has the requisite credentials, (c) the expert had an opportunity to investigate the matter, (d) the matter is not controversial among experts, and (e) there is no special reason to question this person.

The material summarized here is more or less standard fare in the critical thinking literature, although there might be disagreement about some of the details. Each point in the above summary could be elaborated in considerable detail, and its application illustrated in a variety of particular situations.

Understanding these points is rightly taken to be a necessary condition for the intelligent appraisal of the warrant of other people's affirmations.

A critical thinker will know these points and be able and disposed to apply them to particular situations. What is entailed in that knowledge, ability, and disposition? Since there are several groups of points made about assessing the credibility of sources, and since some seem likely to be different in character from others, it is advisable to examine each group separately.

ABILITY TO ASSESS OBSERVATION REPORTS

Norris (1984) has identified several principles to be followed in appraising the credibility of observation reports. These pertain (a) to the reliability of the observation in question, and (b) to the credibility of the observer's report of that observation. Among the former are such requirements as that the observer possess the background knowledge needed to identify what is observed; that there be sufficient time to make an accurate observation; and that the surrounding conditions be favorable to accurate observation. Among the latter are such requirements as that the report is made or recorded soon after the observation; that the observation statement is made by the person who did the observing; and that the report is not made in response to a leading question. These six principles are selected to illustrate the sorts of items included in advice about assessing observation reports.

Consider now whether such principles are generalizable. Note first that the principles are already stated in general form. They apply indifferently to observation reports of songbirds, cloud formations, body language, the commission of crimes, vehicle accidents, sports referees' penalty assessments, crowd size, new comets, the contents of microscopic slides, and restaurant meals. The principles are not restricted to particular kinds of observations.

Does familiarity with these general principles decrease the likelihood of accepting noncredible observation reports and rejecting credible ones? That is an empirical question. Anecdotal evidence suggests that initially being made aware of these principles impedes judgment, but that experience with their use improves judgment. Becoming self-conscious about the principles embedded in an activity is well-known to impede the activity. On a 1989 Canadian Broadcasting Corporation television program about her career, retiring prima ballerina Karen Kain spoke of how analyzing her dancing initially caused her to lose her spontaneity. However, she also contended that when her spontaneity returned, the understanding that had resulted from the analysis enabled her in the long run to be a better dancer. It is to be expected that attention to the mechanisms of an activity impedes its exercise, and there is no reason to expect mental or intellectual skills to be any different from physical skills in this respect. The empirical testing of the hypothesis that awareness of the principles governing credible observation reports improves the quality of the assessment of such reports should therefore not take place until these principles have been internalized. Testing done immediately following the critical thinking courses in which these principles were taught would not therefore be expected to be valid.

Suppose that valid testing shows that observation report assessment improves with an understanding of the general principles of reliable observations and reporting. Can the application of the observation report credibility principles be taken to be completely generalizable? No, they cannot. For one reason, just understanding that background knowledge is needed for a reliable observation does not give anybody the knowledge they need to make or assess observations in some particular situation. Moreover, obviously the knowledge needed in one particular type of situation will be different from what is needed in other types of situations. The background knowledge necessary to discover new insect species, to note the key events in a traffic accident, or to reliably report what people wore to a party is different in each case. Just as the general principles governing observation reports are by definition generalizable, so these particulars are by definition not generalizable across types of situation.

Moreover, the more someone knows the specifics of the situations in which a particular type of observation is made, the more competently can the person be expected to apply the general principles to it in assessing the reports of such observations. For the person then knows not just the general questions that need to be asked—for example, does the observer have the requisite background knowledge?—but also the specific answers to be sought in that situation—for example, does that bird-watcher know how to tell the difference between a tern and a gull? Yet it also seems plausible to expect that the critic will in due course learn how to move from specifics back to the general. Having learned, for instance, that gulls and terns look alike to the inexperienced eye, the critic might be expected to generalize that knowledge, and in other cases of species identification to wonder whether there are two or more similar-looking species that the inexperienced observer might fail to distinguish. The habit of seeking such generalizations might itself be taught.

It also seems likely that one will be best led to understand the general observation-report principles, and best prepared to apply them intelligently, if one learns them in the context of specific applications. The principles can be memorized, but they will be known only as empty formulas unless there is some experience in applying them to particular cases where the learner has the relevant background knowledge. On the other hand, if one does learn how to ask the right specific questions in more than one type of familiar situation, then one should as a result have an appreciation of how the principles are supposed to be applied, and so know what questions to ask when applying them in unfamiliar situations. The broader one's experience of deploying the principles, the richer are one's resources for seeking analogues for the application of the principles in novel situations. Hence we can hypothesize that the relevance of specific questions used in applying the principles to unfamiliar types of situation will increase with an increase in the types of situation to which a person has already learned to apply them.

What can be concluded about generalizability on the basis of this examination of the critical assessment of observation reports? The principles governing credible observation reports are inherently general. The application of those principles to particular observation reports is inherently specific to types of context. Whether learning the principles improves one's ability to assess critically particular observation reports, or specific types of observation reports, are empirical questions. Two things should be kept in mind in setting up tests to try to answer these questions. One is that the process of learning the principles might temporarily diminish the quality of a person's critical judgment. The other is that how people learn the principles seems likely to affect their ability to apply them generally. It is plausible to predict that learning them in application to specific situations with which one is thoroughly familiar will make it more likely that one will be able to apply them appropriately to unfamiliar contexts, than would be the case if one had learned them in abstraction from any particular context or in application to unfamiliar situations. Can students be taught to apply the principles intelligently in unfamiliar contexts in a way that improves their critical assessment of the credibility of observation reports in general? Since some people are remarkably skilled at making such assessments, and since the ability is not likely to be innate, it clearly can be learned. Without assuming that everything that is learned can be taught, given the components of this ability just described, it seems on the face of it plausible to believe that it can be taught, one way or another.

DISPOSITION TO ASSESS OBSERVATION REPORTS

What about the disposition to deploy this ability—can it be generalized? Generalization in this context can mean two different things, so in fact there are two questions to be asked. First, will someone who learns how to raise appropriately critical questions about observation reports tend to exercise that ability—to raise appropriately those questions after the ability has been acquired—either in the types of situation in which it was learned or in others where it applies? Will the student apply the knowledge outside the classroom? Second, will someone with the ability to raise appropriately critical questions about observation reports in contexts of one type tend to raise appropriately such questions in the other types of context to which they pertain? Will the critic of crowd counts be equally a critic of fish stock counts?

These questions may appear to be straightforward, but because the relationship between ability and disposition can take different forms, they are not. We need to notice three of these different forms of the relationship between ability and disposition.

First, consider what are skills, abilities, and dispositions. To have an ability is to be able to do something; to have a skill is to be able to do it well. I am able to skate, but I am not a skilled skater. A disposition is a tendency to engage in something—be it the exercise of an ability or of a skill (or any of the many other things to which dispositions apply).

Now, consider the differences between swimming, playing the violin, and spelling. Someone can know how to swim but not be disposed to swim (because they are too busy, or allergic to pollen in the water, or bored by swimming in a pool). But one never forgets how to swim. So clearly an ability to swim is quite distinct from a disposition to swim. In such cases the ability and disposition are logically and causally independent. In the case of playing the violin, because it is such a difficult instrument to play, in order not only to acquire but also to retain the ability, one must constantly practice. If one is not disposed to keep in practice, one will lose the ability to play. The disposition to play the violin is a causally necessary condition of the ability to play the violin. In cases like this, while the disposition is logically distinct from the ability, the two are causally related.

The case of spelling is different again. Someone who has the ability to spell in a language has learned how to spell correctly a large number of the words of that language, has learned its main principles of spelling, and automatically applies this knowledge. One can imagine situations in which someone who can spell might deliberately make spelling errors—perhaps to disguise his or her identity—but an able speller just is someone who normally and habitually spells correctly a high percentage of the words he or she writes. The disposition, in this respect, is logically inseparable from the ability. A comparison with physical abilities helps to clarify this case. The able skier or paddler automatically skis or paddles competently, and must concentrate in order to perform poorly—must make an effort to disguise or hide the ability.

There appear to be, then, at least three different types of relationship between an ability and the disposition to exercise it, as shown in Figure 9.1. Does the disposition to exercise the ability to assess observation reports critically correspond to one of these three ability/disposition models? From one point of view it looks more like the disposition related to the ability to spell than like either of the other two. In acquiring an appreciation of the principles

Figure 9.1. Relationships between abilities and the disposition to exercise them.

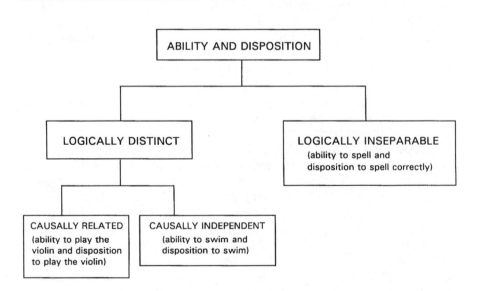

governing credible observation reports, one has learned to recognize that certain kinds of reports are just not credible, while others are highly credible. One has learned that certain questions must be answered before a judgment of an observation report's credibility can be made. It might seem unlikely that, knowing and appreciating these things, a person could fail to use or apply that knowledge and appreciation. However, in applying the principles there are many questions that need to be asked, and, consequently, a conscious effort is required to pursue them all. When it is necessary to take pains in order to accomplish a result, there is scope for backsliding, laziness, or oversight. The disposition to resist these lapses does not seem to be a built-in feature of the ability to assess critically observation statements. It seems likely, therefore, that having the ability and being disposed thoroughly and conscientiously to deploy it are logically distinct traits: the presence of the first would not be expected to guarantee the presence of the second.

If this analysis is correct there will be two tasks to be achieved in teaching the discriminating use of the principles governing credible observation statements. One is to instill the ability. The other is to motivate its exercise. Consequently, we should not expect to find that the ability is generally deployed unless an effort has been made to instill an active inclination to deploy it.

Let me return to the two questions raised about the generalizability of the disposition to exercise the ability to assess critically the credibility of observation reports. The first question was whether someone who has acquired this ability will be disposed to use it, either in similar or in different sorts of situations from those in which it was learned. Will the skill generalize in the sense of being carried forward and exercised in the future? Our answer consists of the following empirical hypothesis: There will be correlations between the extent to which the skill is exercised after its acquisition, and (a) the extent to which the motivation to exercise the skill has been instilled, and (b) the degree of familiarity with the skill's application in the given type of situation.

The second question was whether someone with the ability to assess observation reports will be disposed to carry out such assessments in contexts other than the one(s) in which the skill was learned. Assuming (i) that the principles were taught *as general principles,* not as guidelines applying exclusively to the learning context(s), and (ii) that there was teaching to transfer, it is to be expected that the applications of the principles to other contexts will vary (a) with motivation and (b) with degree of acquaintance with the situation. While under some circumstances these principles might be applied appropriately to novel, unfamiliar situations, they will tend to be applied more readily and with more assurance and relevance in situations in which their application is familiar—for the reason that the specific questions they raise will be known in the second case but not in the first.

A GENERAL PROBLEM FOR TESTING

One of the difficulties facing current attempts to discover how far the learning of abilities and dispositions will generalize is that it is not clear what is demonstrated by a negative result on our testing instruments. Such a result might show any of three different things: that the skill does not generalize, that the instrument is inadequate, or that we do not yet know how to teach the skill for generalization. If students who do a good job of raising critical questions about the credibility of observation statements in a situation they know well also do poorly at raising such questions in novel situations, that might be due to faulty teaching or to a poor test, and not to the fact that these skills are not generalizable.

OTHER ASPECTS OF SOURCE ASSESSMENT

So far the discussion has been limited to the generalizability of the ability and disposition to assess observation reports appropriately. As the sketch quoted at the outset shows, that is but one of a number of ability/disposition sets associated with the critical appreciation of the sources of information, all of which are needed for sound belief management. A partial list would include the abilities and dispositions to assess judiciously, among other things, the following: newspapers; news magazines; other general readership magazines; television news and other information programming; dictionaries and their entries; the pronouncements of experts; reports of polls, surveys, and studies; textbooks; monographs; popular science books and articles; product instructions; advertisements; and regulations. Fortunately, it will not be necessary to work through each of these items in fine-grained detail in order to be able to say something in general about the generalizability of the ability and disposition to assess information sources critically.

First, the extremely general guidelines mentioned in the quoted summary of Pinto and Blair (1989) apply equally to every one of these cases. That is, the credibility of any source depends on the opportunity the source had to know what is claimed, the source's ability to understand or interpret the claim, and the trustworthiness of the source. This rule might seem of minimal use in particular situations, but it is not useless. It is analogous to some of the general principles of morality—more specific than, "Do good and avoid evil," and about on a par with "Be benevolent and just." That is, it does not tell us what to do, but it does tell us the direction in which to look to figure out what to do. If the only change to people's critical thinking behavior was that they began habitually to check these three general criteria of source credibility, I would predict significant improvement in their critical judgments.

Second, the information sources just listed can be organized into groups, with the members of each group having enough in common that the same principles will apply to all of them. For example, the different sources of information about current events have a lot in common, even though there are also important differences between (and among) newspapers, television news, television current events programming, news magazines, specialty magazines, and so on—with which one needs to be familiar in order to be fully sensitive to the merits and flaws of each of them as a source of news. Various sorts of reliance on experts would be another area with a lot of overlap but also important differences between different types of expert and subject matter.

Third, there seems no reason to expect any of these other sources to be different from observation reports when it comes to the importance of particularized knowledge for the application of general principles to particular situations. The greater the amount of particular knowledge and the more specific the knowledge, the better able the critic should be to assess information from a source.

The need for particularized knowledge is not due to different standards of knowledge applying in different fields, subjects, or domains, but rather it is because the principles get instantiated differently when the concrete particulars to which they apply are different. The bird-watcher needs to know birds, whereas the media-watcher needs to know networks. Differences in evaluative criteria are a function of the logical type of the statements made by the source—for example, theory-thin observation statements (for example, "That is a herring gull") *versus* theory-rich interpretations (for example, "The Moscow regime received a serious blow to its authority within the Soviet Union as a result of the Armenia-Azerbaijan conflict"). These differences will occur as much within any given field as they do between different fields, a conclusion that Siegel (this volume) also has reached.

Fourth, it is reasonable to expect that the sorts of empirical hypotheses yielded by an examination of the specifics of the critical evaluation of observation reports will have direct parallels when it comes to the assessment of other kinds of information sources. In general, it seems likely that a combination consisting of (a) mastering general principles, (b) learning their applications in several particular types of context with which the student is familiar, and (c) practicing their application in unfamiliar contexts (that is, teaching to transfer), is likely to increase the extent and sophistication with which the student applies them beyond the classroom and in novel contexts. It is also probable that motivation will be an important variable where the ability in question and the disposition to deploy it are logically distinct.

The points made about generalization connected with the credibility of sources may not apply to all aspects of critical thinking, though I believe they do apply quite generally. To the extent that the disposition and ability to assess sources critically are paradigmatic components of critical thinking, the answer to the question whether critical thinking is generalizable must be mixed. In some respects, probably, generalization tends to occur, and in other respects, probably, it tends not to occur; in either case it is a matter of degree.

SUMMARY

In this paper I have approached the question of whether critical thinking can be generalized by considering a paradigm component of critical thinking: the critical assessment of sources of information. Most of the discussion has been focused more narrowly on one specific type of information source, namely observation reports. There are general principles governing credible observation reports which are beneficial to know and apply across the board, however it seems likely these will be understood and applied more intelligently if they are learned by being applied in particular contexts already well understood by the student, and if there is teaching to transfer. The disposition to apply these principles seems likely to be partly a function of the ease of doing so, partly a function of the motivation to do so. These are empirical questions, and one aim of the paper has been to generate testable hypotheses about them. In testing such hypotheses we should keep in mind the possibility that negative results could be due to unsuccessful teaching or invalid testing instead of lack of generalizability.

NOTE

1. The conception of critical thinking that emphasizes the *proper management* of belief systems as central is due to Robert C. Pinto.

REFERENCES

Canadian Broadcasting Corporation (1989, September 17). Karen Kain: Prima ballerina. Ottawa: CBC.

Code, L. (1987). *Epistemic responsibility*. Hanover and London: University Press of New England.

Ennis, R. H. (1981). Rational thinking and educational practice. In J. F. Soltis (Ed.), *Philosophy and education* (Eightieth Yearbook of the National Society for the Study of Education) (pp. 143–183). Chicago: NSSE.

Ennis, R. H. (1987). A taxonomy of critical thinking dispositions and skills. In J. B. Baron, & R. S. Sternberg (Eds.), *Teaching thinking skills: Theory and practice* (pp. 9–26). New York: W. H. Freeman.

Hardwig, J. (1985). Epistemic dependence. *The Journal of Philosophy, 82,* 335–349.

Norris, S. P. (1984). Defining observational competence. *Science Education, 68,* 129–142.

Norris, S. P., & Ennis R. H. (1989). *Evaluating critical thinking.* Pacific Grove, CA: Midwest Publications.

Pinto, R. C., & Blair, J. A. (1989). *A reasoner's handbook.* Windsor, Ontario: University of Windsor.

Siegel, H. (1988). Rationality and epistemic dependence. *Educational Philosophy and Theory, 20*(1), 1–6.

10 The Generalizability of Self-Regulatory Thinking Strategies

Linda M. Phillips
Memorial University of Newfoundland

Humans think about their thinking. They ask and act upon such questions as: (a) Should I consider more evidence? (b) Was my previous conclusion consistent with my most recent one? (c) Should I consult an expert on this point? (d) Should I change my mind on such-and-such belief? and so on. When they do this, we can say that humans are regulating their thinking. This chapter compares the self-regulatory thinking strategies used by adult and young readers, by readers and mathematics problem solvers, and by readers of narrative text and readers of expository science text. The conclusion is that across each of these boundaries, self-regulatory thinking strategies are the same. Thus, at least to this extent, such strategies are generalizable.

I will begin by exploring briefly the historical basis of contemporary conceptions of reading, culminating in the hypothesis that reading well is thinking well with written language. From there, I shall examine some empirical research that bears on this hypothesis. In particular, I will present research on readers' text understanding that points to general strategies readers use, and to how use of general strategies relates to readers' background knowledge. Finally, I will present some evidence on the generalizability of the strategies across subjects and across text genres.

EVOLVING CONCEPTS OF READING

Early theories of reading proposed, more or less, that one reads first and thinks later. Plato, for instance, maintained that reading is distinguishing the separate letters, both by eye and by ear, in order that when one hears them spoken or sees them written one will not be confused by their position (Jowett, 1942). This theory was used to base an alphabetic, or ABC, method of reading instruction consisting of instruction in the letter names. The method was used in Greek and Roman times and enjoyed almost universal application until the nineteenth century (Beebe, 1990). The alphabetic methods expanded to include the learning of letter sounds—the phonics approach (Thornton, 1790)—followed by the learning of whole words—the look-say approach (Mann, 1843). Davis (1968, p. 501) recounts a story about reading based on a fluent translation of letter sounds observed in a school visited by Horace Mann. Mann asked one of the students to read from a newspaper that he happened to have with him. The student read each line all across the page, paying no attention to the fact that the page was divided into several columns. This experience prompted Mann to argue for the use of the word method, thinking that a focus on whole words would put an end to the phenomenon he had witnessed.

The effectiveness and efficiency of the alphabetic method, and the related phonics and look-say methods, was not challenged until the advent of research on eye movements by Cattell (1886) and Erdmann and Dodge (1898). Even then, the challenges were directed toward views of the mechanics of reading, that is, the basic perceptual habits, and not towards how comprehension was conceived. Comprehension was thought to be a concomitant of engaging the mechanics.

Regardless of the preferred method, comprehension was secondary in the pronouncements of prominent educators. In 1916, Otis stated that reading involves nothing more than the correlation of a sound image with its corresponding visual image (p. 528). Some theorists, however, began to challenge this misapprehension of reading on the grounds that it ignores meaning. Huey (1908, p. 349) remarked "that a false ideal has taken hold of us, namely, that to read is to say just what is upon the page, instead of to think." Thorndike (1917) urged that reading is reasoning, likening comprehending a written paragraph to solving a problem in mathematics. Albert Korzybski (1933), a philosophical linguist, proposed that reading is the reconstruction of the events behind the symbols—an interaction between the reader and written language through which the reader attempts to reconstruct a message from the writer.

The works of Huey, Thorndike, Korzybski, and others prompted much discussion on how people turn marks on a page into meaningful ideas. Nonetheless, at the same time as Korzybski was concerned about meaning, Bloomfield (1933) was wondering about all the fuss over meaning, because, he maintained, if you taught a child what each letter stands for, then the child could read. For Bloomfield and others, reading meant *oral* reading, wherein understanding was assumed when pronunciation was correct and natural. When it became evident that such an assumption was erroneous, the idea of critical reading was proposed as the ideal that should be sought (Betts, 1946).

Critical reading was defined as evaluating the relevancy and adequacy of what is read. This critical function in reading was endorsed by reading theoreticians (Gray, 1960; Robinson, 1964; Smith, 1965; Wolf, King, & Huck, 1968), because they believed that the thinking processes used in *reacting to what was read* fulfilled the purpose of reading. That is, critical reading was seen as an extension of reading beyond the literal and interpretive levels. Critical reading so conceived could involve internal and external critical evaluation. Internal evaluation is the process of arriving at a judgment of the worth of a selection by examining the extent to which its content, form, and style achieve an author's desired purpose. External evaluation is the process of judging the worth of a selection by comparing it to other selections that are similar in purpose and of known quality (Harris & Hodges, 1981, p. 74).

Empirical research guided by a conception of reading as understanding rather than as merely knowing the words was not evidenced until the 1960s (Beebe, 1990). Since that time, it has become widely accepted that reading well involves more than knowing the correct pronunciation of the words, knowing their individual meanings, and being able to locate information in printed material. Current reading theory defines text comprehension as meaning constructed by a reader through strategic and principled integration of textual information and background knowledge. In fact, the majority of scholars in the field now agree on the nature of reading: reading is the process of constructing meaning from written texts (Anderson, Hiebert, Scott, & Wilkinson, 1985).

Nevertheless, despite convincing arguments based on the study of knowledge acquisition and the mental skills involved in reading, there are people who maintain that there are separate phases of reading, marked by such activities as decoding written symbols into sounds and concatenating the meanings of individual words. For instance, Daniels appears to subscribe to this view in his discussions of reading as saying (1970), reading as comprehending (1979), and reading as thinking (1982). In the case of reading as saying, reading is taken to be a sensory and perceptual process in which recognition of particular letters and words and their identification are prerequisites to comprehension (1970, p. 81). Reading as comprehending is discovering what the string of words means using grammar as a clue to meaning (1979, p. 154). Reading as thinking, the ultimate sense of reading, "involves following an argument, pursuing apparent errors in reasoning, searching for hidden premises, evaluating reasons and a host of other activities" (1982, p. 313).

Daniels portrays reading as a stratified process in which the saying sense is a necessary, though not sufficient, condition for comprehension; and comprehension is prerequisite to, but not sufficient for, reading as thinking. He argues that in addition to recognizing and using the phonetic system, readers must have some degree of competence with the lexical system. So, reading is not only matching sounds with a string of printed words but, "having somehow learned a grammar and acquired a vocabulary, children can generate and follow sensible sentences" (1979, p. 153). Comprehension demands *using* the grammar as a clue to the meaning.

While Daniels's view of reading may present a coherent picture of the logical relations between letter-sound correspondence, word recognition, and comprehension, it is in no sense an adequate psychology of reading. Decoding (knowing the words) and comprehension (determining the meaning) go hand-in-hand (Phillips, 1989b). True, readers must know some words by sight to get off the ground in reading. However, comprehension facilitates decoding. For instance, no amount of decoding, thought of as phonic analysis, will enable a reader to decode or know how to say the word "wind" without also comprehending the context in which it is used. Whether "wind" should be decoded as "wĭnd" or "wīnd" depends on whether it means moving air or to encircle, and its meaning must be judged on the basis of comprehending the specific context in which the word appears.

In his three papers, Daniels reinforces what Martin has referred to as the "literacism" of our society, in which reading ability is seen as a criterion for success rather than as a tool for achievement (Kipp Nelson, 1982). Analyses of reading, such as that done by Daniels, bolster a far too common view that reading is something to be mastered as an end in itself, rather than as a means for achieving new knowledge or pursuing other interests. Daniels's work requires emendations from many perspectives, not the least of which is his linear conception of reading in which thinking is presumed to take place after comprehension. This linear conception is incorrect.

In contrast to theories such as Daniels's, current theory recognizes the seemingly obvious point, overlooked for many centuries, that to understand text one has to think! Consider these four sentences:

1. Jennifer will be here.
2. Will Jennifer be here?
3. I warn you Jennifer will be here.
4. I bet you Jennifer will be here.

Each sentence has the same propositional content, "Jennifer will be here," but a different illocutionary force. Sentence 1 usually has the force of an assertion; sentence 2, the force of a request for information; sentence 3, the force of a warning; and sentence 4 the force of a commissive. When the illocutionary force is not indicated by the words of text or by the syntactic structure of the sentence, then the reader must infer the force from the context. Readers' knowledge of the constitutive and regulative rules of language enables them to make such inferences. In reading, the visual input (text) is supplemented by the reader's knowledge of what the text must mean based upon the context.

The context tells one what to expect, and suggests plausible interpretations of what is being perceived.

Inferring in this way is a constructive thinking process, because a reader expands knowledge by proposing and evaluating competing hypotheses about the meaning of the text in an attempt progressively to refine understanding. Inference is the basis of understanding because it often involves transforming, extending, and relating information (Markman, 1981). It requires the thoughtful use of strategies and principles (Collins, Brown, & Larkin, 1980; Phillips, 1988a, 1988b; van Dijk & Kintsch, 1983), evaluative criteria, intelligent judgment (Ennis, 1969; Norris & Ennis, 1989; Phillips, 1989a), and necessitates the use of relevant text information and background knowledge. Background knowledge is important to inferring for at least three reasons. First, an inference in reading involves the interaction of information provided in the text and background knowledge. In other words, neither textual information nor background knowledge alone is sufficient to make good inferences about text meaning. Second, it is background knowledge that enables the generation of alternative hypotheses in inferring. Third, without background knowledge one cannot evaluate the strength of inferences to generalizations and explanations (Govier, 1985).

The upshot of this history of ideas is the proposal that reading well is thinking well with written language. I shall now examine some empirical work designed to test this hypothesis. I shall proceed first to review the findings of some seminal work by Collins, Brown, and Larkin (1980) on the inference strategies used by adults in text understanding. Thence, I shall present the findings of some of my work on inference strategies used by younger readers. The evidence suggests that the inference strategies are generalizable across both groups and across topics, and have an effect on comprehension independent of readers' background knowledge.

EMPIRICAL RESEARCH ON HOW GOOD THINKING IS EVIDENT WHEN READING

The Collins, Brown, and Larkin Theory of Text Understanding

On the basis of a study of four skilled adult readers, Collins, Brown, and Larkin (1980) contend that readers progressively refine models of the text until they are satisfied that the one they have is plausible. This refinement process consists of a number of problem-solving strategies, much like those used to solve crossword puzzles. If a word is too long or does not fit with other clues, then *rebind,* that is, think of another word. If rebinding does not work, *then question the default interpretation,* for instance, think of the word as a verb rather than as a noun. If the new word conflicts with a crossing word, then question the crossing word or the words that led to it. If none of this works, then *shift focus* to a crossing word to add a constraint, and hence a clue, to one of the slots. Thence, analyze the possible words to fill the remaining slots, try the most likely words, and finally converge on the best word.

In all, Collins, Brown, and Larkin proposed five strategies: rebinding, questioning a default interpretation, questioning a direct or indirect conflict, near or distant shifting of focus, and analyzing and assigning cases. Moreover, they concluded that adults evaluate their models or interpretations of text by:

1. Judging the plausibility of the assumptions and consequences of their models against their background knowledge;
2. Judging the completeness of their models against information in the text;
3. Judging the interconnectedness of their models by weighing the fit of their models with their background knowledge and information in the text; and
4. Judging the match of their models to the text by weighing how well their assumptions and consequences fit particular aspects of the text.

You will note that the four tests used in this progressive refinement model appeal to evaluative criteria that comprise various models of critical thinking (Ennis, 1969; Norris & Ennis, 1989). So, then, this initial evidence suggests that what good readers do is to follow the principles of critical thinking while interpreting texts.

Young Readers' Inference Strategies

Building on the research of Collins, Brown, and Larkin (1980), I conducted a study to identify the inference strategies used by young readers to see whether or not they also followed principles of critical thinking. The results were significant because what was found was that readers' choice of strategy differentiated among good and poor readers, while their background knowledge on the topic did not. Good readers used strategies in accord with theories of critical thinking; poor readers used strategies that violated principles of critical thinking.

Eighty sixth-grade children, forty low-proficiency and forty high-proficiency readers, were studied. Equal numbers of students were assigned randomly to read either three passages on topics familiar to them, or three passages on unfamiliar topics, and to report verbally their thinking as they constructed interpretations. The verbal reporting approach arises out of a desire to gain direct evidence on the hypothesis that reading well is thinking well. In the absence of such an hypothesis, there was no particular interest in studying what readers think, and hence the centuries of *a priori* speculation on symbol-sound correspondence. Two complete verbal report protocols are available in Norris and Phillips (1987).

From the reports of the children's thinking, ten inference strategies were identified as described in Table 10.1. These strategies represent the general procedures that the students used to deal with the text information. The strategies are general in the sense that they were applied to texts regardless of content. In principle, the strategies are also applicable to all text genres. The study itself, however, researched only narrative text. Whether the strategies actually do generalize to expository, poetic, and to other genres, is a question currently under investigation.

On the basis of generally acceptable epistemological standards found in the critical thinking literature (Ennis, 1969; Siegel, 1988), the strategies were classified as either productive or counterproductive. The productive strategies are those that would plausibly contribute to the construction of an acceptable interpretation: (a) Rebinding, (b) Questioning a default interpretation, (c) Shifting focus, (d) Analyzing alternatives, (e) Confirming an immediate prior interpretation, (f) Confirming a nonimmediate prior interpretation, and (g) Empathizing with the experiences of others. These seven strategies are plausibly productive because they lead to interpretations that do not conflict with relevant information, that are able to explain all the relevant information, and that are more consistent and explanatory than alternative interpretations (Ennis, 1969). Such standards are basic to all rational thought.

The counterproductive strategies plausibly would detract from an acceptable interpretation: (a) Assigning an alternate case, (b) Assuming a default interpretation and transforming information, and (c) Withholding or reiterating information. These three strategies are plausibly counterproductive because they either violate recognized standards of rational thought (for example, misconstruing information just to make it fit an interpretation), or clearly lead nowhere, for example, repeating what has been said.

Comparison of Adult and Young Reader Strategies

The results of my study suggest that young readers use up to four strategies to arrive at a similar interpretation as adults achieve in one strategy. Young readers might first raise alternatives but not select one until more information is available. They might then temporarily think about one of these alternatives (Analyzing Alternatives), if subsequent information does not allow

Table 10.1 Young Readers' Inference Strategies

Strategy	Description
Rebinding	A reader suggests a possible interpretation, *immediately* realizes that this interpretation conflicts with previous information, and then substitutes another interpretation.
Questioning a Default Interpretation	A reader questions a *previous* interpretation and/or accompanying assumptions, rather than questioning the current interpretation, when subsequent information is in conflict.
Shifting Focus	A reader addresses related questions that have not yet been considered when the immediate textual information cannot be readily resolved within the reader's interpretation.
Analyzing Alternatives	A reader does not settle on any one interpretation of the data, but raises more than one possibility and remains tentative until more information is available.
Assigning an Alternate Case	A reader temporarily digresses from the ongoing interpretation when new textual information cannot be interpreted to fit within it and subsequent information does not provide a solution.
Confirming an Immediate Prior Interpretation	A reader confirms an interpretation on the basis of information immediately following it.
Confirming a Nonimmediate Prior Interpretation	A reader considers alternate interpretations to the one already made but, on the basis of subsequent information, reverts to the earlier interpretation, confirming it as the choice.
Assuming a Default Interpretation	A reader makes an incorrect interpretation and then misconstrues new data presented in an attempt to confirm that interpretation in spite of inconsistencies.
Withholding or Reiterating Information	A reader either is silent in response to requests for information or rephrases a previously made interpretation without the addition of any new information.
Empathizing with the Experiences of Others	A reader projects himself or herself into the situation and experiences another's condition, and makes this projection part of his or her interpretation without a loss of focus or the introduction of inconsistencies.

them to choose among the alternatives. Subsequently, they might withhold comment until more information is available or just reiterate a previous interpretation (Withholding Information). Finally, they might confirm one of the alternatives on the basis of new information (Confirming Immediately or Nonimmediately). The research by Collins, Brown, and Larkin (1980) and by Collins and Smith (1982) suggests that adults continuously confirm and disconfirm interpretations by evaluating their plausibility, completeness, interconnectedness, and match to the text. It seems that the confirming immediately and nonimmediately strategies are used more automatically by adults than young readers.

The deliberateness of the young readers and the automaticity of the adults is consistent with differences between novices and experts on other sorts of tasks. For example, Larkin, McDermott, Simon, and Simon (1980) report that expert physicists solve problems more automatically, flexibly, and directly than novices. Novices tend to be more conscious, rigid, and indirect. Morales, Shute, and Pellegrino (1985) found similar differences between older and younger children in solving mathematics word problems.

There is undoubtedly an extensive difference in the knowledge accessible by adults and by young readers. Walker (1987) proposes that because experts have greater knowledge they are more sophisticated reasoners, and that because they are more sophisticated reasoners they have greater access to knowledge. This may account for why children are slower to question default assumptions. Nevertheless, the young reader strategies exhibit considerable overlap with the adult strategies, and both groups of readers tend to use a common set of strategies for all topics studied. Where differences exist, they seem to involve the automatic use of strategies by adults that children use quite deliberately.

The Relationship Between Strategy Use and Prior Knowledge

The analysis of the quantitative data collected on the young readers showed that prior knowledge and reading proficiency, defined by vocabulary and comprehension scores on the Canadian Tests of Basic Skills (King, 1981) and teacher judgment, interacted in determining strategy use. Figure 10.1 helps illustrate how this interaction occurred. Position along the vertical line represents the type of strategies used. The closer to the bottom of the line that a student falls, the more the student uses the assuming defaults and withholding information strategies, both counterproductive strategies. The closer to the top of the line, the greater the use of the four productive strategies listed near the top of the figure. The ordered pairs in parentheses to the left of the vertical line represent four categories of student in the studies: (a) those with high prior knowledge of the topic and who had high reading proficiency, (b) those with low prior knowledge of the topic and who had high reading proficiency, (c) those with high prior knowledge of the topic and who had low reading proficiency, and (d) those with low prior knowledge of the topic and who had low reading proficiency.

The figure illustrates that high proficiency readers (regardless of level of prior knowledge of the topic) tended to use the productive strategies more than low proficiency readers. Students of low proficiency (regardless of their level of prior knowledge of the topic) tended to use counterproductive strategies. That is, high proficiency led to greater productive strategy use even in the absence of prior knowledge of the topic, and high prior knowledge of the topic contributed to productive strategy use only in the presence of high proficiency.

A number of conclusions and suggestions arise from these findings. The first conclusion is that thinking strategies are operationally detectable in the verbal reports of people's reading. Second, these strategies were used generally across the several topics that have been studied by Collins, Brown, and Larkin, and by me. The question of genre-generalizability still needs to be addressed, though some preliminary findings are discussed in the following section regard-

Figure 10.1. Plot of group centroids on discriminant function 1.

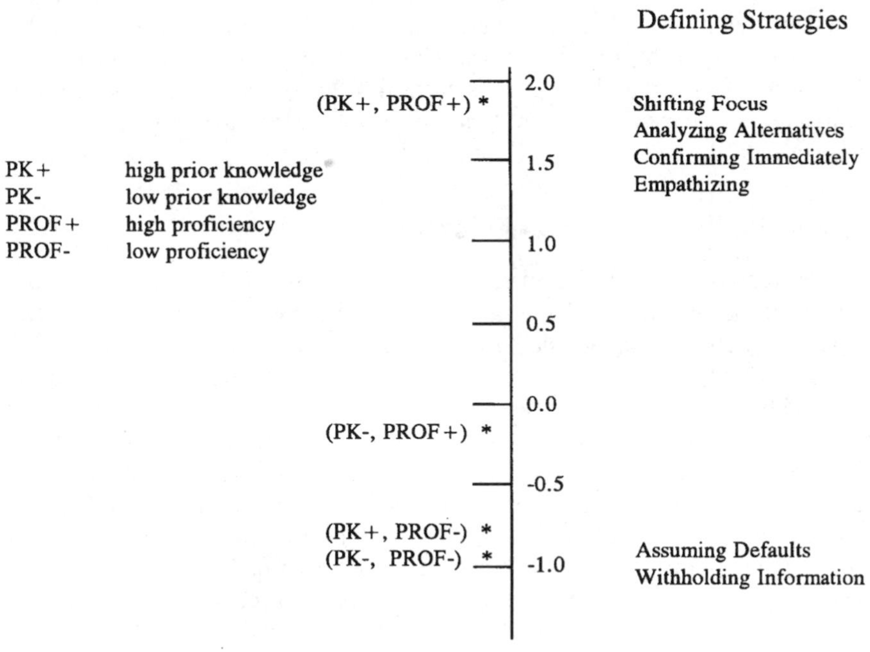

Defining Strategies

(PK+, PROF+) *   — 2.0

PK+   high prior knowledge   — 1.5   Shifting Focus
PK-   low prior knowledge   Analyzing Alternatives
PROF+   high proficiency   Confirming Immediately
PROF-   low proficiency   — 1.0   Empathizing

                                        — 0.5

                                        — 0.0
(PK-, PROF+) *

                                        — -0.5

(PK+, PROF-) *
(PK-, PROF-) *   — -1.0   Assuming Defaults
                                        Withholding Information

ing the comparison of narrative and expository text. Third, the strategies, though general, are strong, despite McPeck's claim that any general strategies are hollow and truistic (1984, p. 39), and Resnick's that general strategies are weak (1987, p. 46). They are strong enough to differentiate more proficient from less proficient readers, something that differences in background knowledge cannot do. This latter finding suggests that knowledge by itself is not enough—it requires general critical thinking strategies to be used effectively. If this is true, there is evidence to support the claim by Siegel (1988), Ennis (this volume), and others that, while knowledge might be necessary for thinking critically in a subject, it is not sufficient.

GENERALIZABILITY OF STRATEGY USE ACROSS SUBJECTS AND TEXT GENRES

There is mounting evidence that episodes of thinking have much in common. Baron (1985, p. 84) claims that each thinking episode calls for the consideration of possibilities, the seeking of evidence, and the setting of goals. Consider the case of an individual interpreting a poem and a mathematical problem. In both cases, the individual should consider the possibilities of interpretation and seek evidence to test the plausibility of each. This means that each piece of evidence can be weighed relative to each possibility. Goals are governed by how disposed a person is to seek the most acceptable resolution in an episode of thinking. In the case of the poem or mathematical problem, some people may have the disposition to ensure that they have worked thoroughly, whereas others may be disposed merely to come up with an answer regardless of the strength of the evidence.

Generalizability Across Subjects

Max Wertheimer in his classic monograph *Productive Thinking* (1959/1945) reports on the "parallelogram problem." He observed a teacher prove to a geometry class, using parallelograms in standard position (that is, longer left to right than top to bottom, with the base of the parallelograms parallel to the top and bottom of the page; see Figure 10.2a), that the area of a parallelogram is equal to the product of the length of its base and its altitude. The teacher illustrated how to find the area first by labeling the corners a, b, c, d, and dropping perpendiculars from d to intersect the base at e, and from c to intersect an extension to the base at f (see Figure 10.2b). This showed that the area of the parallelogram could be represented by the area of a rectangle, e–f–c–d, and, since the students knew how to find the area of a rectangle, it was an easy step to conclude that the area of a parallelogram is equal to the product of the base by the altitude. Repeated numerical examples of finding the area of parallelograms of different sizes, sides, and angles were done by the students and ultimately they did quite well on a quiz.

However, when Wertheimer presented a parallelogram in nonstandard position (original figure turned on its end as illustrated in Figure 10.3), he found one student who flatly refused to try it, saying, "We haven't done that yet," and others who repeated rotely the procedures of the proof they had learned and were stymied when it did not work out. The majority of students dropped perpendiculars from the two upper corners and extended the base line as illustrated in Figure 10.4a. Since the resultant figure did not resemble the one they had seen before, they did not know how to proceed. Other students sat perplexed altogether and wrote the formula "the area is equal to the base times the altitude." A few students either extended the parallelogram as in Figure 10.4b, or turned their papers through forty-five degrees as illustrated in Figure 10.4c, and solved the parallelogram problem.

While Wertheimer's problem was exactly the same as the one given by the teacher, students were unable to solve it because they focused on the steps of the solution that they had memorized, rather than on the properties of the parallelogram, that is, how to draw auxiliary lines to make a rectangle. Most of the geometry students failed to *question their default interpretations* about the steps of the solution, to *shift their foci* from the solution steps to the prop-

Figure 10.2a. Parallelogram in standard position.

Figure 10.2b. Extensions to parallelogram in standard position.

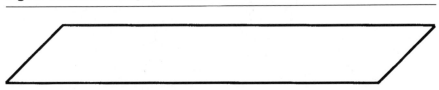

Figure 10.3. Parallelogram in nonstandard position.

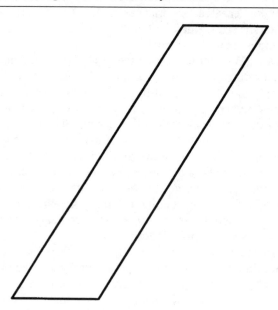

Figure 10.4. Students' extensions to parallelogram in nonstandard position.

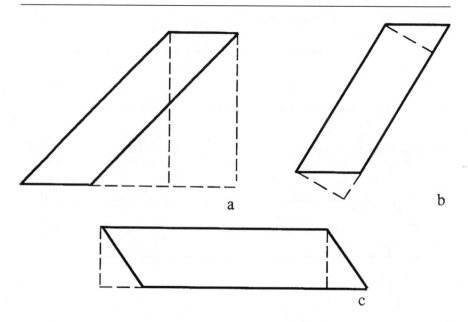

erties of the parallelogram, and to *analyze alternative ways* to solve Wertheimer's problem. The thinking strategies required to solve the parallelogram problem are fundamentally no different from those required to determine the most appropriate meaning for a word in a story. Compare the example reported by Norris and Phillips (1987) in which a sixth grade student forces "a department store" as the meaning of the word "bay" in a story that discusses such things as strong winds, heavy seas, and the splitting and gutting of fish. Just as the geometry students considered one and only one way to solve the new parallelogram problem, the reading student considered one and only one meaning for the word.

Building on Wertheimer's work, Schoenfeld (1989), almost fifty years later, commented that, while much has changed technologically and in other ways in schools, little has changed in how we teach mathematics. The power in learning mathematics lies not in blindly employing procedures, or using procedures in exactly similar circumstances, but in having the ability to use what is learned in circumstances other than those in which it was taught. Such generalization requires understanding the ideas behind the procedures. Schoenfeld summarized how a pair of students attempted to solve a mathematical problem after they had taken his problem-solving course. He reported that "after reading the problem, they jumped into a solution attempt that, unfortunately, was based on an unfounded assumption [that is, Assumed a default interpretation]. They realized this a few minutes later [that is, Shifted focus], and decided to try something else [that is, Analyzed alternatives]" (1989, p. 98). He goes on to say that the students' solution was not expert-like because they rushed into explorations without careful analysis. Furthermore, it was not until they had followed several false starts that they managed to arrive at the best solution, whereas experts quickly truncate false starts.

Note that Schoenfeld's findings are highly similar to the findings about adults and young readers' inference strategies. The results are similar in at least two ways: (a) some of the strategies used in mathematics are similar to those used in reading, and (b) the differences between the expert and novice mathematicians and the expert and novice readers are similar in the time and manner taken to arrive at the best solution. These results suggest that while there may be differences in the specifics of each subject area, there are underlying thinking strategies that are generalizable. Schoenfeld concurs that "there are strong analogies between competent performance in mathematics and competent performance in reading and writing" (1989, p. 87).

Generalizability Across Text Genres

Looking to another subject, science, the counterproductive strategies described previously and used by the less proficient young readers reading the narrative texts are similar to strategies used by poorer students reading science texts that are expository. Roth (1985), for example, found that when students are reading science texts, they often tend to rely too heavily on either their background knowledge or the text; they tend to memorize facts as they appear in the text and fail to relate them to what they know; they rely on prior knowledge to the extent that often they distort or ignore text information to make it fit; and they tend to change their prior knowledge too readily to make it fit with text information.

Researchers in science education have conducted much work on the misconceptions students bring to tasks (Anderson & Smith, 1984). One of the examples reported by Anderson and Smith deals with a series of lessons on light. The science text reads as follows:

> Have you ever thrown a rubber ball at something? If you have, you know that when the ball hits most things, it bounces off them. Like a rubber ball, light bounces off most things it hits.
>
> When light travels to something opaque, all the light does not stop. Some of this light bounces off. When light travels to something translucent or transparent, all the light does not pass through. Some of this light bounces off. When light bounces off things and travels to your eyes, you are able to see. (Blecha, Gega, & Green, 1979, p. 154)

In a two-year study of science teaching at the fifth-grade level, Anderson and Smith (1984) identified students' preconceptions about science and described how these often prevented students from both understanding what they read in their science textbooks and what their teachers taught. In the particular case described, they found that out of more than two hundred fifthgraders, fewer than a quarter of them understood the passage. To explain this failure, Roth, Anderson, and Smith (1983) found that students' preconceptions about light and how vision occurs is at odds with the science text. The majority of students did not have the belief that light must be reflected from the object in order for them to see it, as presupposed in the passage. Moreover, Anderson and Smith (1984) found that even in the face of instruction where counterevidence, examples, and challenges to students' misconceptions were presented, demonstrated, and explained, they persisted in their false beliefs. They concluded that "most fifth-grade students lack self-monitoring ability and sensitivity to dissonance between their own belief systems and the content of written texts (p. 188). The science students, just as those in geometry and reading, failed to question their assumptions about how they see, shift their foci away from how much light there is to the direction that light is reflected, and analyze alternatives in order to explain how light works.

It seems that the strategies used by students in science are in fact highly similar to those used in mathematics and reading, and that there are underlying similarities in how students think. Note also, that inconsiderate science texts (Armbruster, 1984) may be part of the problem. The text says twice that "all light does not pass through" which means that no light passes through. However, the authors really meant to say that some light passes through and some is reflected, that is, that "not all light passes through." Consideration for text comprehension must rest with writers as well as readers.

CONCLUSION

Much research in cognition has pointed to the domain-specificity of subject-matter learning, that is, to the fact that there are different problem-solving strategies in mathematics, reading, writing, and science. However, there is growing additional evidence to suggest that at the self-regulation level, that is, at the level where people direct their thinking, there are similar strategies used across various boundaries. It seems that, regardless of the task, strategies like shifting focus when you realize that you are not making headway, creating and analyzing alternative ways of doing something, weighing the evidence and deciding upon the best alternative, and confirming your choice, are generalizable. The degree of their generalizability still needs exploration. In this paper, I have shown similar self-regulation strategy use between adults and children, between narrative reading and mathematics problem solving, and between narrative reading and expository reading of science.

Many of the strategies identified indicate either a flexible or inflexible use of knowledge and information. When knowledge and information are used inflexibly, alternatives are not considered, negative evidence is not heeded, and presuppositions are not questioned. Such approaches are unproductive in most contexts. This is why the evidence shows, in accord with the theoretical arguments of Ennis (this volume), Paul (1982), Norris and Phillips (1987), and Siegel (1988) that having knowledge and information is not sufficient for good thinking. In addition, individuals need to follow specific strategies in the use of knowledge and information. The evidence shows that the self-regulation thinking strategies discussed in this paper are generalizable and are neither trite nor weak, but the failure to follow productive ones explains why many children read, solve mathematic problems, and learn science poorly.

ACKNOWLEDGMENT

Preparation of this manuscript was supported by grants from the Social Sciences and Humanities Research Council of Canada, grant numbers 410-85-1321 and 410-88-0778.

REFERENCES

Anderson, C. W., & Smith, E. L. (1984). Children's preconceptions and content-area textbooks. In G. G. Duffy, L. R. Roehler, & J. Mason (Eds.), *Comprehension instruction* (pp. 187–201). New York: Longman.

Anderson, R. C., Hiebert, E. H., Scott, J. A., & Wilkinson, I. A. (1985). *Becoming a nation of readers*. Washington, DC: National Institute of Education.

Armbruster, B. B. (1984). The problem of "inconsiderate text." In G. G. Duffy, L. R. Roehler, & J. Mason (Eds.), *Comprehension instruction* (pp. 202–217). New York: Longman.

Baron, J. (1985). *Rationality and intelligence*. New York: Cambridge University Press.

Beebe, M. (1990). Literacy theories informing the teaching of reading: The transition to whole language instruction. In S. P. Norris & L. M. Phillips (Eds.), *Foundations of literacy policy in Canada* (pp. 153–170). Calgary: Detselig.

Betts, E. (1946). *Foundations of reading instruction*. New York: American Book Company.

Blecha, M. K., Gega, C., & Green, M. (1979). *Exploring science* (2nd ed.). River Forest, IL: Laidlaw.

Bloomfield, L. (1933). *Language*. New York: Henry Holt & Company.

Cattell, J. M. (1886). The time it takes to see and name objects. *Mind, 11,* 63–65.

Collins, A., Brown, J. S., & Larkin, K. M. (1980). Inference in text understanding. In R. J. Spiro, B. C. Bruce, & W. F. Brewer (Eds.), *Theoretical issues in reading comprehension* (pp. 385–407). Hillsdale: Erlbaum.

Collins, A., & Smith, E. E. (1982). Teaching the process of reading comprehension. In D. K. Detterman & R. J. Sternberg (Eds.), *How and how much can intelligence be increased* (pp. 173–185). Norwood, NJ.: Ablex.

Daniels, L. (1970). The concept of reading (Part 1: Reading as saying). *The Journal of Education, 16,* 73–84.

Daniels, L. (1979). The concept of reading (Part 2: Reading as comprehending). *Philosophy of Education, 34,* 151–161.

Daniels, L. (1982). The concept of reading: Reading as thinking. *Philosophy of Education, 37,* 309–317.

Davis, F. B. (1968). Research in comprehension in reading. *Reading Research Quarterly, 3,* 499–545.

Ennis, R. H. (1969). *The logic of teaching*. Englewood Cliffs, NJ: Prentice-Hall.

Erdmann, B., & Dodge, R. (1898). *Psychologische untersuchungen uber das lesen auf experimenteller grundlage*. Halle: M. Niemeyer.

Govier, T. (1985). *A practical study of argument*. Belmont, CA: Wadsworth.

Gray, W. S. (1960). The major aspects of reading. In H. M. Robinson (Ed.), *Sequential development of reading abilities* (pp. 8–24). Chicago: University of Chicago Press.

Harris, T. L., & Hodges, R. E. (1981). *A dictionary of reading*. Newark, DE: International Reading Association.

Huey, E. B. (1908). *The psychology and pedagogy of reading*. New York: Macmillan.

Jowett, B. (Trans.) (1942). *The Dialogues of Plato* (2 vols). New York: Random House.

King, E. (Ed.). (1981). *Canadian tests of basic skills*. Don Mills, Ontario: Thomas Nelson.

Kipp Nelson, B. (1982). The pedagogy of reading: Reading as reception. *Philosophy of Education, 37,* 318–322.

Korzybski, A. (1933). *Science and sanity: An introduction to non-Aristotelian systems and general semantics*. Lancaster, PA: The Science Press Printing Company.

Larkin, J., McDermott, J., Simon, D., & Simon, H. (1980). Expert and novice performance in solving physics problems. *Science, 208,* 1335–1342.

Mann, H. (1843). Seventh Report of the Secretary of the Massachusetts Board of Education.

Markman, E. (1981). Comprehension monitoring. In P. Dirkson (Ed.), *Children's oral communication skills* (pp. 61–84). New York: Academic Press.

McPeck, J. (1984). Stalking beasts, but swatting flies: The teaching of critical thinking. *Canadian Journal of Education, 9,* 28–44.

Morales, R. V., Shute, V. J., & Pellegrino, J. W. (1985). Developmental differences in understanding and solving simple mathematics word problems. *Cognition and Instruction, 2,* 41–57.

Norris, S. P., & Ennis, R. H. (1989). *Evaluating critical thinking.* Pacific Grove, CA: Midwest Publications.

Norris, S. P., & Phillips, L. M. (1987). Explanations of reading comprehension: Schema theory and critical thinking theory. *Teachers College Record, 89,* 281–306.

Otis, A. (1916). Considerations concerning the making of a scale for the measurement of reading ability. *Pedagogical Seminar, 23,* 525–535.

Paul, R. (1982). Teaching critical thinking in the strong sense: A focus on self-deception, world views, and a dialectical model of analysis. *Informal Logic Newsletter, 4*(2), 2–7.

Phillips, L. M. (1988a). Young readers' inference strategies in reading comprehension. *Cognition and Instruction, 5,* 193–222.

Phillips, L. M. (1988b). Improving inference ability in reading comprehension. *Journal of College Reading and Learning, 21,* 137–150.

Phillips, L. M. (1989a). *Developing and validating assessments of inference ability in reading comprehension.* Technical Report No. 452. Champaign, Il.: University of Illinois, Center for the Study of Reading (ERIC Document Reproduction Service No. ED 303 767).

Phillips, L. M. (1989b). Specific content knowledge is not necessary for good reading. *Philosophy of Education, 45,* 163–167.

Resnick, L. (1987). *Education and learning to think.* Washington, DC: National Academy Press.

Robinson, H. M. (1964). Developing critical readers. In R. G. Stauffer (Ed.), *Dimensions of critical reading: Proceedings of the annual education and reading conferences, 11,* 1–12.

Roth, K. (1985). Conceptual change learning and student processing of science texts. Paper presented at the annual meeting of the American Educational Research Association, Chicago.

Roth, K., Anderson, C. W., & Smith, E. E. (1983). Teacher explanatory talk during content area reading: Case studies in science teaching. Paper presented at the annual meetings of the National Reading Conference, Austin, Texas.

Schoenfeld, A. (1989). Teaching mathematical thinking and problem-solving. In L. B. Resnick & L. E. Klopfer (Eds.), *Toward the thinking curriculum: Current cognitive research* (pp. 83–103). Alexandria, VA: North Central Regional Education Laboratory.

Siegel, H. (1988). *Educating reason: Rationality, critical thinking, and education.* London: Routledge.

Smith, N. B. (1965). *American reading instruction* (Rev. ed.). Newark: International Reading Association.

Thorndike, E. L. (1917). Reading as reasoning: A study of mistakes in paragraph reading. *Journal of Educational Psychology, 8,* 323–332.

Thornton, A. (1790). Treatise on written language. *Common School Journal,* Vol II.

van Dijk, T., & Kintsch, W. (1983). *Strategies of discourse comprehension.* New York: Academic Press.

Walker, C. H. (1987). Relative importance of domain knowledge and overall aptitude on acquisition of domain-related information. *Cognition and Instruction, 4,* 25–42.

Wertheimer, M. (1959). *Productive thinking.* New York: Harper & Brothers. (Original work published 1945)

Wolf, W., King, M. L., & Huck, C. S. (1968). Teaching critical reading to elementary school children. *Reading Research Quarterly, 3*(4), 435–498.

III Challenges to Generalizability

Jane Roland Martin presents a different slant on the generalizability question in Chapter 11. She asks whether critical thinking should be a general aim of education, in the sense that everyone should be taught to think critically. She comments that, after inspecting much of the critical thinking found in the world, she is not sure whether it is necessarily a good thing. Thus, in answer to one of Johnson's rhetorical questions, Martin would challenge the assumption that goodness is a property semantically related to "critical thinker," and indeed would challenge the appropriateness of many of the properties associated with critical thinkers in theorizing on the matter.

In the first place, she points out, critical thinking demands that the thinker establish distance from the problem under consideration. But when creating distance means that an appropriately caring, compassionate, or concerned response is not given, then the critical thinking is discredited. In fact, Martin wonders why a distance from one's objects of study is to be valued when there are ample traditions in the social sciences and humanities that endorse just the opposite approach. She points to work that argues that the separation of subject from object is not appropriate even in the natural sciences.

As Martin sees it, critical thinking theory focuses on rationality, logic, propositional knowledge, and theoretical understanding; not on friendship and love, intimate knowledge, and integrative intuition. Under current critical thinking theory, the uniqueness of individuals and real situations are problems to be overcome, and personal feelings must not be allowed to stand in the way of objectivity. That this approach does not represent the style of many thinkers is used by Martin to call into question its appropriateness as a general goal of education.

However, if intimacy, love, and the merging of the self with others are to be seen as parts of critical thinking, then the gender barrier is encountered. In the public world, traditionally a world that belonged to men and the world for which the schools are supposed to prepare students, Martin points out that the characteristics of rationality, logic, and distance hold sway. Therefore, she reasons that in order for theories of critical thinking to represent all styles of critical thinking, education itself is going to have to break the gender barrier.

According to Martin, the crucial question we must ask is whether our society is served well by spectator citizens of the type that traditional critical thinking theory would have us produce. Of course, we would produce critical spectators, and these are valuable. But they are valuable for judging the passing scene, and not as participants in it. The problem with this approach is that it limits school children's experience to theoretical inquiry, and, unfortunately, proper thought does not lead necessarily to proper action. The best thinking in the world is no good for people who are not willing and disposed to act upon it.

David R. Olson and Nandita Babu begin Chapter 12 by asking whether the word "critical" serves as a classifier or as an emphasizer in the expression "critical thinking." If it is a classifier, it serves to define a particular domain of thinking, much like "mathematical" in mathematical thinking. They opine, however, that it is an emphasizer, serving a function similar to the word "good" in "good morals." This issue is crucial to whether "critical thinking" is to be treated as a nominal or natural kind term as discussed in Chapter 1.

Olson and Babu then charge that theorizing about critical thinking rests on a defunct psychology that posits the existence of abilities, skills, and dispositions. Such terms have no explanatory power, in their view. The central issue that should be guiding critical thinking research is not what abilities, skills, and dispositions people have, but how people represent situations. Olson and Babu attribute the problem to the fact that much of the critical thinking discourse is philosophical rather than psychological, and that therefore it should be no surprise that it represents ideals better than it characterizes human behavior.

Their next charge is that critical thinking discourse embraces a defunct pedagogy. The idea of teaching general principles of thought and hoping thereby to improve thinking is outmoded. Such general principles may be useful in theoretically characterizing how people ought to think, but it is a mistake to infer from this that they represent the rules by which people do think.

Olson and Babu thence propose a stipulative definition of critical thinking. They suggest that critical thinking is reflection and analysis on what people have said. More specifically, they equate critical thinking with literacy: critical thinking is the interpretation, analysis, and criticism of written texts.

Having offered this stipulation, Olson and Babu argue that the tools for such interpretation, analysis, and criticism are the concepts expressed in such speech act and mental state terms as "say," "mean," "intend," "infer," "assume," and the like. Such terms are used to characterize our own thoughts and the thoughts of others. Therefore, an analysis of the meaning and function of these terms would provide a theory of critical thinking, and an explanation of how the associated concepts are acquired would constitute a promising psychology of critical thinking. Furthermore, Olson and Babu argue, such concepts are general in that they apply to all fields of inquiry.

In terms of pedagogy, Olson and Babu propose that the concepts mentioned above should be seen as the *language* of instruction, but not as the *object* of instruction. The pedagogy appropriate for instruction in the basic set of critical concepts should be based upon two principles: (a) basic concepts are acquired by children before they come to school, and (b) children ought to be encouraged to take a critical stance toward texts by learning to talk about utterances from a theoretical point of view.

Having been one of the strongest critics of critical thinking generalizability, and having faced many equally strong objections to his view, John McPeck takes the opportunity in Chapter 13 to clarify some of his previous conclusions, to reargue some points, and to draw some further conclusions from his antigeneralizability position. McPeck concludes that, because of the plasticity of language, many of the central terms used to talk about critical thinking are vague, and that this vagueness affects the generalizability debate. For instance, if we take the expression "general thinking skill," it is not clear what degree of generality is intended, or how to separate having different skills at a variety of tasks from having the same skill for a variety of tasks. Thus, McPeck feels that the charge that his antigeneralizability position suffers from vagueness in its central terms is a charge that applies equally well to the opposite view. His suggestion is that the vagueness can be less troublesome when discussion about generalizability refers to specific subjects and to critical thinking skills being used within specific contexts.

Furthermore, McPeck takes issue with the question of whether critical thinking learned in the context of school subjects will transfer to everyday life. The dichotomy implied in this question between every-day life and school subject knowledge is false, he maintains. School subject knowledge is studied precisely as preparation for everyday life. The distinction has nothing to do with generalizability, he believes, because it does not address the essence of the transfer problem, which is about whether learning one task helps with learning others. Focus-ing on the relevance of school knowledge to everyday life is to narrow illegitimately the concerns over transfer.

McPeck agrees that some general skills exist, but that their useful-ness is limited. The most useful skills tend to be limited to narrow domains. A distinction that McPeck urges as worthwhile is between skills and their domains of application. Some skills, such as counting, may seem quite narrow, but their domains of application are quite extensive. Thus, the skill as such is not general, but its domain of application is. Other skills may be quite general, but be only narrowly applicable. This point is similar to one made by Blair in Chapter 9.

Charles V. Blatz argues in Chapter 14 that the idea of standardized testing of critical thinking ought to be abandoned in favor of contextu-alized testing. This conclusion is supported on the grounds that critical thinking abilities and dispositions are highly context bound. In particu-lar, contextual variance arises from two categories of differences: (a) differences in community of discussion, and (b) differences in informa-tional context.

A community of discussion exists where there are commonly understood background assumptions and procedures of reasoning. From one community of discussion to another, background assump-tions differ about what exists, and how existents behave. Procedures also differ for determining what is the case and what is to be taken as problematic, and for providing possible solutions to problems. Further-more, procedures for acting upon what is the case also differ. Blatz concludes that critical thinkers are accountable for constraining their reasoning to some community of discussion or another.

Within any community of discussion, differences in informational context occur over time. As common knowledge changes, the expecta-tions for what individuals should know as part of their common knowl-edge also changes. Critical thinkers will be held accountable for what they do not know from this store of common knowledge.

The upshot of these differences, Blatz argues, is that critical think-ing testing can be judged valid only within particular communities of discussion and informational contexts. Any attempt to standardize the community of discussion or the informational context will constrain seriously what is being tested by limiting it to some preferred modes of thought. This result, however, is contrary to critical thinking, on Blatz's view.

None of this is to say that there are no general, abstract patterns and principles of reasoning that individual acts of thinking instantiate. However, just because someone's thinking instantiates some more general pattern or principle of thinking, Blatz holds, in a position closely related to McPeck's, this does not mean that the ability of that person is operationally general. People can be taught to think in general ways, that is, in ways that are free of the constraints of all communities of discussion and informational contexts, and such thinking can be tested. However, learning to think in ways that are general in this sense does not guarantee that someone will have learned to think generally in the sense of being able to think well in ways that are constrained by different contexts of community and information. The upshot, however, is that testing that is true to the highest ideals of critical thinking will likely be localized, nonstandardized testing that relies on information gathered on students over long periods of time in many contexts.

11 Critical Thinking for a Humane World

Jane Roland Martin
University of Massachusetts, Boston

Is critical thinking the same across subjects? Which features of it are generalizable? Does it involve general competencies? These are the issues that spring to mind when the question of the generalizability of critical thinking is raised. Should critical thinking be made a goal of every subject in the curriculum of our schools? Or, what is not the same thing, a goal of that curriculum as a whole? Does the critical thinking taught and learned in school transfer to life on the outside? If so, is that an outcome to be applauded? Whose thinking does the construct "critical thinking" represent anyway? To put it another way, just how universal is it? Should everyone be taught to think critically? If so, does this mean that everyone should be taught the same critical thinking skills, dispositions, and so forth? These are also generalizability questions. That they do not automatically spring to mind suggests that we take their answers for granted. Should we?

DANGEROUS DISTANCE

Should critical thinking be a general aim of education, however that notion is to be construed? I used to assume the answer was an unqualified yes, that of course critical thinking should be taught and the more the better. But after inspecting the critical thinking one finds in the world, I am no longer so sure that it is an unalloyed good.

In a 1984 lecture at the Harvard Divinity School, Robert Coles told a story about himself. While sitting in the officer's dining room in a Mississippi air force base, he watched a crowd of blacks gathering on the beach. It was the early 1960s and they were protesting segregation. But Coles knew that beach. And he said to himself, "Why do they bother? The water's too warm. There are no dunes. If it were Cape Cod it would be a different matter, for that is gorgeous. But this beach is nothing." Transforming a real life problem of racial segregation and oppression into a theoretical issue of aesthetics, he made it easy to solve. He also made it easy for himself to sit there in the air conditioned dining room and watch the action down below.

Coles was questioning the morality of a kind of abstract critical thinking that is all too common. At a national conference of educators I attended not long ago, a noted historian told his audience that instead of speaking on the advertised topic he would deliver a lecture based on an incident of rape that had recently occurred on his university campus, for he had learned a great deal from this. What exactly had he learned? The rape, he said, had caused him to rethink the history of the university. Once again an urgent, real life problem of human suffering—it was a gang rape of a female student by several male undergraduates—had been transformed into an interesting intellectual question. When in the discussion period another noted historian asked him why in a speech about a rape he had not talked about gender, he answered that gender was not relevant. The audience was shocked but in a sense he was right. Just as Coles had neatly conceptualized his problem so that the oppression of blacks by whites was not germane to its solution, this historian had framed his problem so that the violence that men do to women was also not germane. And the similarities between the two cases do not stop there. As Coles's exercise in critical thinking allowed him to sit tight while others joined the fray, this man's exercise let him watch Take Back the Night marches from the library.

One does not have to attend esoteric lectures or conferences to encounter critical thinking gone awry.[1] One need only look at public policy discussions on nuclear war where hawks and doves alike transform a problem of the fate of life on earth into questions of military technology and strategy about which they exercise their considerable powers of critical thinking. It is to be found also in discussions of medical ethics where expert physicians and philosophers turn real cases of birth and death that bring catastrophe into the lives of family members into abstract questions of "the patient's best interest."

Once, in speaking with an anthropologist about the problem of teaching the 3Cs of care, concern, and connection to liberal arts students, I remarked that since her field uses the method of participant observation it must be an especially good vehicle for this purpose. "Not at all," she replied. "We're taught in graduate school to maintain our distance from the people we study. I teach my undergraduates to do this too for they need to learn to think critically about their material." Distance from one's subject matter is precisely the issue here. On the one hand it is what critical thinking seems to demand.[2] On the other, it is what discredits both the thinker and the thinking in the examples I have adduced.

"He has got no good red blood in his body," says Sir James to Mrs. Cadwallader in George Eliot's *Middlemarch* as they discuss Dorothea Brook's impending marriage to Mr. Casaubon. "No," replies Sir James's friend, "somebody put a drop under a magnifying-glass, and it was all semicolons and parentheses" (1956, p. 52). A man who spends his waking hours collecting and classifying material for the Key to all Mythologies he is always writing and never finishing, Mr. Casaubon "dreams footnotes and they run away with all his brains. They say when he was a little boy, he made an abstract of 'Hop o' my Thumb,' and he has been making abstracts ever since. Ugh!," Mrs. Cadwallader adds (p. 52). When, on their wedding trip to Rome, Dorothea asks her husband if he would care to see Raphael's frescoes, he replies, "They are, I believe, highly esteemed. Some of them represent the fable of Cupid and Psyche, which is probably the romantic invention of a literary period, and cannot, I think, be reckoned a genuine mythical product" (p. 146). At this point, even Eliot who tries valiantly to enlist her readers' sympathies with the unlovable Casaubon is moved to comment on how depressing is "a mind in which years full of knowledge seem to have issued in a blank absence of interest or sympathy."

What about a mind in which years of abstract critical thinking have had this same issue? Coles's physical distance from the people on the beach was matched by his emotional distance from their hopes and fears, frustrations and desires. That he soon began to see the world through their eyes and to share their sense of injustice—that in his books (for example, Coles, 1967) he also began to help the rest of us white people to do this too—does not change the fact that from the distance he stood from his subject matter he could not see what was there. As for our historian, he stood at such a distance from the rape victim's pain, shame, and anger that he could not comprehend the pain, shame, and anger his apparent callousness to her suffering caused members of his audience.

WHOSE THINKING IS IT?

If distance has its dangers, is not a radical separation of subject and object nonetheless essential to critical thinking? In one of his talks to students, William James said:

> The spectator's judgement is sure to miss the root of the matter, and to possess no truth. The subject judged knows a part of the world of reality which the judging spectator fails to see, knows more while the spectator knows less, and, wherever there is conflict of opinion and difference of vision, we are bound to believe that the truer side is the side that feels the more, and not the side that feels the less. (1958, p. 150)

Agreeing with James that their "objects" of study are subjects in their own right who actively give meaning to the worlds in which they live, many practitioners of the social or human sciences make a systematic effort to get "inside" those other minds. Historians try to capture the feel of times past and enter into the thoughts of their historical subjects, or at least reconstruct their conceptual frameworks and their reasons for acting. Psychologists try to discover how the individuals they study see others and themselves. Anthropologists try to understand other cultures from the point of view of the people in them. Of course, no matter how hard these researchers work at adopting the standpoint of their subject matter, their success will be a matter of degree since mere human inquirers can never shed all the preconceptions of their own time and place, let alone comprehend those of another. Still, in view of this methodological precept, one wonders why it is supposed that to think critically one must stay at a distance from one's objects of study.

If the social sciences with their emphasis on "Verstehen" do not serve as the model for our theories of critical thinking, do the humanities? Whereas their practitioners exercise the willing suspension of disbelief, analysts of critical thinking like John McPeck stress the suspension of belief (1981, pp. 6, 37, 157). Perhaps, then, the natural sciences serve as the model just as they have in the past for our theories of knowledge.

Although it is generally assumed that when your subject matter is an atom or cell or chromosome there is no alternative to the separation of thinker from object or thought, two analytic studies of women scientists suggest otherwise (see Martin, 1988, pp. 129–130, for more detail). When it was published, Evelyn Fox Keller's *A Feeling for the Organism* (1983) was widely reviewed as a biography of Barbara McClintock. To read it solely in this light is, however, to miss the fact that it reveals a way of doing science that our dominant metascientific theories do not capture. A rigorous sophisticated theoretician, McClintock's research is nevertheless grounded in the concrete life and times of the corn plants she studies. Seeking a holistic understanding that will honor the complexity she sees in nature and the individual uniqueness of the organisms she studies, McClintock establishes what, except for the absence of reciprocity, is best described as a personal or intimate relationship with the corn ears, kernels, and cells she grows and observes.

"Well, you know," a colleague recalls McClintock saying, "when I look at a cell, I get down in that cell and look around" (Keller, 1983, p. 69). Telling Keller that the more she worked with chromosomes the bigger and bigger they got, McClintock says,

> When I was really working with them I wasn't outside, I was down there. I was part of the system. I was right down there with them, and everything got big. I even was able to see the internal parts of the chromosomes—

actually everything was there. It surprised me because I actually felt as if I were right down there and these were my friends. (Keller, 1983, p. 117)

As in cases of friendship between humans, McClintock feels affection for her materials and pays attention to the individuals constituting it as individuals. "No two plants are exactly alike. They're all different," she tells Keller. "I start with the seedling, and I don't want to leave it. I don't feel I really know the story if I don't watch the plant all the way along. So I know every plant in the field. I know them intimately, and I find it a great pleasure to know them" (p. 198).

The personal knowledge of her subject matter McClintock possesses, the intimate relationship in which she stands to her corn at all levels of analysis, the merging of self and objects of study, her holistic intuitions: these are also central features of the scientific practice described by Goodfield in *An Imagined World* (1981). For five years, Goodfield monitored the thought and work of a Portuguese scientist named Anna Brito who, for most of that period, headed a cancer research laboratory in New York City.

In a letter to Goodfield, Anna writes:

We T- and B-lymphocytes travel most of the time in journeys of blood and lymph, and we rest from time to time: in the spleen, the lymph nodes, and Peyer's patches. We don't mix much in obvious ways, but naturally we talk to each other infinitely more than people who look at us realize. In times of great distress—such as when some of us are killed by antilymphocyte serum—the fact that normally we interact becomes more apparent. And when some of us, T-cells, are killed a great increase in the number of pairs of B-cells and of B- and T-cells is observed. (Goodfield, 1981, p. 62)

In conversation she says, "Most importantly, of course, you must identify with what you're doing. You must identify totally. If you really want to understand about a tumor, you've got to *be* a tumor" (p. 226). "You fall in love with a thing," she continues.

Here is a cell. It has been going round all the time, and nobody has taken any notice of it. Suddenly you fall in love with it. Why? You, the scientist, don't know you're falling in love, but suddenly you become attracted to that cell, or to that problem. Then you are going to have to go through an active process in relationship to it, and this leads to discovery. First, there is the building up of the attraction, and the object of your attention eludes you. Then you must try to do things to gain its attention with your concepts. (p. 229)

Compare the images of scientific practice conveyed in Keller's and Goodfield's research with those embedded in our metascientific theories. Philosophers of science focus on rationality and logic, not friendship and love; on propositional knowledge and theoretical understanding, not intimate knowledge and integrative intuition. The uniqueness and complexity of individuals are viewed as problems to be overcome by science, not as irreducible aspects of nature; personal feelings and relationships are taken to be impediments to objectivity, not ingredients of discovery. Were McClintock and Anna social scientists, their concern for concrete individuals and their experiences of merging with the things they study would be considered routine by at least some metatheories of their domain. But they are experimental scientists who study corn, chromosomes, and cells, not human beings and human societies. As such, the fundamental premise upon which "Verstehen" theories rest, namely that of the identity—the shared humanness—of scientist and subject matter is violated.

I have called the cluster of attitudes, assumptions, and experiences that Keller and Goodfield have uncovered "a different style" of doing science (Martin, 1988), on the clear understanding that to mark its existence is not in any sense to prejudge the question of either its prevalence or its association with gender. Just as Carol Gilligan acknowledged that the different voice she was describing "is characterized not by gender but by theme. Its association with women is an empirical observation" (1982, p. 2), so we must await further research before drawing conclusions about the gender specificity, or lack thereof, of the different style. From the studies of Goodfield and Keller one cannot even infer that the different style characterizes the scientific practice of anyone besides McClintock and Anna. It should be noted, however, that Stephen Jay Gould has claimed McClintock's style of doing science as his own (1984). Furthermore, according to Gould, "McClintock's style is not uncommon; it just isn't widely used in her own discipline—evolutionary and taxonomic biology" (p. 6). Gould's comments leave no doubt that the different style is neither a figment of Keller's and Goodfield's imaginations nor an invention of McClintock and Anna. Moreover, since the latter does not fit into the category of naturalist in which Gould places himself and McClintock, one cannot but suspect that this different style is more common to science than even Gould's remarks suggest.

Like our metascientific theories, analyses of critical thinking focus on rationality and logic. Like them, they consider the uniqueness and complexity of individual people, situations, and events as problems to be disposed of, and personal feelings and relationships as obstacles to be overcome.[3] Yet McClintock and Anna do not switch off their critical thinking powers in order to indulge their feelings and become intimate with their chromosomes and cells. Their relationship to their subject matter is an integral part of their critical thinking.

THE GENDER BARRIER

I used to assume that as Aristotle's rules of logic captured the way people actually think—at least when they are thinking logically—what educators call critical thinking was supposed to represent the way people think when they are thinking critically. That it does not adequately represent the different style of Anna, McClintock, and many many other critical thinkers raises questions about the status of the construct of critical thinking itself as well as about the wisdom of making it as it stands a general goal of education. Yet it must be acknowledged that the principles of selectivity that have allowed central elements of the different style to drop out of the picture also make it possible for critical thinking to be incorporated into the goals of education.

Although in his review of Keller's *A Feeling for the Organism,* Gould quoted a passage from the book that makes reference to the relation of intimacy in which McClintock stands to her subject matter, he did not explicitly claim this aspect of her style (see Martin, 1988). Focusing on her intuitive mode of reasoning and her interest in the development of concrete individuals, he allowed her feelings for the organisms she studies to drop out of the picture. How are we to explain this gap in his account? Is it that when science is viewed as a fundamentally epistemological enterprise, intimacy, friendship, and love are seen as complications to be avoided? Since Gould is someone who honors complexity in nature, this does not explain how he could possibly have excluded it from his description of the study of nature. Let us not forget, however, that intimacy, the merging of self and other, and the love that involves these are considered in our culture to be feminine traits or characteristics (Kaplan & Bean, 1976; Kaplan & Sedney, 1980; Martin, 1988). Wanting the different style to be appreciated, and believing correctly that to the extent that it was associated with femininity it would be denigrated, Gould had added reason to ignore these aspects of it.[4]

Acknowledge that intimacy, love, and a merging of self and other have important roles to play in critical thinking and one immediately encounters the gender barrier. The rationality and logic that according to standard accounts lie at the very heart of critical thinking are considered masculine in our culture (cf. Keller, 1985; Harding, 1986). Since a field's "persona" derives not only from the attributes of its practitioners but from the gender assignment of its various elements, critical thinking itself is perceived as a masculine endeavor. It is not one of these "soft" subjects like art or literature. It is a "tough" minded, "hard" headed one like science and mathematics. Because masculinity and femininity are construed as polar opposites, to introduce into accounts of critical thinking elements that are labeled feminine would be to detract from the field's masculinity. This step would also court denigration, because what is seen as feminine in our culture tends to be devalued.

But critical thinking would not only suffer "a loss of masculinity" and a consequent loss of status if its standard analyses were to incorporate elements considered feminine. It would also be inconsistent with what is assumed to be the function of education. Briefly, in our culture, school and college are expected to prepare people for life in the "public" or "civic" world by making them capable of being economically self-sufficient and responsible citizens of a democracy (see Martin, 1985). Since, historically speaking, that public world belonged to men, it is considered to be the place where the presumed "masculine" attributes of rationality and logic, distance and disconnection hold sway, even though women have long since entered it. It is also assumed that the so-called "feminine" attributes of intimacy, love, and the 3Cs of care, concern, and connection are irrelevant to the activities and processes that occur there. Not surprisingly, their place is considered to be the world of the private home. In relation to this cluster of assumptions about education, gender, and the "two worlds," it is downright irrational to expect schools to teach a critical thinking that stresses love and replaces distance with intimacy and connection. It makes no sense at all to foster a kind of thought appropriate to the private home, if the function of school is to prepare young people for life in the world beyond, and the two worlds are taken to be polar opposites.

No matter how deeply one believes that our theories and analyses should represent the whole range of critical thinkers, this goal will be difficult, if not actually impossible, to achieve unless the gender barrier standing in the field of critical thinking is broken. No matter how much one deplores the examples introduced earlier, as educators we can do little about them unless we are willing to go through the gender barrier that stands as high in education as it does in the domain of critical thinking. It can be done. The assumptions that the sole function of education is preparation for the public world; that the public world and the private home are separate and opposite realms; that intimacy, connection, and the like are appropriate only in the one world, can be disputed. The construction of masculinity and femininity as polar opposites, the assumption that biological males and females who fall at the "wrong" end of the continuum are unnatural or abnormal, the value hierarchy that places the masculine end above the feminine can all be rejected. Since these beliefs are so deeply rooted in our cultural consciousness that we are barely aware of them, the first and one of the most difficult steps in the process of breaking the gender barrier is to acknowledge its existence. But even when this step is accomplished, the question arises of whether the exclusion of intimacy, connection, and the like is not a small price to pay to make acceptable an educational goal, that, in Harvey Siegel's words, is "reflective of a commitment to liberation and empowerment" (1988, p. 76).

EDUCATION FOR CRITICAL SPECTATORS

A critical thinking premised on distance is consonant with the goals of education today not only because it cuts reason off from love and the 3Cs and divorces self from other, but because it separates mind from body and thought from action (see Martin, 1992). Confessing that she is sorry for Mr. Casaubon, Eliot says:

> It is an uneasy lot at best, to be what we call highly taught and yet not to enjoy; to be present at this great spectacle of life and never to be liberated from a small hungry shivering self—never to be fully possessed by the glory we behold, never to have our consciousness rapturously transformed into the vividness of a thought, the ardour of a passion, the energy of an action, but always to be scholarly and uninspired, ambitious and timid, scrupulous and dimsighted. (1956, p. 207)

In far less passionate prose John Dewey told school people not to separate mind from body, thought from action, reason from feeling and emotion, self from other. Yet this is precisely what our schools and colleges today are expected to do and it is what the goal of critical thinking, as this is usually understood, does.

"I am a whole human being. Help me to form myself in my wholeness and let me develop my real potential" (Bloom, 1987, p. 339). In *The Closing of the American Mind,* Allan Bloom, who admits to having no use for Dewey's philosophy, put those Deweyan words in a student's mouth. Savoring the memory of his own undergraduate days at the University of Chicago and taking it for granted that the development of a human being's "real" potential and the development of that person's mind are one and the same, Bloom has asked us to place the "Great Books" at the center of the college curriculum. That way students can address the "great questions that must be faced if one has to live a serious life" (p. 227). What kind of life is that? Judging from his account of what he considers to have been one of the significant triumphs of his teaching career, it is a life of spectatorship.

A few years after Coles sat in that officers' dining room looking down at the civil rights protest, the students where Bloom was teaching were engaged in mass political protests that encompassed critiques of the university itself. Bloom himself stayed in the classroom reading Plato's *Republic* with twelve or so freshmen. "They were really more interested in the book than the revolution," he has reported with satisfaction. Indeed, they "were rather contemptuous of what was going on, because it got in the way of what they thought it important to do. They wanted to find out what happened to Glaucon during his wonderful night with Socrates. They really *looked down* from the classroom on the frantic activity outside, thinking they were privileged, hardly a one tempted to join the crowd" (p. 332). As Bloom later discovered, some of his students had run off copies of a passage from the *Republic* and distributed them to the protesters. "They had learned from this old book what was going on and had gained real distance on it, had had an experience of liberation," he says (p. 333). The passage? It is one in which Socrates warned against joining exactly the kind of action taking place down below because in a crowd one loses one's judgment and is swept away.

Acute as are Socrates's and Plato's insights into mob psychology and the dangers of uncritical emulation, the question we need to ask is not, "Which students were right, the ones down below or those up there in the classroom?" but, "Is a democratic society well served by spectator-citizens, even ones who are accomplished critical thinkers?"

Bloom, of course, was concerned only with the curriculum of the denizens of the Ivy League, the University of Chicago, Stanford, and the like in *The Closing of the American Mind*. Echoing the principle Plato enunciated in the *Republic* that only the special few are capable of thinking about the great philosophical questions, he recommended a spectator's life not for all but for that small number without whose presence "no society...can be called civilized." As Plato held that only those educated for a life of reason are qualified to rule the state, Bloom said that only those whose education he was discussing would become "the models for the use of the noblest human faculties" and hence "benefactors to all of us, more for what they are than for what they do" (p. 21).

Before her marriage, Dorothea Brooke thought that Mr. Casaubon was one of those models. But upon close acquaintance she changed her mind, preferring those like her husband's physician, Lydgate, who tried, however unsuccessfully, to make the world a better place in which to live. In defense of spectatorship Bloom might say that Mr. Casaubon had too small a mind—or perhaps a too poorly trained one—to ponder the great questions. Were that maker of abstracts as *self*-critical as he was critical of the scholarship of others, he would tell us that one big question Bloom himself needed to ask and did not is how education can inform life—as almost everyone says it should—if it is only devoted to turning out spectators thereof.

Spectatorship is not just built into the Great Books curriculum that Bloom would proffer our most academically talented undergraduates. It stands at the very heart of the one that is prescribed for undergraduate liberal education in general. It stands also at the core of the curriculum that educators today believe our elementary and secondary schools should provide to all.

The natural sciences, the social and behaviorial sciences, the humanities: these are the bodies of knowledge that our elders tell us should in one form or another constitute the liberal curriculum of our higher education. Simplified versions are also held to be the main components of "lower" education. Carving up the world into separate domains, treating selected aspects of the one they claim to study, asking their own specialized questions of their subject matter, and using their own technical languages, the various fields or disciplines of knowledge that fall under these three broad categories have spectatorship built into them from the start. Theirs is not to do or die. It is to tell the reason why the world is the way it is, or at least to describe what it is like and how it works. Thus, to base the curriculum of our nation's schools and colleges around these studies—as most critics want our schools to do—is to teach our young *about* the world, to "produce" observers *of* it, not participants *in* it.

Of course, in developing their theories scientists do much more than observe. Conducting experiments, they tamper with nature as they study it and interrupt natural processes to learn more about them. Yet their interventions are for the sake of gaining knowledge or understanding of the world, not acting in it. As they themselves tell us, the uses of science, not to mention its abuses, are not their business *qua* scientists although they may be *qua* citizens. Thus, when educators say that students should be taught those organized bodies of knowledge we call science, they implicitly recommend that our young learn to see through the lenses of one or another spectator. When some of them add that, since scientific knowledge is not God-given but a human construction, physics, chemistry, biology, and the rest should be taught also as fields of human inquiry, they are saying that students should acquire not merely the knowledge of one or more observers of nature but the corresponding attitudes and methodologies as well.

Add the goal of critical thinking to an education in spectatorship and one does not get agency. One gets critical spectatorship. True, critical thinking involves agency in that the student must exercise complex skills, exhibit certain tendencies, and use good judgment (Ennis, 1981). But it is directed toward judging or evaluating the passing scene, not participating in it. Insofar as this can be said to reflect commitments to liberation and empowerment, it is to the liberation and empowerment of thought, not action.

LETTING LIFE HAPPEN

Even if analyses of critical thinking incorporated the care and connection, intimacy and love of the different style, an education in critical thinking would still support spectatorship. The different style of doing science requires, if not an absolute merging of researcher and object of inquiry, at least a genuine attempt to identify with the object of study. But although the distance between the observer and the observed is so greatly reduced that the judging spectator may not miss the root of the matter after all, the end is still understanding. The theories gained still serve as conceptual lenses through which to see the world. Other stances toward nature than that of spectator are possible, however. Like the members of a Cape Cod bird walk, one can acquire the kind of familiarity with it that we usually reserve for our friends and acquaintances. Like Henry David Thoreau, one can think of oneself as living in it. Like many of our first settlers, one can seek to subdue rather than understand it. Like environmental activists today, one can work to guard it from human destruction (see Martin, 1992).

It is often said that the difference between the natural and the human sciences is that only in the latter is it possible to adopt the standpoint of one's object of study. However, the different style of McClintock and Anna suggests otherwise. Think about the school and college curriculum instead of methodology, however, and a clear difference between the natural and the human sciences emerges. Because the latter takes human beings and their activities as their domain of study, students can get inside their subject matter not just to see the world from another's standpoint. They can get inside to *learn* human activities as well as *learn about* them. In other words, besides teaching our young about drama's historical development, its societal function, and its aesthetic qualities; besides trying to get them to see the world as Shakespeare or Euripides did; it is possible to teach them to write, perform, and produce dramatic works. In addition to conveying knowledge about voting patterns, alternative models of democracy, the history of revolutions, and the intricacies of parliamentary government, educators can teach their students to run for office, lobby legislative bodies, participate in political campaigns, and work on the staffs of elected officials.

The curriculum of "choice" casts young people in the single role of spectator of life. Even the exceptions to this rule prove it. Insofar as that curriculum initiates students into the methodologies of the various disciplines as well as transmitting to them the bodies of knowledge arrived at by those fields of inquiry, it does teach our young to engage in a human activity—theoretical inquiry. However, that privileged kind is itself a form of spectatorship. Insofar as that curriculum fosters the activity of critical thinking, it teaches an especially sophisticated type of spectatorship.

In education, as in life, participation in a human activity is not always a desirable goal, of course. If history, psychology, and physics are worthwhile activities for students to engage in; if occupations like drama and politics—or at least selected aspects of these—are too; if health care, protecting the environment, and preparing nutritious meals are valid additions to our list, then drug dealing and rape, polluting our air and rivers, abusing young children and battering their mothers, denying jobs and housing to people of color and persecuting them and other minorities are not.

The trouble with an education for spectatorship is not that all forms of human activity and behavior belong in our children's education and only one—theoretical inquiry—is included. It scarcely needs saying that we should avoid teaching pickpocketing and mugging, extortion and terrorism. Its problem is that it leaves no curriculum space for the enormous range of ways of acting and forms of living that the young of any nation need to learn and that are especially required by those in our condition. Supplying students with different kinds of lenses for different occasions—now those of a physicist, now those of a historian, a psychologist, a philosopher—and also with lenses of different strengths so that a slice of life past and present can be seen from a distance or close up, this program turns them into more versatile spectators of the world than Mr. Casaubon was. But although there are many views from outside and although glasses for distance as well as close work have their rewards, an education that favors spectatorship over participation—that is devoted almost exclusively to the former—is not an appropriate one for the young of any society, certainly not ours.

Adopting the standpoint of a teacher of a book-centered curriculum Bloom remarked, "Life will happen to his students" (1987, p. 21). There is no doubt about that. The most academic study in the world will not keep them from living some kind of life or other. Yet this brute fact makes a mockery of an education devoted wholly to spectatorship. Since as human beings students are and continue to be experiencers, doers, agents, performers—in other words, participants in living—and since they are not born knowing how to do the things and perform the activities that constitute human life, it is wholly perverse to teach our young to be only competent watchers, perceivers, observers, and assessors. In the best of scenarios—those that include the goal of critical thinking—an education solely for spectatorship teaches students to lead bifurcated lives. Instructing them to apply their intelligence in observing the world, it teaches them by default if not design to be unthinking doers—people to whom life just happens. In the worst of scenarios it consigns them to the nasty, brutish, and short life Hobbes attributed to the state of nature.

Mindless imitation is the easiest path for one to follow who has not been trained to bring intelligence to bear on living. In the United States, where the violence in our public places matches that in our private homes, the evil that Socrates inveighed against is doubly dangerous, because the ideas and the behavior that are most conspicuous and therefore the easiest to emulate are also the most destructive.

EXPANDING THE CIRCLE OF CONCERN

Does not the critical thinking learned in the classroom transfer to life on the outside? The examples I introduced earlier suggest that it sometimes does; that just as in school critical thinking is an abstract intellectual exercise to be performed on prepackaged subject matter, in the world it is a game to be played with whatever materials are at hand. However, if we are genuinely interested in having critical thinking inform life, we must think about how to teach it without separating thought and action. Perhaps if we can figure out how to make it inform life in classrooms, we will discover the key to generalizing it to the world beyond.

The integration of critical thought and action will not in itself accomplish what critical thinking's advocates claim for it, however. I used to assume, as Siegel does, that critical thinking "has ramifications undesirable for the fascist, since the attitudes, traits, dispositions, habits of mind, and skills to be fostered according to that ideal would tend to undermine the authority of any fascist leader and similarly would tend to undermine the subservience of the citizenry on which a fascist (and many another) regime depends" (1988, pp. 69–70). Yet history does not bear this out. Werner von Braun has to have been a good critical thinker to have accomplished what he did in World War II. Those officers who worked out the final solution had to think long and hard to devise such an efficient system for carrying out a brand new idea. True, there were flaws in the design of the experiments done by Nazi doctors but that hardly suggests that they did not do their fair share of critical thinking before turning human skin into lampshades.

It is tempting to say that those who supported the Third Reich were not critical thinkers in that they did not subject the basic assumptions of Nazi ideology to critical scrutiny. However, the thesis that they could not have done this and continued to support the regime presupposes not only that all critical thinkers will reach the same conclusion about a given question but that critical thought guarantees appropriate action. Even if the first assumption is correct, the second is not. The thesis also assumes that to think critically about some issue, one must question all relevant assumptions. The truth of the matter, however, is that, like all thought, critical thinking is necessarily selective. One of the tendencies Robert Ennis has told us a rational thinker displays is to "Take into account the total situation" (1981, p. 145). Yet one cannot think critically about everything at once: some things must be assumed so that others can be scrutinized critically. Indeed, in an entire lifetime one cannot think critically about everything: there is too much to be thought about and, in any case, there is always something new. Whether the goal of critical thinking has undesirable implications for the fascist will at the very least, therefore, depend on *what* is thought about critically. Think critically about alternative proposals for attaining a final solution but not about the end itself, and the consequences will be desirable for fascism, not undesirable. Think critically about how the state can best be served but not about whether to obey a superior, and the fascist leader's authority will be maintained, not undermined.

The political ramifications of critical thinking will also depend on *how* the thing in question is thought about. Keep a sufficient distance from the human suffering at issue and one will not be outraged by racism and rape. Nor will one question the commands of an authority. One of the main lessons of Stanley Milgram's studies was that the further removed the subjects were from their "victims," the easier it was for them to deliver what they thought were strong electric shocks (1974). In their case, out of sight really did mean out of mind. We do not know how the subjects would have behaved had they known their "victims" and cared about them. But we do know that one does not literally have to see the people to whom one feels closely connected in order to feel their suffering and refrain as best one can from doing them harm. We know too that one does not have to be literally acquainted with a person in order to exhibit care, concern, and connection. *Lest Innocent Blood be Shed* is the remarkable story of "how goodness happened" in Le Chambon during World War II. It happened there because the inhabitants of that French village cared so much about the victims of Nazis—people they did not know personally—that they did not merely feel their pain. They gave them shelter. When in 1942, nine thousand French police remained indifferent to the rounding up of twenty-eight thousand Jews in an arena in Paris from whence they were shipped to concentration camps, Magda Trocmé had already said to a stranger, a German Jew who had knocked at her front door, "Naturally, come in, and come in" (Hallie, 1979, p. 120).

I began by saying that the distance that critical thinking seems to presuppose is a dangerous thing. Am I now suggesting that closeness is an unalloyed good? Traveling in North Carolina, William James was struck by the destruction of the forest. "No modern person," he mused, "ought to be willing to live a day in such a state of rudimentariness and denudation" (1958, p. 151). He changed his mind quickly, however, when he asked a mountaineer about the new clearings. "I instantly felt that I had been losing the whole inward significance of the situation," he said. And he added:

> When *they* looked on the hideous stumps, what they thought of was personal victory. The chips, the girdled trees, and the vile split rails spoke of honest sweat, persistent toil and final reward. The cabin was a warrant of safety for self and wife and babes. In short, the clearing, which to me was a mere ugly picture on the retina, was to them a symbol redolent with moral memories and sang a very paean of duty, struggle, and success. (pp. 151–152)

James concluded that he had been "blind to the peculiar ideality of their condition" (p. 152). A century later we who watch the destruction of rain forests, think about the consequences for the planet, and then appreciate its meaning for those engaged in the denudation, must think twice before agreeing with him that the subject's judgment is always to be preferred and the spectator's necessarily misses the root of the matter.

If keeping one's distance from a situation prevents one from seeing some of its central aspects and feeling its force, standing up close can make one myopic. In *The Making of the Atomic Bomb,* Richard Rhodes (1988) has reported Robert Oppenheimer's November 1945 response to the question of why scientists built the bomb the United States had dropped on Japan only three months earlier. Oppenheimer cited the fear that Nazi Germany would build it first, the hope that the war would be shortened, and the motives of curiosity and a sense of adventure. "When you come right down to it," the head of the Los Alamos Project said, "the reason that we did this job is because it was an organic necessity. If you are a scientist you cannot stop such a thing. If you are a scientist you believe that it is good to find out how the world works; that it is good to find out what the realities are...." (Rhodes, 1988, p. 761). Oppenheimer was so close to the project he had carried brilliantly to completion that he managed to transform a question about death and destruction, war and peace, into one about the inviolability of scientific curiosity. Yet, although he did not have enough distance from his object of thought, the remedy for his myopia is not distance *per se.* Because it is so easy to be swayed by special interests and pleadings when one identifies with one's object of thought, we tend to equate closeness with bias or partiality and distance with objectivity. But Oppenheimer, who was his own object of thought, needed to distance himself from himself and his project *in order to decrease his distance from the bomb's victims.* Too little distance from the project prevented him from drawing into his circle of concern those whom it harmed.

McPeck has said that "learning to think critically is in large measure learning to know when to question something, and what sorts of questions to ask" (1981, p. 7). If the links to democracy that have been ascribed to the goal or ideal of critical thinking are to be forged, critical attention will have to be paid to the questions that children are encouraged to ask in school, and thought and action will have to be integrated. The best thinking in the world is of little avail if a person has not acquired the will, the ability, the skill, the sensitivity, and the courage to act on it. If the critical thinking they learn in school is to inform a *humane* democracy, it will also have to include a large measure of learning to feel connected to others, a goal that brings us right up against the gender barrier. But in any case, if the goal of critical thinking is to reflect a genuine commitment to the liberation and empowerment of both sexes, the gender barrier will have to be crossed. There is by now enough evidence to suggest that when critical thinking adopts a masculine persona, education in it may have ramifications undesirable for girls and women (Gilligan, 1982; Gilligan, Ward, & Taylor, with Bardige, 1989; Belenky, Clinchy, Goldberger, & Tarule, 1986). If the field of critical thinking is going to address these, it will have to get enough distance on itself to draw into its circle of concern the people it might otherwise harm. This also will involve facing barriers other than the gender one, such as those of race and class.

Should critical thinking be a general aim of education? Definitely yes, if instead of being taught to keep their distance from their objects of study, students learn to expand their circle of concern. But even when it incorporates the different style, critical thinking is still thinking, and no matter how much one values thought, education encompasses far more than that.

NOTES

1. In contrast to the case cited by Passmore (1967, p. 193) of a person who automatically questions every assertion, the instances of critical thinking gone awry to which I draw attention are cases of critical thinking as that has tended to be defined.

2. I use "seems" here because my point is to show that critical thinking does not demand this kind of distance.

3. Siegel (1988, Ch. 2) maintains that critical thinking involves emotions but the emotions he cites have epistemic objects; for example, the critical thinker loves truth and rationality. McClintock and Anna may love truth but the relevant point here is that they love their subject matter or objects of inquiry.

4. It should be noted that this point about the gender association of elements of the different style is different from the one made above that whether the different style is associated predominantly with women scientists is an empirical question. It does not follow from the fact that a given trait is considered feminine in a culture that only or primarily women will display it.

REFERENCES

Belenky, M. F., Clinchy, B. M., Goldberger, N. R., & Tarule, J. M. (1986). *Women's ways of knowing*. New York: Basic Books.

Bloom, A. (1987). *The closing of the American mind*. New York: Simon & Schuster.

Coles, R. (1967). *Children of crisis* (Vol. I). Boston: Atlantic-Little, Brown.

Eliot, G. (1956). *Middlemarch*. Boston: Houghton Mifflin.

Ennis, R. H. (1981). Rational thinking and educational practice. In J. F. Soltis (Ed.), *Philosophy and education* (Eightieth yearbook of the National Society for the Study of Education) (Part I, pp. 143–183). Chicago: University of Chicago Press.

Gilligan, C. (1982). *In a different voice*. Cambridge: Harvard University Press.

Gilligan, C., Ward, J. V., & Taylor, J. M., with Bardige, B. (1989). *Remapping the moral domain*. Cambridge: Harvard University Press.

Goodfield, J. (1981). *An imagined world*. New York: Harper & Row.

Gould, S.J. (1984). Review of Evelyn Fox Keller: *A feeling for the organism. New York Review of Books, 31*, 3.

Hallie, P. (1979). *Lest innocent blood be shed*. New York: Harper & Row.

Harding, S. (1986). *The science questions in feminism*. Ithaca, NY: Cornell University Press.

James, W. (1958). On a certain blindness in human beings. In *Talks to teachers*. New York: Norton.

Kaplan, A. G., & Bean, J. P. (Eds.). (1976). *Beyond sex-role stereotypes*. Boston: Little Brown & Co.

Kaplan, A. G., & Sedney, M. A. (1980). *Psychology and sex roles*. Boston: Little Brown.

Keller, E. F. (1983). *A feeling for the organism*. San Francisco: W. H. Freeman.

Keller, E. F. (1985). *Reflections on gender and science*. New Haven, CT: Yale University Press.

Martin, J. R. (1985). *Reclaiming a conversation*. New Haven, CT: Yale University Press.

Martin, J. R. (1988). Science in a different style. *American Philosophical Quarterly, 25*, 129–140.

Martin, J. R. (1992). *The schoolhome*. Cambridge, MA: Harvard University Press.

McPeck, J. E. (1981). *Critical thinking and education*. New York: St. Martin's Press.

Milgram, S. (1974). *Obedience to authority*. New York: Harper & Row.

Passmore, J. (1967). On teaching to be critical. In R. S. Peters (Ed.), *The concept of education* (pp. 192–211). New York: Humanities Press.

Rhodes, R. (1988). *The making of the atomic bomb*. New York: Simon & Schuster.

Siegel, H. (1988). *Educating reason: Rationality, critical thinking, and education*. New York: Routledge.

12 Critical Thinking as Critical Discourse

David R. Olson
Ontario Institute for Studies in Education
Nandita Babu
Utkal University

Yes Virginia, there is such a thing as critical thinking and it can be taught, practiced, and exercised. But, like Santa Claus, the original object of Virginia's question, critical thinking may not be quite what it is ordinarily taken to be. What it is taken to be varies somewhat as the writings of McPeck (1981), Resnick (1987), and Ennis (1989) make clear. For present purposes, it is enough to note that the expression is commonsensically taken to refer to a kind of thinking that is characterized by abstractness, systematicity, appropriateness, and validity. Further, it is taken to consist of a set of principles or rules which could be taught and which could, therefore, be usefully specified in a curriculum devoted to the development of "critical thinking skills and dispositions." The first part of this paper is devoted to a criticism of these assumptions; the second part towards a theory of subjectivity and reflectivity that could help give content to such a notion as "critical thinking."

There are three fundamental, perhaps fatal, limitations to the "critical thinking movement." First, "critical thinking" seems not, at least not yet, to have a content or domain of its own. At issue is the meaning or use of the term "critical" in the phrase "critical thinking." An adjective such as "critical" may serve either of two functions. One function is that of an *emphasizer* such as the "good" in the phrase "good morals"; or as the adjectives "quick," "sound," or "clear" modifying "thinking" in which role they emphasize the goodness or virtue or value of thinking. Such adjectives carry little semantic value; there is no difference between the request to "think about p" and to "think clearly or critically about p." The second function is that of a *classifier*, such as the adjectives "mathematical" or "musical" in the phrases "mathematical thinking" and "musical thinking." The adjective here classifies a domain and defines a particular content.

The first issue, then, is the function of the adjective "critical" in "critical thinking." My suspicion is that it is an emphasizer similar to "good," "sound," "clear" when modifying the gerund "thinking." If critical thinking is intrinsically good thinking then it would seem to be an emphasizer; if it is a particular kind of thinking, applying to a particular set of objects, for example, it could be a classifier. No such set of objects has yet been defined, although Ennis's (1989, p. 4) suggestion "the correct assessing of statements" and theories of metacognition seem to be promising. I shall return to those suggestions in the second half of the paper. "Critical" thinking either has a distinctive content or it has none at all.

The second limitation is that discourse about critical thinking and the teaching of critical thinking is typically framed in psychological terms such as "skills," "abilities," and "dispositions": In order to be a critical thinker, a person must have...certain attitudes, dispositions, habits of mind, and character traits (Siegel, 1988, p. 39). Yet, almost a half-century of psychology has gone into disabusing us of the explanatory value of such notions as traits, abilities, and dispositions. Nothing is added by the term "skill" in the phrase "critical thinking skill"; this is mere hypostatization—creating an entity by adding the noun "skill." Consequently, critical thinking is not explained by saying that someone has critical thinking abilities or dispositions. It is not an explanation of why someone took the money to say that he is larcenous or has a disposition to larceny. Furthermore, the theory of dispositional traits has been found to be ungeneralizable; whereas an observer may be tempted to describe another's missing the train by saying that the person is tardy or slothful, the subject of the description usually rejects the description, pointing rather to situational factors such as inability to find an umbrella. This pattern of erroneous description is referred to as the "fundamental attribution error" (Ross, 1977). To see this point in the present context let us consider the concept of intelligence, a central trait and dispositional term in what may be regarded as a defunct psychology.

Intelligence was traditionally taken to be a quantitative variable, an underlying trait or ability that could help to explain what people could or could not do. Thus, Binet's contribution was to devise a set of test items that was diagnostic of the degree of intelligence a person possessed. Of course, the IQ test was, and continues to be a useful device, but the theory of abilities it gave rise to is dated if not obsolete. The decisive shift occurred when Piaget took many of the same test items or problems that Binet had used to determine the degree of ability people possessed, and used them to show that when children failed such items it was not because they lacked some intellectual ability but because they represented—(roughly) thought about—the item in a different way. Thus, children failed the water level task not because they lacked an ability but because they represented water level in terms of the axis of the bottle rather than the gravitational axis. Their reasoning followed precisely from the representation they had assigned (Olson & Bialystok, 1983). It is not a matter of a person having more or less or an underlying ability or disposition, but rather a matter of how the subject represents a situation, what the subject takes the purpose or goal to be, and what operations are available to transform the represented situation into the goal situation (Olson, 1986).

To build a theory or a pedagogy of critical thinking on the development of skills, abilities, and dispositions is, then, to embrace an obsolete psychology. It is to assume that generalizability arises from all-purpose skills rather than from particular concepts or ideas.

It may be worth noting that much of the critical thinking discourse is philosophical rather than psychological—a discourse appropriate for describing ideals rather than for correctly characterizing human behavior. The claim that in order to be a critical thinker one must have a critical spirit (Siegel, 1988, p. 39) is such a statement. It may be ideally true or worth striving for; the fact that there are no persons who possess such a spirit is presumably neither here nor there for such discourse. But the question then arises as to the function that such ideals play in policy and practice.

The third limitation is that much of the critical thinking discourse embraces a traditional, and to a large extent, defunct pedagogy. That pedagogy is a simple, commonsensical one: characterize the behavior in terms of good or bad general rules, teach the rules, and give learners practice in using them and in applying them to new contexts. It is a pedagogy which works to some extent in a discipline such as algebra (although there is much criticism of the approach even then), but which works not at all on a subject such as grammar or logic. Take grammar: One can characterize the competence of a native speaker in terms of a set of abstract rules relating entities like noun phrase, verb phrase, and the like. Once the linguist characterizes the basic rules of the language in these terms, the pedagogue is tempted to teach these rules and show children how to apply them. This historic approach to grammar is known to be seriously limited. The problem arises from a failure to distinguish between behavior produced by following a rule and producing behavior that may be characterized by a rule, a distinction advanced by Wittgenstein (Kripke, 1982). The question here is whether the rules for right reason or for critical thinking are of the former or the latter type. Like grammar, the rules for critical thinking may characterize thought *but do not constitute the rules for thinking.* To anticipate the second part of this paper, there may be virtue in learning to talk about how people think, but it is a mistake to believe that discourse about thinking constitutes rules or procedures that people think with, or to believe that thinking is the application of such rules. The point here is that the enterprises of the grammarian and logician, valuable as they are, are at best only indirectly related to the speaking and thinking practices of people. The principles of grammar, many now believe, are innate; the same may be true of the principles of logic (MacNamara, 1986).

WHAT THEN IS CRITICAL THINKING?

Let us see if we can reconstruct the issues on somewhat different grounds. We have argued that critical thinking is not in itself a way of thinking, or a form of rethinking, or a form of intelligence, or a skill, ability, disposition, or trait. What then is it; rather, what could it be? Is there a possible way of viewing the concerns expressed under the rubric of critical thinking that would give the enterprise a content, a psychology, and a possible pedagogy? Let us begin with Ennis's (1989, p. 4) suggestion that critical thinking includes "the correct assessing of statements." The important property of this definition is that it focuses on statements rather than on thinking. Statements are expressions of thought. A theory of thinking may be concerned with thought and how it comes to have expression in action or utterances. Critical thinking, on the other hand, is concerned with the analysis of those products; it is a piece with criticism—literary criticism, film criticism, architectural criticism, or what have you. That would give the enterprise a distinctive content.

However, we may note that the expression "assessing of statements" misrepresents the problem somewhat in that it fails to highlight the relations between thoughts, statements, and utterances. Statements are not thoughts, although they may express thoughts, and statements are not utterances. Utterances are speech acts consisting of the statement of a propositional content together with some propositional attitude of the speaker to that content. In the simplest cases one may *assert* that such and such is the case, *assume* that it is, *claim* that it is, and so on. Similarly we may *think* it is the case, *know* it is, *infer* it is, and so on. Nonetheless we may generalize that notion to say that critical thinking is not an account of thinking but a description of the ways of reflecting on someone else's, or one's own, thinking. Critical thinking, then, is thinking about thinking, what some have referred to as metacognition.

But even that is to miss the target somewhat. The usual indication of what one thinks is what one says. To think about someone's thinking is to think about what someone has said. Critical thinking, then, is thinking about saying. It is a piece with interpretation and commentary. Critical thinking, then, involves the reflection and analysis of what oneself or others have said.

But again, it is extremely difficult to preserve what others have said and so turn it into an object of reflection and criticism in the absence of a written record of what was actually said. The primary forum for critical thinking, indeed, the context in which one learns how to think critically is in the analysis of written texts. That is why critical thinking is essentially synonymous with literacy. So here is our stipulative definition: The interpretation, analysis, and criticism of written texts is what critical thinking is and what it is for. Admittedly, once one learns how to criticize texts, that is, once one has acquired the conceptual tools for the criticism of real verbal texts, it turns out that those tools are suitable for the criticism of everything else that may be treated as a text. Thus the tools shaped for the interpretation of texts are the tools required for the interpretation of nature. All that is required is the assumption that nature, like Scripture, constitutes a text that may be deciphered and interpreted. This, of course, was a guiding principle in the rise of early modern science (Olson, 1987).

TOWARDS A PSYCHOLOGY OF THINKING CRITICALLY

What then are these conceptual tools, how do they develop, and how may their development be encouraged?

The tools for analysis of and reflection on what others have thought and said are the concepts expressed through speech act and mental state terms such as "say," "mean," "intend," "infer," "assume," "understand," and the like. An appropriate semantic analysis of these terms would provide a suitable foundation for a theory of critical thinking. And an account of the acquisition and use by children of these concepts would constitute a promising theory of the development of critical thinking.

Let us consider how these concepts are involved in critical thinking. Suppose that Sam asserts that Saint John is the capital of New Brunswick. Critical thinking would involve analysis of and commentary on Sam's assertion. Note that a statement may be used to express an assertion, a lie, an assumption, or a question. The purpose of the analysis is to determine the interpretation of the content (that is what is usually called comprehension), and to determine the speaker's attitude to that content *from the perspective of the critic.* That is why we defined critical thinking as the analysis or interpretation of assertions rather than as the analysis of statements. Does Sam *believe* it or is he lying? Does Sam *mean* it or is he joking? Does Sam *know* it or does he merely *assume* it since it is the only New Brunswick city he has heard of? Or did he *infer* it from the fact that Moncton and Saint John are the only two cities of New Brunswick that he knows, and he knows Moncton is not the capital so Saint John *must* be? And how could Sam *know* it when in fact it is not the case? But does Sam *think that he knows* it because he heard it from a reliable source? And so on. Characterizing the thoughts, assertions, and texts produced by oneself and others in terms of thinking, meaning, intending, assuming, inferring, knowing, seeing, understanding, and the like defines or constitutes critical thinking.

Thus we have two properties of critical thinking to analyze. First, it involves ways of characterizing the thought, talk, or writings of oneself or others and, second, it does this characterizing by means of epistemic speech act and mental state verbs combined with modal auxiliaries. Critical thinking is, therefore, discourse about discourse. Our concern in this paper is with children's understanding and use of these cognitive and metalinguistic concepts.

The research we shall discuss examines children's acquisitions and use of a few of these concepts, in particular those that may be labeled epistemic—those that have to do with knowledge claims: *think, know, infer, assume, conclude.* Their more elementary forms of expression involve modals: *might be, must be, could be.* Expressions involving modals are more elementary in that complex epistemic concepts may be analyzed into these more elementary forms. Thus *infer* may be equivalent to *thinks it must be* and *interpret* may be equivalent to *thinks it means,* a suggestion first made by Astington (Astington & Olson, 1990).

Two points before we turn to empirical issues: First, the best known test of critical thinking, the Watson-Glaser test (Watson & Glaser, 1980), attempts to measure people's understanding of two of the above-mentioned concepts, namely, assumptions and inferences. Assumptions and inferences are vital to any form of discourse. Critical thinking, however, has nothing to do with making assumptions and inferences; it has to do only with recognizing assumptions as assumptions and inferences as inferences. Such recognition matters. The rule in explicit, systematic, prosaic discourse is that if it is an assumption it should be acknowledged; if it is an inference it should be warranted. Tests of thinking processes are often disguised tests of subject's knowledge of just these concepts and rules.

Second, the issue of whether critical thinking skills are tied to particular subject matter areas or whether they are general across disciplines may be seen as a conceptual issue rather than an empirical issue. Thus, concepts such as *assumption, definition, inference,* and *assertion,* being ordinary language concepts, are general; they may be used in any field of inquiry. Yet their general utility is not often noticed; the glossaries for junior high school science texts that have been examined (Olson & Astington, 1990) contain entries for genes and molecules but not for assumption and inference. The same is true of those advanced under the banner of cultural literacy (Hirsch, 1987). But the propositional content that is to be assigned to the category of assumption or of inference depends upon the particular discipline involved. "Oxygen has an atomic number of 6"—is that a definition or an observation? To answer that demands that one know something about chemistry; to pose the question does not. Just how these concepts develop and how they are applied to diverse domains are empirical questions that we have recently begun to examine.

THE DEVELOPMENT OF CRITICAL DISCOURSE

Our interest in children's understanding of what others say and think took root in recent developments in what has come to be called "children's theories of mind" (Astington, Harris, & Olson, 1988). In the precedent-setting experiment reported by Wimmer and Perner (1983) it was found that children in Western societies understand for the first time when they are about four years old that others may hold a belief that may not be true. They begin to say of persons holding a false belief, "He thinks the candy is in the drawer." "Think" is used first to characterize a belief discrepant from the speaker's belief. It is therefore the first step in characterizing the thoughts and utterances of other people. Interestingly, it turned out that if children can use verbs like "think," "knows," "remembers," or the like to characterize the talk and thought of others they can also use them to apply to themselves (Astington & Gopnik, 1988). We shall discuss briefly two studies that examine aspects of this development.

In one study (Babu, 1989), children were told stories in which a character makes either a warranted or an unwarranted assertion, and the child subjects were asked first to describe the character's assertion and then to retell the story. The story has the following logical form. One character tells a second character that an object is in either A, B, or C. The second character then looks in A, and, in one of the conditions, asserts: "It must be in C." That of course is an assertion based on an unwarranted inference. How do children represent that assertion? The subjects are asked a series of questions including "Did he know that the object was not in B?" Children aged four to six years respond, "No." Examples of eight-year-olds' responses include:

1. "I think he guessed."
2. "I guess he forgot to open that box."
3. "He just guessed that it's not in there."
4. "He thought his mother probably forgot to put it in there."
5. "Yes...well, I think she thought if it's not in that cupboard, it must not be here (the other cupboard) and maybe mother forgot."
6. "He said probably in his head, it's not in here. He thought it's not there."
7. "No, maybe somehow he figured it out that it's not there."
8. "Well, he just assumed it's not there."

Notice that even four- to six-year-olds correctly acknowledge that the speaker could not *know* that the object was not in B because he had not looked in B. By the time they are eight years old they offer reasons why he may not have looked including "he guessed," "he thought," "he just guessed," "he said probably," "he figured," and most interesting "he just assumed." This last child characterizes the action as based on an assumption. Furthermore most six- and eight-year-olds when asked if the speaker knew it was in C after claiming "It must be in C" asserted that he could not know it was in C because he had not checked B, whether or not it turned out actually to be in C. They recognized that the assertion was not warranted. This is paradigmatic thinking about thinking—the critical thinker, rather than merely remembering and reporting the assertion, characterizes that assertion in the light of how the speaker came to make the assertion and of what the reporter knows about the true state of affairs. We refer to this activity as that of characterizing an utterance from a theoretical point of view.

Secondly, child subjects were asked "Why did he say that it must be in C?" Children's answers to this request for an explanation fall mainly into three categories: (a) empirical explanations, (b) intentional explanations, and (c) deductive explanations.

Empirical explanations are exemplified by the following: because the chocolate is in the purse; because dad took the chocolate. Intentional explanations were of two types: (a) intentional (action) explanations (because he *wants* to play with his car); and (b) intentional (belief) explanations (he thought it might be up there; because he knew his car is there; she guessed it is there; he forgot about the other box). The deductive explanations were also of two types: (a) deductive (action) explanations (it's because he looked in this cupboard, it wasn't there, then he looked in the cupboard, it wasn't there, so he opened the purse); and deductive (belief) explanations (because if it wasn't in those cupboards it *must be* in the purse; after opening the cupboards she *thought it would be* in the paper bag, because that's the only place to look at; because his mother said "If I forget to put it in the cupboard, it will still be in

Figure 12.1. Percentage of empirical, intentional, and deductive justifications for speaker's expressions of inference offered by children at three age levels.

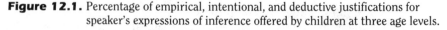

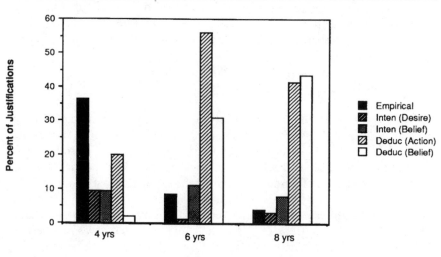

the purse," Jim checked the cupboards, it wasn't there, so *it has to be* in the purse).

The percentages of each type of explanation given by children in the three age groups are shown in Figure 12.1. The youngest children tended to give empirical explanations, reporting some aspect of the empirical rather than the inferential or mental facts, such as, "Because the chocolate is in C." Most common among the six-year-olds was an appeal to the logical implications of the actions: "Because he looked in the cupboards and it wasn't there." The eight-year-olds appeal to the same logic, the logic of necessity, but they mark the necessity not in terms of action but in terms of thought and beliefs using modals such as "must be," "has to be," and "knew."

The acquisition of this knowledge for characterizing the assertions of others shows up in the second method utilized in this study. Children were asked to retell the story that they had just been told. Interestingly, the initial version was a simple narration of action—he looked at A, it was not there, and so on. Children, as they grow older, increasingly retell the story by appeal to the intentional states, the beliefs, knowledge, and desires of the characters in the story. Using a distinction first advanced by Bruner (1986), children's retellings were scored in terms of "the landscape of action," that is, the doings and happenings of the characters; or "the landscape of consciousness," the thoughts, desires, and intentions of the characters. Figure 12.2 shows the distribution of these types of story as a function of age. Even if the original story made no ref-

Figure 12.2. Percentage of action and belief stories retold by children at three age levels.

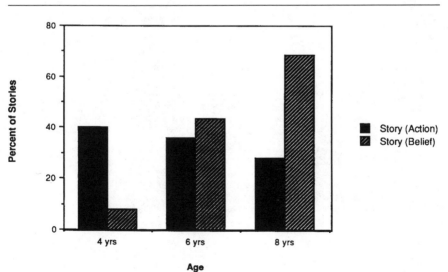

erence to the intentional states of the characters, by eight years of age most children explain both action and utterances of characters by characterizing the mental states and the logical necessity or lack of necessity of the inferences using such expressions as "he knew it must be in C."

Finally, it is interesting to note that only the older children thought it important to report the assertion that serves as the major premise of the inferential reasoning (See Figure 12.3). We infer that as they get older they increasingly recognize that the story could be characterized not merely as one of hunting for the hidden object but as the testing of hypothetical possibilities and logical implications of the initial premise. They represent that logic in their description of the actions and utterances of protagonists.

Generally, such evidence suggests that by the time they are eight or nine years old, children have mastered the basic concepts they need to represent utterances as inferences (figure out), as assumptions (guess), warranted assertions (must be), true assertions (know), and false beliefs (think). What more is there?

In a second line of research, Astington and Olson (1990) examined senior elementary and high school students' knowledge of a more elaborate set of concepts for characterizing the speech acts and mental states of others. These concepts have an interesting history; they are largely Latinate, introduced into English in the fourteenth to sixteenth centuries as English became the lan-

Figure 12.3. Percentage of children at three age levels who in retelling a story recount the logical basis of the character's actions.

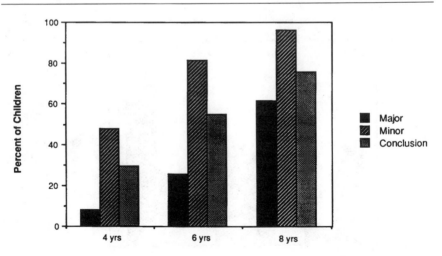

guage of science, philosophy, literature, religion, and government in England. They are, we may say, part of the literate standard if not the vernacular language. In particular, we examined children's knowledge of the verbs "infer," "hypothesize," "concede," "interpret," "conclude," "assume," "doubt," "remember," "assert," "imply," "predict," "confirm," using items such as the following:

> Jane and Kate are arguing about which is the best place to eat. Jane thinks Harvey's is best but Kate thinks McDonald's is. Kate says that McDonald's is nearer, but Jane still thinks Harvey's is the best one to go to because the burgers taste better. *She says to Kate, "It's true McDonald's is nearer,* but I'd rather go to Harvey's."
> A. Jane contradicts Kate's point.
> B. Jane doubts Kate's point.
> C. Jane claims Kate's point.
> D. Jane concedes Kate's point.

> Bob is reading a scene from one of Shakespeare's plays for English homework. He comes to the lines: "that she may feel how sharper than a serpent's tooth it is to have a thankless child." He knows the words but he doesn't understand it, so he goes to ask his mother. *She says it means* "King Lear wants Cordelia to know how painful it is to have a child who is ungrateful."
> A. Bob's mother understands the lines.
> B. Bob's mother interprets the lines.
> C. Bob's mother criticizes the lines.
> D. Bob's mother defines the lines.

> Last week in science class Mr. Jones showed Dave that acid solution turns litmus paper pink. This week there's a test. The first question says "What color will litmus paper be when you dip it in acid solution?" *Dave thinks that it will be pink.*
> A. Dave remembers that it will be pink.
> B. Dave hypothesizes that it will be pink.
> C. Dave infers that it will be pink.
> D. Dave observes that it will be pink.

The percentage of children correctly answering these three items is shown in Figure 12.4.

Figure 12.4 makes clear that some of these concepts are sorted out well in the high school years. Secondly, performance in choosing some verb to characterize the utterance of another depends upon the context and the alternatives available. All of these verbs are elaborated forms of the verbs "say" and "think" which even the youngest children know. But the poor performance for the verb "remember" (see Figure 12.4) is a function of the distracting alternatives available. The content of that item is science, so many of the younger children are distracted by the alternative "hypothesis." Our conclusion is that while the basic concepts are in place, children have a considerable amount to learn about characterizing the utterances and beliefs of themselves and others, a form of learning that proceeds over the school years.

It is worth mentioning that in addition to testing children's knowledge of the metalinguistic and cognitive concepts, we also gave subjects a reading vocabulary test and the Cornell Critical Thinking Test (Level X, Parts III and IV) (Ennis & Millman, 1985). The pooled within-cell correlations (which control for the effects of age) between our test and the above were 0.45 for reading vocabulary and 0.49 for critical thinking. Both were significant. Those results suggest that children's acquisition of these metalinguistic and cognitive verbs is partly, but not entirely due to the general increase in vocabulary during these years. The correlation with a test of critical thinking suggests that the concepts expressed by this vocabulary are important to critical thinking (see Astington & Olson, 1990 for full details). Again, our point is that an analysis of

Figure 12.4. Percentages of childern at four grade levels who correctly select the appropriate speech act verb in describing a mental event.

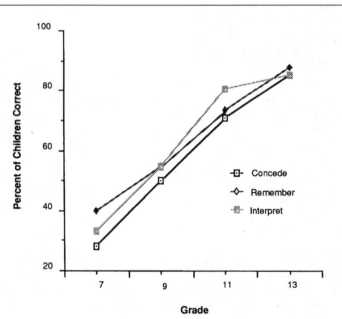

how people go about talking about discourse could help to make clear just what is distinctive about critical thinking beyond reference to some general or generalized skill.

THE PEDAGOGY OF CRITICAL DISCOURSE

In our conversations with teachers, we have noticed two attitudes towards the concepts we have discussed above. Some teachers claim to use these concepts consistently in their discussions with students. For them it is the language of instruction; it is not the object of instruction. The concepts are used to characterize utterances; they are not taught as a body of knowledge. The second attitude we have encountered is that of rejecting these concepts as "secondary" or "bookish"; teachers want their students to think rather than to learn words for talking about thinking. We believe this latter view is fundamentally mistaken. In our view, critical thinking is characterizing the utterances of others in terms of the truth, warrant, and attitude of the speaker to his or her utterance. The language of speech acts and mental states is the language for so characterizing utterances. To learn to think critically about another's utterances is therefore to learn a language for talking about and, hence, for thinking about those utterances.

How then is such a language to be taught? Not as word lists, clearly, but rather as useful devices for characterizing particular utterances and texts employed in various everyday and subject-matter contexts. Children in literate households often acquire these concepts through everyday discourse. In school, this language is widely exploited in the humanities but is often ignored in the sciences. As mentioned earlier, however, it is a language of general applicability. The fact/theory distinction, like the observation/inference distinction, is fundamental to modern discourse in both the arts and the sciences. And both teachers and textbooks ignore these concepts to the detriment of the welfare of their students.

The pedagogy appropriate for the acquisition of this set of concepts for talking about talk and thought could be based on two general principles. First, the basic concepts are in place by the time children come to school. While children do not know the concept *inference,* they do know the concept *think-it-must-be;* while they don't know *interpret,* they do know *think-it-must-mean.* The more abstract and analytical concepts, then, need not be simply learned or taught, but related to what the children already know, a valid pedagogical principle.

But if children know so much about these concepts when they come to school, why do they have such formidable difficulty with schooled tasks? In line with the preceding argument, we suggest that the difficulty is not to be found in children's limited thinking abilities nor is it always to be found in the esoterica of particular subject matters but, rather, the difficulty is found in the peculiarities of literate discourse. Consider the by now famous report of the reasoning habits of traditional or nonliterate subjects made by Luria (1976) following the lead of his teacher Vygotsky. A typical anecdote follows.

> The following syllogism is presented: **In the Far North, where there is snow, all bears are white. Novaya Zemlya is in the Far North and there is always snow there. What color are the bears there?**
> "There are different sorts of bears."
> *Failure to infer from syllogism.*
>
> The syllogism is repeated.
> "I don't know; I've seen a black bear, I've never seen any others...Each locality has its own animals: if it's white, they will be white; if it's yellow, they will be yellow."
> *Appeals only to personal, graphic experience.*
>
> **But what kind of bears are there in Novaya Zemlya?**
> "We always speak only of what we see; we don't talk about what we haven't seen."
> *The same.*
>
> **But what do my words imply?** The syllogism is repeated.
> "Well, it's like this: our tsar isn't like yours, and yours isn't like ours. Your words can be answered only by someone who was there, and if a person wasn't there he can't say anything on the basis of your words."
> *The same.*
>
> **But on the basis of my words—in the North, where there is always snow, the bears are white, can you gather what kind of bears there are in Novaya Zemlya?**
> "If a man was sixty or eighty and had seen a white bear and had told about it, he could be believed, but I've never seen one and hence I can't say. That's my last word. Those who saw can tell, and those who didn't see can't say anything!" (At this point a young Uzbek volunteered, "From your words it means that bears are white.")
> **Well, which of you is right?**
> "What cock knows how to do, he does. What I know, I say, and nothing beyond that!"

A nonliterate member of a traditional society is presented with a syllogism of the form: "All As are B. X is an A. Is X a B?" The correct answer, presumably, is yes. The subject interviewed in this episode refuses to grant that X is B.

Could the failure be a lack of critical thinking ability, perhaps a failure to apply the rule of modus ponens, or the laws of syllogistic reasoning? If we look carefully, we see that the subject's second response has a fully formed syllogism in it: "Each locality has its own animals; if it's white, they will be white; if it's yellow, they will be yellow." In a word, there is nothing wrong with his reasoning ability. Why then cannot he "solve" the problem? Perhaps he cannot transfer his ability; he can reason syllogistically one moment but not the next. That seems unlikely as he transferred his syllogism from Novaya Zemlya to "each locality."

Something more serious has happened. The subject has failed to grant the premise. Cole and Scribner (1974) in repeating such tasks with the Kpelle of Liberia found that subjects "failed to accept the logical task" (p. 162), answering the questions as if they were factual questions. Indeed, they concluded that the main sources of error for the Kpelle were the same as those Henle (1962) had found with American college students. These consisted not of logical flaws but of failing to recognize the "genre." Scribner (1977) has characterized such failures by unschooled subjects in terms of their tendency to treat such problems as empirical rather than theoretical problems. We would go further and suggest that the difficulty springs from a peculiarity of written language.

Writing provides a medium for preserving statements independent from utterances. That is, the content can be preserved without an acknowledgement of the attitude of the speaker to the content, or for that matter, who the speaker is. In the case of the syllogism in question, the statement "In the Far North, where there is snow, all bears are white" does not indicate who the speaker is or the form of the speech act. The written form has not marked the speaker's attitude to the statement: Is it a hypothetical assumption, or is it an empirical claim? The writer intended, we suppose, that it be taken as the former. Luria's subject took it as the latter. Hence, he disputed the claim. Is that a failure of reasoning? Again, it appears that the reasoning is appropriate—what is lacking is familiarity with the conventions of written discourse. For if the premise was marked as a hypothetical assumption, whether through intonation, context, or an explicit marker, we may expect that our subject would have done much better. In fact, Scribner (1977) has reported just such data.

What about children in our culture? Again, children appear to be competent in assessing the utterances of others when they know the attitude of the speaker to his or her utterance. Difficulties arise when dealing with written texts. The difficulties are of two types. First, the attitude is often unmarked as in such practice syllogisms as: All men are mortal; Socrates is a man; Therefore, Socrates is mortal. School children can fail such items because they don't know how to take the first statement. If it is an empirical claim, it is false, given such notable counterexamples as Jesus Christ. Similarly, textbooks, especially science texts, may not indicate how particular claims are to be taken. The student has nothing to go by in deciding whether to represent a statement as a claim, a definition, an assumption, or whatever. If that difficulty is a failure, it is a failure either of the textbook writer or teacher, or a failure to understand the conventions of written discourse. Indeed, it would not be incorrect to claim that the literate tradition has not been aware of its peculiar assumptions (such as hiding the speaker's attitude to his propositions) and consequently has explained the failure of children and less literate adults by ascribing irrationality to them.

To introduce children to these conventions, it would seem appropriate to encourage them to not simply learn and remember what the text says, or even what it means—the focus of the recent emphasis on comprehension—but also to adopt a critical stance to those texts. That critical stance involves learning to talk about utterances and texts in a particular way, namely, characterizing the utterances of oneself or another from a theoretical point of view as exemplars of particular speech acts or mental states. This ability to characterize what is said and thought would seem to define a suitable candidate for a distinctive, critical, and for that matter metacognitive, competence.

REFERENCES

Astington, J. W., & Gopnik, A. (1988). Knowing you've changed your mind: Children's understanding of representational change. In J. W. Astington, P. L. Harris, & D. R. Olson (Eds.), *Developing theories of mind* (pp. 193–206). Cambridge: Cambridge University Press.

Astington, J. W., Harris, P., & Olson, D. R. (Eds.). (1988). *Developing theories of mind.* Cambridge: Cambridge University Press.

Astington, J. W., & Olson, D. R. (1990). Metacognitive and metalinguistic language: Learning to talk about thought. *Applied Psychology: An International Review, 39,* 77–87.

Babu, N. (1989). Children's understanding of the validity and truth of mental representations. Unpublished doctoral dissertation, University of Toronto, Ontario Institute for Studies in Education, Toronto.

Bruner, J. S. (1986). *Actual minds, possible worlds.* Cambridge, MA: Harvard University Press.

Cole, M., & Scribner, S. (1974). *Culture and thought: A psychological introduction.* New York: John Wiley & Sons.

Ennis, R. H. (1989). Critical thinking and subject specificity: Clarification and needed research. *Educational Researcher, 18*(3), 4–10.

Ennis, R. H., & Millman, J. (1985). *Cornell Critical Thinking Test, Level X.* Pacific Grove, CA: Midwest.

Henle, M. (1962). On the relation between logic and thinking. *Psychological Review, 69,* 366–378.

Hirsch, E. D. Jr. (1987). *Cultural literacy.* Boston: Houghton Mifflin.

Kripke, S. A. (1982). *Wittgenstein on rules and private language*. Cambridge, MA: Harvard University Press.

Luria, A. R. (1976). *Cognitive development: Its cultural and social foundations*. Cambridge, MA: Harvard University Press.

MacNamara, J. (1986). *A border dispute: The place of logic in psychology*. Cambridge, MA: Bradford Books/MIT Press.

McPeck, J. (1981). *Critical thinking and education*. New York: St. Martin's.

Olson, D. R. (1986). Intelligence and literacy: The relationships between intelligence and the technologies of representation and communication. In R. J. Sternberg & R. K. Wagner (Eds.), *Practical intelligence: Nature and origins of competence in the everyday world* (pp. 338–360). Cambridge: Cambridge University Press.

Olson, D. R. (1987). Interpreting texts and interpreting nature: The effects of literacy on hermeneutics and epistemology. *Visible Language, 20*(3), 302–317.

Olson, D. R., & Astington, J. W. (1990). Talking about text: How literacy contributes to thought. *Journal of Pragmatics, 14,* 705–721.

Olson, D. R., & Bialystok, E. (1983). *Spatial cognition: The structure and development of mental representations of spatial relations*. Hillsdale, NJ: Erlbaum.

Resnick, L. B. (1987). *Education and learning to think*. Washington, DC: National Academy Press.

Ross, L. (1977). The intuitive psychologist and his shortcomings: Distortion in the attribution process. In L. Berkowitz (Ed.), *Advances in experimental social psychology,* (Vol. 10, pp. 173–220). New York: Academic Press.

Scribner, S. (1977). Modes of thinking and ways of speaking: Culture and logic reconsidered. In P. N. Johnson-Laird & P. C. Wason (Eds.), *Thinking: Readings in cognitive science* (pp. 483–500). Cambridge: Cambridge University Press.

Siegel, H. (1988). *Educating reason*. New York: Routledge.

Watson, G., & Glaser, E. M. (1980). *Watson-Glaser Critical Thinking Appraisal*. Cleveland, OH: The Psychological Corporation.

Wimmer, H., & Perner, J. (1983). Beliefs about beliefs: Representation and constraining function of wrong beliefs in your children's understanding of deception. *Cognition, 13,* 103–128.

13 Thoughts on Subject Specificity

John E. McPeck
The University of Western Ontario

Today, most educators and informal logicians who are interested in teaching critical thinking are aware of the dispute over whether or not there exists a set of so-called "critical thinking skills" that transfer, or generalize across subjects. Theorists such as Robert Ennis, Michael Scriven, Richard Paul, Trudy Govier, Harvey Siegel, Ralph Johnson, Tony Blair, and others, believe that there does exist a set of "critical thinking skills" that can be applied to a broad range of problems and problem types which cut across subject boundaries. On the other side, arguing against this point of view, are theorists such as Mortimer Adler, Paul Hirst, Francis Schrag, E. D. Hirsch, Charles Blatz, and myself, who contend that this view is fraught with both conceptual and empirical difficulties. One of these difficulties, which this volume is committed to exploring, revolves around the question of the generalizability of these putative skills. That is, in what sense can it be claimed that the *same skill* is being used in two different domains or subject areas? Does reasoning to a conclusion in science require the same or a different skill as reasoning to a conclusion in ethics?

The view I have maintained is that what might be *logically* general (for example, the rule of modus ponens) is not necessarily *cognitively* generalizable. And I have charged proponents of logic and critical thinking courses with having confused these different things, or with merely assuming that the one follows from the other. My own view has been that one's ability to think critically, or to apply the rules of logic in real-life situations, is a direct function of one's familiarity with the kind of subject matter under discussion. Thus I have argued for a view of critical thinking which can be called "subject specific." (Sometimes it is called "domain specific.") It has been a fair question, however, to ask what one might mean precisely by "subject" or "domain?"

There is now a growing literature which is helping to clarify this trouble-some notion of subject specificity. For instance, in calling for clarification on this matter, Ennis (1989, this volume) has raised the level of discussion about the meaning of "subjects," "domains," and even "psychological transfer." No longer can we simply gloss over questions about the precise scope and limits of the putative skills that various critical thinking programs are alleged to pro-mote. Another example of this literature is the recent paper by Perkins and Salomon (1989) which provides a useful historical overview of just how vexing the problem of transfer has been over the past thirty years. These analyses have prompted me to reexamine my own thesis, and in the remainder of this chapter I address some concerns that they raise.

LANGUAGE AND VAGUENESS

Ennis has urged that the central terms used to formulate the subject-spe-cific or domain-specific view (that is, "subject," "domain," and "field") are inherently vague. It is worth mentioning, however, that many of the central concepts in his position, concepts such as "general thinking skill," "critical thinking skill," and the like, are equally vague. Indeed, many of Ennis's own arguments apply with equal force to both sets of terms. We similarly need to ask, for example: How general is general? When is skill at two tasks a general skill, as opposed to two separate skills? What precisely is to be included (and excluded) in the notion of a general thinking skill? What does "general critical thinking" actually mean? I have tried often to show that these central ques-tions raise difficulties which can also be raised about "domain," "field," and "subject" (McPeck, 1981, 1984, 1985).

As one thinks about all of these concepts, it is important to keep in mind that the vagueness which inheres in them is not necessarily the result of bad or confused theorizing on either side of the debate. Rather, vagueness fre-quently reflects the plasticity of language itself. Vagueness is both the strength and weakness of language; it is what makes both poetry and poppycock possi-ble. When isolated from a specific context, the concepts indeed are vague. The particular *use* of them, that is, their contexts and exemplars, always needs to be supplied to reduce vagueness. It is this fundamental insight about lan-guage, in fact, which prompted Wittgenstein's oft-quoted dictum, "Do not ask for the *meaning* of a word, ask for its *use*."

Thanks largely to Wittgenstein, we know now that neither scientific terms nor ordinary language will stand still, as it were, such that their meaning is always clear, uniform, and definitive. Notice, for example, that Ennis intro-duces the term "topic" to differentiate further certain discourse under a "subject." Presumably, a topic is more specific than a subject—I'm not sure. Under many circumstances, however, this distinction is of little help since a "topic" can also be a "subject." Again, as Wittgenstein pointed out, the circumstances of a particular *use* determine what is meant.

Elsewhere (McPeck, 1981), I have criticized the notion of generic critical thinking and critical thinking courses that claim to teach general critical thinking. This is because I think that there are almost as many different kinds of critical thinking as there are different kinds of things to think about. And the criteria for applying and assessing critical thinking derive from the thing (call it a "topic," "subject," "field," or "domain") being discussed or thought about at the time. Because I recognize that the thing being thought about could be something very general (for example, the laws of physics) or something very specific (who will win the Kentucky Derby), I intentionally use such phrases as "thinking about X" or "some specific subject X." Here, the notion of "subject" or "X" can range from very specific subjects (if that is the word) to the very general. The subject may be something that is taught in school classrooms or it may not. The point is that it doesn't matter; my general thesis still holds. I thus view this vagueness as a strength of the analysis, not a weakness. This is not to sanction ambiguity, intentional vagueness, nor having words mean anything one wants. It does suggest, however, that precision cannot always be supplied in advance. As often as not, specific cases of subjects and/or skills have to be examined in context to determine more precisely what we are dealing with.[1]

THE TRANSFER PROBLEM

Recent discussions of the critical thinking transfer problem are particularly welcome, because many critical thinking programs simply assume that the skills taught in these courses will be readily applicable in diverse problem areas. The critical thinking courses that teach logic, both formal and informal, frequently have made the boldest transfer claims. However, both Evans (1982) and Glaser (1984) have shown that the transfer of logical skills is just as problematic as it is for many other skills. Logic is not exempt from the transfer problem. (Though logical transfer can, of course, be done from time to time.)

Also, within the critical thinking literature, one often finds a rather odd and confusing way of construing the transfer problem as that which may exist between school-subject knowledge and everyday knowledge, as though the two, like oil and water, have nothing to do with one another. For instance, Ennis (this volume) construes the transfer problem as bridging the supposed gap between these two when he asks:

Will the learning in the individual fields transfer to daily life? If the transfer principle of domain specificity is correct, then immersion will not result in transfer to daily life (the content of which is not much taught in school subjects), because teaching for transfer does not occur in the immersion approach. (pp. 31-32)

And elsewhere he predicts that:

If the domain-specificity transfer principle is correct, immersion in a subject-matter area, which, let us assume, includes ability to think in the area, probably will not lead to critical thinking in everyday life (except perhaps for the gifted students), since immersion is not accompanied by explicit attention to general principles of critical thinking. (pp. 25-26)

This is a decidedly unhelpful way of framing the transfer problem for several reasons. The first is that knowledge is not necessarily limited or constrained by where it is learned. The schoolhouse, firehouse, museum, playground, and library are all wonderful places to learn things. And the knowledge gained cannot, for example, be clearly divided into playground knowledge as opposed to museum knowledge—whereupon we must then bridge between the playground and museum.

Secondly, school-subject knowledge is not isolated from, nor distinct from, nor irrelevant to everyday life. Rather, that is precisely *what it is about.* School knowledge is not studied for its own sake or for preparation for a life on Mars, nor is it meant to be uselessly stored away in the back of one's mind, as in an attic. (This view of school knowledge, parenthetically, is what sanctions the use of the pejorative phrase "merely academic knowledge.") The whole point of school-subject knowledge is to enlighten people about their everyday world for this everyday life. In fact, school subjects had their historical origins in everyday life, and that is what they continue to be about no matter how theoretical or esoteric the study might become at times. The dichotomy between everyday life and school-subject knowledge is a false dichotomy; it misrepresents the nature of the transfer question. Lauren Resnick (1987) manifests much of this same confusion about the nature and purpose of school-based knowledge. To her credit, however, she is careful not to treat her discussion as an analysis of the transfer problem.

The transfer question is about whether learning a particular task helps or hinders the learning of another different kind of task (for example, does learning to hit a baseball help or hinder learning to play golf?). This is the structure of the transfer problem as initially treated by Thorndike and Woodworth (1901), and as it continues to be understood by contemporary psychologists (see Perkins & Salomon, 1989). The difficulties inherent in Ennis's notion of transfer become evident in the following discussion:

> There are, of course, many topics which are not school subjects and are not included in the study of the school subjects to which a person considering these topics is exposed. For example, the topic stabbing, which was considered in a murder trial for which I was on the jury, was *not part of any school subject that any of us had studied in school or college.* Yet that was a topic about which we were supposed to think critically. (this volume p. 24, italics mine)

Apart from the fact that there are over thirty stabbings in just four of Shakespeare's more popular plays (*Hamlet, Macbeth, Romeo and Juliet,* and *Julius Caesar*), not to mention a dozen more in *Antigone, Oedipus Rex,* and *West Side Story,* I doubt if the jurors' difficulties resided in understanding stabbing, no matter what school they might have attended. Indeed, it is arguable that learning the meaning of "stabbing" comes with learning one's native tongue. The problem for jurors is determining whether a defendant is guilty of stabbing, which is a different kettle of fish because this involves understanding a complicated network of evidence and counterevidence, claims and counterclaims, in a legal context in which most people will have no experience. It is difficult to see how a course or two in critical thinking could eliminate these particular difficulties. In any event, such problems are not clear cases of a lack of transfer of training.

GENERAL THINKING SKILLS

Critical thinking, like any thinking, is necessarily connected to particular objects of thought. And because objects of thought can and do differ enormously in scope, quality, and variety, I claim that there can be no one general skill or limited set of skills (including formal logic) that could do justice to this wide variety of objects of thought. This is the reason that there can be no completely general set of thinking skills. I think the work of Stephen Toulmin (1958), among others, also supports this point of view.

I believe there are, in fact, some very limited general thinking skills. As I have argued elsewhere (1984), however, these skills offer little to get excited about for two reasons. First, there is an inverse relationship between the usefulness of such skills and their generality. The more general they are, the more trivially obvious they are—for example, not contradicting oneself, not believing everything one hears, and so forth. Conversely, the truly useful thinking skills tend to be limited to specific domains (pardon the word!) or narrower areas of application (see also Glaser, 1984).

Secondly, there is the problem which Evans (1982) documents, namely, that even when a person possesses a skill that might be applicable in a new or different situation, there remains the problem of seeing or recognizing that the skill applies in *this* situation. We do not possess an executive skill, as such, which guides the appropriate choice for different instances. Notice, in this regard, what Piaget claims about his concepts of conservation and reversibility: he says that they are very broad, logical concepts. Well, indeed they are very broad, logical concepts, but this does not entail that the child comes to understand these concepts in all of their full-blown generality, or broadness. On the contrary, the evidence shows (Egan, 1983) that conservation and reversibility must be learned anew with each new kind of subject matter or material. For example, if (and when) children learn conversation with respect to weight or mass, they must learn again, with independent experience, that conversation also applies to volume, and again to length, and again to number. Indeed, numerous studies have shown that there can be as much as a four-year lapse (on average) between learning conservation of mass and then conversation of volume (Egan, 1983). Children do not learn conservation simpliciter, and automatically know that it applies equally across different phenomena—this, despite the *logical* generality of "conservation." That we, looking back after the fact can "see," so to speak, that the phenomena are all instances of conservation, says nothing about transfer, nor about what the child sees, nor about whether this accumulated knowledge of conservation constitutes one ability or several.

These considerations would seem to argue against transfer, or general reasoning skill, not in favor of it. This same kind of difficulty plagues adult applications of logic as well (Evans, 1982). An agent's choice to apply some general principle such as conservation, reversibility, or a principle of logic seems more reasonably attributable to direct acquaintance with the particular phenomena in question than it does to the application of a generic skill. This problem, incidentally, is never treated, yet looms large, throughout the Perkins and Salomon discussion of the generality of thinking skills as well (Perkins & Salomon, 1989).

Looking inwardly for a moment, I might ask whether I have acquired general critical thinking abilities associated with logic. I have, after all, taught logic (both graduate and undergraduate) for a number of years, and thus have more than a little familiarity with it. In addition, the literatures on thinking and thinking skills have been an academic specialty of mine for some time. In short, I have developed a certain amount of expertise in these two subject areas. Thus, it is not at all surprising that I have developed some abilities within these relatively narrow confines. However, I have no confidence that I could apply these same critical abilities to work done in physics, engineering, mathematics, law, poetry, or foreign languages. So just how general is this ability of mine? It is obviously neither completely general, nor perhaps even very general—and from a certain perspective it might even be considered quite narrow.

It is worth making a more general point about the various relationships that hold between skills, abilities, and domains of application. Some skills, and their accompanying abilities, might be very narrow when looked at as a skill, per se, yet the domain to which the skills apply could be very broad. For example, counting, or even adding, are very narrow skills, *qua* skills, but their domains of application are virtually unlimited. Thus the skill, as such, is not general; the domain of application is. Similarly, we could discuss all the permutations and combinations of general skills for narrow domains, and narrow skills for narrow domains (for example, wiggling one's ears), and so forth. It seems to me that my particular ability to apply formal logic to a specific area of my academic interest is a relatively narrow ability applied to a relatively narrow domain of expertise.

NOTE

1. One small correction: Ennis has categorized my position as the "immersion" approach. This is incorrect. I have made it clear elsewhere (McPeck, 1984, 1985) that when it comes to the teaching of school subjects, I favor an explicit emphasis on those epistemological questions that undergird the various school subjects. I also agree with Glaser (1984) that the crucial epistemic questions tend to vary among domains and subjects. In any case, it would be more accurate to describe my position, along with Glaser's, as the "infusion" approach—though I don't like the term.

REFERENCES

Egan, K. (1983). *Education and psychology.* New York: Teachers College Press.

Ennis, R. H. (1989). Critical thinking and subject specificity: Clarification and needed research. *Educational Researcher, 18*(3), 4–10.

Evans, J. St. B. T. (1982). *The psychology of deductive reasoning.* London: Routledge & Kegan Paul.

Glaser, R. (1984). Education and thinking: The role of knowledge. *American Psychologist, 39,* 93–104.

McPeck, J. (1981). *Critical thinking and education.* New York: St. Martin's Press.

McPeck, J. (1984). Stalking beasts, but swatting flies: The teaching of critical thinking. *Canadian Journal of Education, 9,* 28–44.

McPeck, J. (1985). Critical thinking and the 'Trivial Pursuit' theory of knowledge. *Teaching Philosophy, 8,* 295–308.

Perkins, D. N., & Salomon, G. (1989). Are cognitive skills context-bound? *Educational Researcher, 18*(1), 16–25.

Resnick, L. B. (1987). Learning in school and out. *Educational Researcher, 16*(9), 13–20.

Thorndike, E. L., & Woodworth, R. S. (1901). The influence of improvement in one mental function upon the efficiency of other functions. *Psychological Review, 8,* 247–261.

Toulmin, S. (1958). *The uses of argument.* Cambridge: Cambridge University Press.

14 Contextual Limits on Reasoning and Testing for Critical Thinking

Charles V. Blatz
University of Toledo

This chapter advances an argument against standardized testing of critical thinking. It proceeds by supporting six claims about the contextual character of our abilities and dispositions to think critically. The argument emerges from a detailed though not radical analysis of critical thinking itself. The overall strategy is to force us to choose between three alternatives for critical thinking testing: (a) such testing that is standardized but has no construct validity, that is, that cannot be certified as testing for what we are interested in, namely, the presence and working of critical thinking abilities and dispositions; (b) such testing that is standardized and has construct validity, but is made possible through an intolerable level of standardization; and (c) testing for critical thinking that is contextualized in ways that remove it from the realm of what is ordinarily called "standardized testing." I argue for adopting the last of these alternatives.

GENERAL ABILITIES AND STANDARDIZED TESTING

The existence of context-free abilities and dispositions of critical thinking would seem to go hand in hand with the possibility, not to say desirability, of standardized testing of critical thinking. If there are such highly general abilities and dispositions, then they should work in context-free ways. If someone can argue to the best explanation, can check the credibility of sources, is generally cautious about taking an authority's word, generally looks for countervailing reasons before settling on a conclusion, is generally open to constructive criticism and the possibility of having made an error in reasoning, then these abilities and dispositions should come into play *whenever* the thinker sees the occasion and seeks to give them play. That is, they should come into play regardless of subject matter, the specific nature of the intellectual task, school programs in which the thinker is a participant, and varying other circumstances. Since it seems to some that there are such general critical thinking abilities and dispositions, and that the exam and exam context can be structured so as to provide examinees all the needed information, cues of proper occasion to exercise particular critical thinking abilities and dispositions, and motivation, then it has seemed to these individuals that standardized critical thinking tests should be possible (Norris & Ennis, 1989; Norris & Ryan, 1987).

But suppose there are no critical thinking abilities and dispositions that operate in such highly general and context-free ways. In that case, there would be no reason why similarly alert and motivated individuals should respond in the same ways to the same questions; no reason why a single set of answers would show the workings of contextually different abilities and dispositions to think critically. Test-takers would see, in ways characteristic of their differing abilities and dispositions to reason through things, the varying intent of test questions, the specifics of information pertinent to them, and the different strategies and standards of proper thoroughness in answering them. Thus, tests could show only the workings of these varying critical thinking abilities and dispositions.

In the discussion that follows I shall make six claims.

Thesis I: Critical thinking is a constructive activity of pursuing well-supported beliefs, decisions, plans, and actions. *Thesis II:* This activity requires care and effort of the thinker to meet certain expectations. *Thesis III:* Some of these expectations constitute paradigms of inquiry and so tests for critical thinking abilities and dispositions are tests for thinking as exercised from within a certain standpoint of inquiry. *Thesis IV:* Other expectations call for the critical thinker to collect and use information with more or less thoroughness and sophistication, so tests of critical thinking are tests of thinking conducted within varying contexts of information management. *Thesis V:* Thus, there are no standardized tests that simultaneously: (a) are tests of true critical thinking abilities and dispositions, (b) are truly revealing for individuals or populations, and (c) avoid being counterproductive with respect to the very critical thinking abilities and dispositions they seek to reveal. *Thesis VI:* Indeed, at an operational level, as revealed by construct valid critical thinking tests, critical thinking abilities and dispositions are highly context bound.

OVERVIEW OF THE NATURE OF CRITICAL THINKING

Critical thinking is understood by Norris and Ennis as "reasonable and reflective thinking that is focused upon deciding what to believe or do" (Norris & Ennis, 1989, p. 1). My own understanding is very close to this: "The process of critical thinking can be understood as the deliberate pursuit of well-supported beliefs, decisions, plans, and actions" (Blatz, 1989, p. 107). In both of these views, the critical thinker is one who moderates and informs belief and action by the use of norm-governed reason. Thus, no case of critical thinking will be without a certain amount of effort, concentration, and self-direction on the part of the thinker.

Although critical thinking is deliberate, it is far from formulaic. The procedures of inference, assumptions of evidence, and modes of investigation that we use in critical thinking do not determine answers to questions, even when combined with the background beliefs a thinker brings to an inquiry. Rather, the thinker has to *employ* these modes of reasoning and assumptions, to select from them, and to combine them in appropriate ways, with proper emphasis, care, and precision. There is no formula to follow, but there are constraining limits. In critical thinking we are accountable to some community for compliance with its standards of reasoning.

Therefore, all cases of critical thinking are episodes of applying reason, in self-moderated ways and constrained by standards of various sorts, to questions we take seriously in some context. Critical thinking tests, then, must check on the presence and strength of abilities and dispositions to engage in such deliberate, constructive, and norm-governed activity. This claim follows from Theses I and II (see Norris & Ennis, 1989; Facione, 1990).

These points should lead us to wonder to what extent there is contextual variance in the expectations critical thinkers are accountable for meeting. If there is such variance, the abilities and dispositions of critical thinkers will be abilities and dispositions to think in ways that are contextually variable and, then, tests for critical thinking abilities and dispositions will be tests for these contextually variable features. In short, if there is contextual variance, then Theses III and IV would be acceptable.

TWO DIFFERENT TYPES OF EXPECTATIONS ON CRITICAL THINKERS

Theses III and IV are tied to two different sorts of contextual differences that critical thinkers face. The labels I shall use are: (a) differences in community of discussion, and (b) differences in informational context. My subsequent discussions of these differences will cast my views partially as a form of what Ennis (1989, this volume) calls "epistemological subject specificity."

Differences in Community of Discussion

These differences show up in background assumptions and procedures (Blatz, 1989). Background assumptions of a community of discussion concern categories of existents and how things in these various categories might behave. Behavior is treated either by generalizations about the regular or law-like natural behavior of the things in question, or by normative expectations on behavior (Blatz, 1989; Körner, 1970; Kuhn, 1970). Together, these assumptions define what possibilities there are for the world as conceived through the community of discussion in question. The assumptions define what can cause or result from what, and what should be expected from whom in various circumstances. They do not tell us what is the case in other than this hypothetical way. But they provide the beginning points and touchstones for determining what is the case.

In addition to these assumptions, the community of discussion agrees generally upon and holds people to account for using certain procedures: (a) procedures for determining what is the case; and (b) procedures for putting the determination of the facts into practice in forming beliefs, decisions, and plans, and in guiding actions in the general area of common interest to the community. The first procedural category includes the various modes of reasoning and investigation employed to determine the kind of problem that is being confronted, and the kinds of options there are for resolving it. The second set of procedures includes those employed to move from a diagnosis of the problem, or a clarification of the question, to an answer. For example, it would include procedures of reasoning to an acceptable plan of medical treatment or urban development, or to a sequence of steps to follow in improving our financial situation.

An example of dramatically different communities of discussion concerned with health care might be helpful here. Suppose that we are attempting to explain the behavior of a child who is rolling erratically about the floor, who seems to be strangling, and who has swallowed her tongue. At one time, one society believed that a possible cause of such behavior was demonic possession. One of the forces at work in the world was the force of the Devil. The Devil's force could be invoked or unleashed by certain people. The way to learn who was able to control the Devil's force was to test individuals for the powers of witchcraft. If they were found to possess the powers, for example by surviving the dunking stool, they could be eliminated and things would once again be set right in the village. There was no provision for the possibility of the behavior being caused by the biochemical problem we now understand as epilepsy. There could not have been, since there was no belief in the existence of the substances biochemists posit, let alone the technology or understanding necessary to study problems with such a cause. Thus, there was no provision for dealing with the problem chemo-therapeutically. That sort of approach was as foreign and inconceivable to the residents of seventeenth century New England as is the possibility of witchcraft and demonic possession to the modern medical community.

Thus, communities of discussion are groups of people who approach a set of questions and problems through commonly understood assumptions and procedures of reasoning. The questions and problems define the area of interest of the community, and the assumptions and procedures define the general outlines of the modes of inquiry and the belief- (or decision-) fixing methods of the group. Further, the members of the group hold each other accountable to follow accepted procedures of reasoning and to stay within the bounds of the group's background assumptions.

To the extent that communities differ on the background assumptions and basic procedures for investigation and solution of problems, differ in ways that would make a difference to the expectations placed on critical thinkers in those communities, there will be different abilities and dispositions to think critically in those communities, and, thus different ways of testing for critical thinking.

Although the witchcraft case gives one example of such a difference, this case might not seem to prove much because many of us today think that only the biochemical approach to the child's problem could be respectable as an example of critical thinking. But there are many other differences in critical thinking that we may see as legitimate. In the history of modern philosophy, for instance, it makes a great difference to explaining why Descartes believed systematic doubt was possible whether we look for an explanation from the standpoint of clinical psychology or from that of philosophy. And within the latter of these domains, it makes considerable difference whether we are analytic philosophers or phenomenologists, and whether we are logical positivists or Wittgensteinians. Each of these differences could be seen as differences between communities of discussion. The community in which we place ourselves in order to address the question at issue would make a difference to the logical and conceptual expectations of the reasoning that constructed our answer, and to what is tested when judging the ability to argue to the best explanation of Descartes' beliefs.

Now, of course, just what differences of background assumptions and procedures there might be, what variance this generates in abilities and dispositions to think critically and, then, what limits there are on critical thinking testing that can claim construct validity, is something which could be answered only at some considerable length. It would involve examining in great detail the various communities of discussion and their areas of concern, assumptions, and procedures. But we do not need to do that in order to make the point against standardized testing for critical thinking.

Critical thinkers will always be accountable for constraining their constructions by some proper subset of the possible logics, geometries, physical theories, cosmologies, and other sets of beliefs and procedures that can enter into inquiry (Blatz, 1989; Perkins & Salomon, 1989). These restricted sets of assumptions and procedures are those that are expected in some community of discussion or another. In other words, critical thinking occurs within the framework of broader or narrower, more or less common, more or less arcane, communities of discussion. This is the reason for Thesis III: Tests for critical thinking abilities and dispositions can have construct validity only within the confines of a particular standpoint of inquiry or community of discussion.

Differences in Informational Context

Inquiry is not static within communities of discussion. Even if the background assumptions and procedures of thinking within communities do not change rapidly, thinkers do often move ahead relatively quickly on specific issues. Thus, there are often changes in what is accepted as received opinion, if not common knowledge, on matters of interest in the community. For example, anthropologists are settling on a small set of favored views of the progenitors of humans, just as geologists have narrowed their attention to a favored set of beliefs about the origins of the continents.

All of this is acceptable enough. But the critical thinking testing implications may not be fully appreciated. As common knowledge changes, or even as the investigation of a matter of community interest progresses, so do the expectations concerning familiarity with and use of the body of common knowledge. Thus, in a variety of more or less evolving and institutionalized ways, expectations will be set concerning just what information to take for granted, what different portions of the body of common knowledge persons at different stages of accomplishment and mastery in the community are supposed to possess and use, what facility should be available to use that common knowledge, what range of tasks and questions should be approached through this knowledge, and what thoroughness should be applied in using epistemic skills. Differences in how these expectations are set will create differences in critical thinking abilities and dispositions. Such differences affect the validity of claims that can be made on the basis of critical thinking tests. In other words Thesis IV is correct: testing for critical thinking must not be limited only to testing for abilities and dispositions of people in a certain community of discussion, but also to testing in a certain context of information management.

The problem Thesis IV presents for standardized critical thinking testing is enormous. Thesis III has severe enough implications, because schools and educators would like to be able to certify simply that students are good or not as critical thinkers, not just as critical thinkers in a certain brand of psychology, or in philosophy, or in one or another community of discussion. However, teachers and administrators will be more frustrated by the implications of Thesis IV. After all, consider what determines how much of common knowledge is available to students: (a) the currentness and accuracy of textbooks or other learning technology and sources of information, (b) the currentness and accuracy of teachers' knowledge, (c) the abilities of teachers to teach, (d) the capacity of particular students to learn and the impact differential capacity has on group progress, (e) the willingness of individual students to learn and the impact differential willingness has on group progress, (f) the particular approach that teachers take, (g) the time available for learning various dimensions of various subjects, (h) the amount of individual assistance available to students, and (i) the specifics of student-teacher negotiated interpretations of individual assignments (Evans, 1989).

It would be incredible if there were not great differences in some of these determinants between every pair of classrooms, let alone between schools, school districts, and regions of a country. And yet, if there are such differences in determinants, then there will be concomitant differences in the abilities and dispositions to think critically in ways that meet expectations created under these determining conditions. Thus construct-valid test results for individual critical thinking abilities and dispositions will at best tell us about the members of a certain class, operating on a certain problem from the standpoint of a certain community of discussion, at a certain time, with respect to certain texts, and so on. One might ask at this point, as indeed John McPeck has (1981), whether testing for critical thinking could be anything other than testing for subject-matter knowledge gained in a particular classroom during a particular period of time.

NO NEED TO STANDARDIZE TESTS FOR CRITICAL THINKING

I have argued that critical thinking abilities and dispositions are contextual in that there are abilities and dispositions to think critically within certain communities of discussion and informational contexts. Tests of how well someone can think critically will check the presence and strength of abilities and dispositions to think in ways meeting such contextualizing expectations. Such tests can take several forms; still the point is the same.

For example, critical thinking tests might be direct, providing the test-taker with the opportunity to think critically about some question or issue and to respond with an answer reflecting that thought. Such a test will have validity only when the best explanation of the test responses is that they are in part the result of the operation of critical thinking abilities and dispositions (Messick, 1989; Norris, 1983; Norris, 1989; Norris & Ennis, 1989). Only in this case would a direct test be able to separate critical thinking responses from responses outwardly identical but resulting merely from a lucky guess, test wiseness, or rote recall. Part of the barrel-over-the-falls fascination of stories about great impostors, impostors who even performed good surgeries, for example, is that these are cases in which the critical thought of the surgeon or other subject of imitation does not come into play, even though things turn out just fine. Thus the answer on a direct test of critical thinking (whether a short answer, a multiple-choice answer, or even an essay answer) can be the same whether or not it really shows the workings of critical thinking abilities and dispositions.

Unless we are willing to adopt a crude behaviorism, according to which just giving the right or keyed answer is the display of a critical thinking ability or disposition, or unless we are willing to adopt a crude functionalism, according to which whatever generates the right or keyed answer is an ability or disposition of critical thinking, then we shall have to insist that construct-valid direct tests of critical thinking are ones where the responses are generated in part by the workings of the critical thinking abilities and dispositions in question (Norris, 1983). Crude behaviorism and crude functionalism do not discriminate between real displays of critical thinking and the mere appearance of such. Since we want only tests that make such a discrimination, we should seek those tests whose construct validity rests on the fact that they elicit responses explainable by the very abilities and dispositions we are testing.

What this means is that, to the extent that there are real differences between abilities and dispositions to meet differing expectations on thinking, direct tests that are valid with respect to each of these different constructs will be needed. Claims of construct-valid test results *will* be limited by contextually differing expectations of reasoning tied to contextually different communities of discussion and informational contexts.

The same point holds true with respect to tests for critical thinking abilities and dispositions that proceed by checking for some property or response of the test-taker that is correlated with critical thinking abilities and dispositions. To establish the correlation, we must find some type of test performance that is correlated with just those contextually bound abilities and dispositions we are testing. Correlation between the results of several different tests does *suggest* that they measure the same thing. However, it tells us *nothing* about *what* each of the tests really measures (Phillips, 1989). The extent to which a test really tests some construct of interest will depend upon how good the correlation is between the test results of interest and the presence and strength of the abilities and dispositions being tested. Since the latter are features of being able to think critically in certain communities of discussion and informational contexts, then the correlation by which we examine someone's critical thinking acumen will be associated with, and will serve as evidence for, such context-limited features.

Even if we decide to test for critical thinking abilities and dispositions by first establishing a criterion that shows them to be present in some degree and then checking the test-taker's performance against this criterion, the point will hold. If the criterion is an invariably sure guide to critical thinking, and not just an arbitrarily stipulated operationalization of a certain critical thinking feature, then it will be a criterion of one of the contextually bound features that enter into and explain a case of critical thinking.

No matter what form the test takes, if it really reveals critical thinking abilities and dispositions, then it will have to reveal abilities and dispositions to think in ways meeting expectations that are different from one community of discussion to another and from one informational context to another.

If we want standardized tests that are not limited in these ways, and we do not want to control for these differences, then it seems we must give up claiming that the tests have construct validity. Without controlling for these variables, the test results might well seem to be telling us that someone has (or lacks) a certain ability or disposition, when really the test performance reflects the operation of an ability or disposition to think in ways meeting a different set of expectations, where this other ability or disposition also leads to the keyed answer.

Ennis (1984) has pointed out certain problems of false confirmation and false disconfirmation, and the need to standardize test-takers' background knowledge as well as the need to consider the test-takers' justification for their answers. Ennis makes these points in criticism of various standardized tests, including one of his own. For example, in testing for the ability to discern legitimate authorities or to check the credibility of claims, Ennis imagines visitors to an alien planet having to say whether it is more reasonable to believe a military officer or health official on the question of the potability of water found there. The critical thinker could respond in either of three contrary ways depending upon what set of background beliefs he or she held about the special knowledge of health officials and military personnel. For example, the health official should know how to check for bacteria and other sources of contamination, while the military person should know how to survive by finding drinkable water (Ennis, 1984; Norris & Ennis, 1989). Here we should standardize or otherwise control for the influence of varying background knowledge, or else we should give up claims to know about critical thinking abilities through such a test question.

The general points I am making are along this same line; it is just that the variables I am considering are both more systemic (in the case of community-of-discussion differences), and apparently more numerous and local (in the case of informational-context differences) than those considered by Ennis.

One option we have is to give up seeking construct-valid tests for critical thinking abilities and dispositions. Such capitulation, I take it, is an intolerable result, because it amounts to giving up the ability to make claims about test-takers' critical thinking. Alternatively, we can try to control for the variables in question. However, this alternative is no better. Note that critical thinking is not just a matter of displaying appropriate permutations and combinations of elements of common knowledge according to the procedures and within the background assumptions of a community of discussion; it is not *just* a matter of this micro-constructiveness mentioned above. There are also constructive and modifying functions performed on the basic elements of communities of discussion and, as was pointed out in passing, on the common body of a community's knowledge on some issue.

Thus, for example, Copernicus and Galileo greatly modified both basic assumptions about the solar system and the procedures by which it should be studied. After Galileo, the Copernican view of the solar system had a much greater purchase, and the same technology appropriate to studying the motion and surface appearances of distant terrestrial objects was found appropriate to studying the same features of celestial objects. After Lavoisier and the revolution in chemistry, the attempt to give partially analogically qualitative explanations of chemical actions was replaced by procedures of strict measurement and the assumption that qualitative differences were explicable in terms of nonanalogical quantitative properties of substances. At least after Pauli, argument to the best explanation without the possibility of immediate backing in experimental testing was admitted as a method of studying the basic physical structure of things. And so it goes. Part of the constructive role of critical thought is sometimes to modify the very underpinnings of a community of discussion, replacing or restating basic assumptions about the possibilities of what exists and how it works, and replacing procedures of studying what is the case with other and sometimes incompatible procedures.

In addition, in this age of interdisciplinary studies, we see many examples of new or renewed combinations of approaches to problems, even though these approaches have their origins in different and heretofore isolated communities of discussion. A recent newspaper article reports the redefinition of "national security" to include, beyond issues of military aggression, such matters as threats to environmental, economic, and cultural survival. And, this is just one example of many new fields and new scholarly, technological, and policy endeavors which have come along through the constructive work of critical thought combining and recombining the constraints of various communities of discussion.

Finally, as noted, the progress of common knowledge in a community's discussion lurches on. This progress calls for us to rethink earlier conclusions and even the adequacy of procedures for thinking about problems that had heretofore been regarded as fully appropriate for the purposes at hand. These changes, like those in the basic elements and working combinations of communities of discussion, will make vast differences to the textbooks, lessons, curricular emphases, grade level expectations, and public debate expectations that our students and their parents will encounter. Just think, for example, of the differences to be made by the recent discoveries concerning Neptune's weather patterns, the age of stone ruins in England and the related views of the seat of civilization, and the discovery of Shakespeare's Rose Theatre in London.

Thus, there are three dimensions of the larger or macro-constructive aspect of critical thinking which make significant differences, both in the community-of-discussion and in the informational-context expectations affecting how to think critically. So, it should be clear that standardizing critical thinking tests so that differences between these expectations are minimized will have an intolerably adverse effect upon critical thinking itself. After all, standardizing these tests in the ways in question would amount to controlling for the influence of any but a preferred set of expectations of thought. And the best way to do that would be to make sure that class presentations, text books, teaching emphases, and the rest *curtail rather than develop* student knowledge and facility in working with any but the approved set of expectations. In other words, it would amount to making sure that students to be tested did not develop the familiarity and facility with alternative communities of discussion and new developments in the mix of and discussion in single communities. As a consequence, standardized critical thinking tests would ensure that students did not develop the macro-constructive dimensions of critical thinking of which we have just been speaking.

This Orwellian result would make the testing of critical thinking abilities and dispositions counterproductive. To test in a neat way with results leading to broad generalities, we would have not just to ignore but, in fact, to work against part of what it is that we should be testing!

Some might find this price acceptable and be willing to put up with the subtle political and intellectual repression needed to pay it. But even for those people, there is something more to say. For it is just a confusion bred of hubris that would lead us to be content in such a pass of events. Notice that there is a real point to the macro-constructive side of critical thinking as just described. We humans do not find ourselves with any clearly reliable, instinctual mode of access to the truth, or to the nature of our world. We must not only learn our way by investigating the particular contingencies we encounter, but also by experimenting with various methods of investigating those contingencies. Of course, we are not entirely ill-equipped to do this. If nothing else, we can, within limits, improve upon our methods as we debate their efficiency and efficacy for our purposes of inquiry (Blatz, 1989). The possibilities of macro-reconstructions that improve our methods and assumptions of inquiry have been and remain crucial to human progress.

Similarly, part of the point of the micro-constructive side of critical thinking is that even as we modify and adjust our methods and assumptions at the level of communities of discussion, we individually must exercise, modify, and adjust their use in specific situations. We must, as we said above in sketching the nature of critical thinking, decide how to combine and to order the appropriate methods, assumptions, and portions of the body of common knowledge in order to construct a solution to the problem at hand. The standardization of critical thinking performance expectations would work against this dynamic dimension of the micro-constructive side of critical thinking. It would standardize what portions of the common knowledge to use and how individuals should use them to get the right answer. Thus, it would call for us to suppress the individual micro-constructive processing that is present in settings where there is some point to critical thinking.

Standardized tests, as we have been speaking of them, will be out of place in settings where critical thinking has some point. Thesis V, is true: We have to choose between tests that lack construct validity, tests that subvert the very thing they seek to measure, or tests that are nonstandardized since what they measure is nongeneralizable in the ways explored. The first two of these alternatives are not welcome. Thus, it seems we should contextualize critical thinking testing. We should limit our claims about critical thinking to claims about abilities and dispositions to think in specific community-of-discussion and informational-context ways. This could involve limiting claims even to the critical thinking abilities and dispositions one has as a member of certain school classes.

UNIVERSAL PRINCIPLES, PARTICULAR PRACTICES, AND CRITICAL THINKING TESTS

Note that I have not argued that there are no highly general principles, patterns of inquiry, and modes of inference for critical thinking. For example, there are the general logical types, instances of which are found in the critical thinking of various communities of discussion and informational contexts (Blatz, 1989). Nor have I argued that we cannot identify or understand these general principles and patterns. We can, and they are studied and debated in formal, informal, and philosophical logic. However, these are claims about the logical patterns to be found in critical thinking, not claims about the abilities and dispositions to operate in ways which, in fact, fit these patterns.

We have to keep separate the generality of an ability or disposition to think in certain ways, and the generality of the abstract logical pattern which that way of thinking instantiates. Four-year-olds are able to think about some features of the world while using a pattern of reasoning that fits the pattern of disjunctive syllogism. They can recognize that either they may hear a story or watch a TV program, and, since they choose not to watch TV, then they may hear a story. But this does not mean that they understand the abstract pattern of disjunctive syllogism, that they can articulate it, or that they can follow it in addressing other problems or in answering the questions of a community of discussion with which they are unfamiliar. For example, it does not mean that they can reason to an elimination of all but the real cause of the tractor's not starting. To do the latter they would have to know not just facts about tractors, tractor engines, and this particular tractor engine, but also they would have to know how to conduct the proper tests needed to eliminate all but the real cause of the problem. All that involves a number of critical thinking abilities and dispositions different from those we use in seeing the consequences of our simple choices of consumption.

Thus abilities and dispositions to think in ways expected and appropriate in a particular community of discussion and informational context will instantiate highly general abstract patterns and principles of reasoning. But the level of the generality of those critical thinking abilities and dispositions, as they operate in a particular community of discussion and informational context, is not to be equated with the level of generality of the most abstract expression of the logic they instantiate. It is a basic error to infer that since the logic of someone's thinking can be described generally, across many communities of discussion and informational contexts, the abilities or dispositions of that individual to think that way are themselves operationally general.

One more disclaimer is important. I am not saying that students cannot develop abilities and dispositions at using logically abstract aspects of critical thinking, nor that we cannot test for the presence and strength of these features. Logic texts are full of both exercises and test questions to check on the presence and strength of these features. Thus, we can develop the abilities and dispositions to use principles, strategies, and modes of reasoning that are specified independently of contextually special epistemic requirements and expectations. And we can test for these features of a critical thinker. Such features are not general, that is, "all purpose," abilities and dispositions of critical thinking. Rather they are abilities and dispositions to think in general ways, that is, in ways free from the constraints of all or virtually all particular communities of discussion and informational contexts.

Standard logic classes, whether classes in formal or informal logic, are not about good thinking in particular communities of discussion and informational contexts. Rather, if they touch thinking in these contexts at all, they are about the logic patterns, pitfalls, principles, and programs of inquiry common to all or many of these varying contexts. Students can become adept at the metalevel analysis involved in identifying and clarifying these common logical aspects. Indeed, they can become adept at checking for compliance with these expectations in a range of cases, from the uninterpreted formal system to a large suite of common-sense examples where there are no significant peculiar contextual demands. In this way, to the extent that the real logic of the community of discussion and informational context in question fits the most abstract patterns of the logic class, the student can become a good critic of the most general structural features of the thinking in those contexts.

However, this does not make the student a good critic of the critical thinking in those contexts! It does not ensure that the student will understand, appreciate the reason for, and be able to judge the accommodations necessary to the specific contextual embodiments of these aspects of logic. Thus, it does not mean that the student will be able to check whether some person is or is not meeting the appropriate set of contextually varying expectations as that person tries to operate with the technology, information sources, and approved programs of inquiry of those contexts. The well-versed logic student might be no more than a partially informed and thoroughly unwelcome gadfly.

Finally, it does not follow from the fact that if someone is a well-versed logic student that the individual can participate with any great sophistication in any community of discussion not specifically concerned with the study of logic. Doing well in logic does not guarantee also doing well in history, economics, or even other areas of philosophy. Critical thinking lessons in particular subject-matter areas do not seem to transfer by themselves (Ennis, 1989; Kennedy, Fischer, & Ennis, 1987; Perkins & Salomon, 1989). Context-independent lessons in how to think well transfer no better, if my students are any indication. The explanation in both cases, I submit, is the very point at issue. Being able and disposed to think well in ways that are paradigm- and common-knowledge-specific, rests on abilities and dispositions to think in ways meeting different, even if only more complex, expectations than those the context-independent thinker must meet in logic classes. And no amount of memorization of the facts of a field will remedy this situation, contrary to the suggestions of other thinkers who believe there are "all purpose" general features of critical thinking—thinkers such as Ennis (1987).

Transfer *seems*, in my theory and experience, best explained by, and best guaranteed when, those expectations of reasoning in the context of previous learning which are the same as those of the next context of learning, are made explicit, and the idiosyncratic expectations of the context of new learning are taught as adaptations of the common or transferring elements. If that is so, and logic classes do teach what truly are common aspects of good reasoning in many contexts, then such classes can aid in the transfer process. However, this does not change the fact that the abilities and dispositions we develop and test in logic classes are not operationally general abilities and dispositions of critical thinking.

CONCLUSION

Nothing I have said runs counter to saying that there are highly general aspects of critical thinking, that we can develop abilities and dispositions to work with these, and that we can test for these features in construct-valid ways. Still, this does not mean that these features are "all purpose" general abilities and dispositions to think well in any context, so that developing them will lead to a development of the contextualized features of critical thinking, or that testing for the former will reveal the latter.

There are a number of ways of testing for critical thinking abilities and dispositions. What I have said is not intended to speak against testing using multiple-choice, short-answer, or essay tests, nor is it meant to restrict us to direct testing or testing through checking for a correlate of critical thinking abilities and dispositions. It *is* meant to restrict us to tests where we can put students' responses into the framework of their thinking—its paradigm- and informational-context expectations—so that we can check to see whether they really have the ability and disposition to think as they are asked to do.

Just telling students to answer from a certain paradigmatic and informational standpoint will not be enough here, because students can think in those ways without being able to identify that they are the ways they are thinking and without being able to follow instructions to deliberately think in these ways. Thus, as Ennis and Norris have said, we frequently will have to test for critical thinking in ways eliciting students' own description of their thinking and assumptions (Norris, 1989; Norris & Ennis, 1989). This approach in itself is fraught with risk, because it can be accomplished only by observing the student over a long period of time and being intimately familiar with the instructional and learning circumstances of the student. Thus, Thesis VI is true: contextualized testing promises also to be localized testing for critical thinking abilities and dispositions. Anything less, however, will be untrue to the nature of critical thinking.

REFERENCES

Blatz, C. V. (1989). Contextualism and critical thinking: Programmatic investigations. *Educational Theory, 39,* 107–119.

Ennis, R. H. (1984). Problems in testing informal logic/critical thinking/reasoning ability. *Informal Logic, 6*(1), 3–9.

Ennis, R. H. (1987). A taxonomy of critical thinking dispositions and abilities. In J. B. Baron and R. J. Sternberg (Eds.), *Teaching thinking skills: Theory and practice* (pp. 9–26). New York: W. H. Freeman and Company.

Ennis, R. H. (1989). Critical thinking and subject specificity: Clarification and needed research. *Educational Researcher, 18*(3), 4–10.

Evans, P. J. A. (1989). The use and abuse of standardized tests. *Field Development Newsletter, 19*(1), 1–15.

Facione, P. A. (1990). *Critical thinking: A statement of expert consensus for purposes of educational assessment and instruction.* Fullerton, CA: California State University, Fullerton.

Kennedy, M., Fischer, M. B., & Ennis, R. H. (1987). *Critical thinking: Literature review and needed research.* Champaign, IL: University of Illinois, Illinois Critical Thinking Project.

Körner, S. (1970). *Categorial frameworks.* Oxford: Oxford University Press.

Kuhn, T. S. (1970). *The structure of scientific revolutions* (2nd ed., enlarged). Chicago: The University of Chicago Press.

McPeck, J. E. (1981). *Critical thinking and education.* New York: St. Martin's Press.

Messick, S. (1989). Meaning and values in test validation: The science and ethics of assessment. *Educational Researcher, 18*(2), 5–11.

Norris, S. P. (1983). The inconsistencies at the foundation of construct validation theory. In E. R. House (Ed.), *Philosophy of evaluation* (pp. 53–74). San Francisco: Jossey-Bass.

Norris, S. P. (1989). Can we test validly for critical thinking? *Educational Researcher, 18*(9), 21–26.

Norris, S. P., & Ennis, R. H. (1989). *Evaluating critical thinking.* Pacific Grove, CA: Midwest Publications.

Norris, S. P., & Ryan, J. (1987). Designing a test of inductive reasoning. In F. H. van Eemeren, R. Grootendorst, J. A. Blair, & C. A. Willard (Eds.), *Argumentation: Analysis and practices* (pp. 394–403). Dordrecht: Foris.

Perkins, D. N., & Salomon, G. (1989). Are cognitive skills context-bound? *Educational Researcher, 18*(1), 16–25.

Phillips, L. M. (1989). *Developing and validating assessments of inference ability in reading comprehension* (Technical Report No. 452). Champaign, IL: University of Illinois, Center for the Study of Reading. (ERIC Document Reproduction Service No. ED 303 767)

About the Contributors

Nandita Babu is lecturer in the Department of Psychology at Utkal University in Orissa, India. She received her Ph.D. from the University of Toronto in 1989. Her dissertation, entitled "Children's Understanding of the Validity and Truth of Mental Representations," has contributed to an understanding of children's earliest concepts of logical necessity, that is, the ways in which children base their beliefs on the decisiveness of evidence.

Sharon Bailin is Associate Professor in the Faculty of Education, Simon Fraser University. Her work is in philosophy of education and drama education. A primary focus of her research has been on creativity, with a particular interest in the relationship between creativity and critical thinking. She is the author of *Achieving Extraordinary Ends: An Essay on Creativity* (Ablex, 1991).

J. Anthony Blair is Professor of Philosophy at the University of Windsor. He is co-author of the texts *Logical Self-Defense* (McGraw Hill Ryerson, 1977) and *A Reasoner's Handbook* (University of Windsor, 1989), and co-editor of the journal *Informal Logic*, the first journal devoted exclusively to informal logic and critical thinking. In addition, he is the author of numerous articles on informal logic and critical thinking.

Charles V. Blatz is Associate Professor and Chairman of the Department of Philosophy at the University of Toledo. His recent work in critical thinking focuses on the nature and pedagogical implications of contextual limits on good reasoning. Current work is on transfer of learning, the nature of reasoning strategies, and the relation between the logic and psychology of reasoning. He also works in ethical theory with applications to agriculture and international development.

Robert H. Ennis is Professor of Philosophy of Education at the University of Illinois at Urbana-Champaign. He has been interested in the conceptualization and assessment of critical thinking since he taught high school science, English, and social studies in the early 1950s. He is co-author (with Stephen Norris) of *Evaluating Critical Thinking* (Midwest, 1989), and has co-authored the Cornell Critical Thinking Tests, Level X and Level Z (with Jason Millman), and the Ennis-Weir Critical Thinking Essay Test (with Eric Weir). He is author of *The Logic of Teaching* (Prentice-Hall, 1969) and is currently completing a textbook in critical thinking.

David Hitchcock is Associate Professor of Philosophy at McMaster University in Hamilton, Ontario. He is the author of *Critical Thinking* (Methuen, 1983), and of articles on non-deductive inference and on Plato. He was the founding president (1983–1985) of the Association for Informal Logic and Critical Thinking.

Ralph H. Johnson is a Professor of Philosophy at the University of Windsor, where he has taught since 1966. He is the author of numerous articles on informal logic and critical thinking. With J. Anthony Blair, he is co-editor of the journal *Informal Logic*, and co-author of *Logical Self-Defense* (McGraw Hill Ryerson, 1977), the third edition of which is now being prepared.

Robert S. Lockhart received his Ph.D. from the University of Sydney. He is currently Professor of Psychology and Coordinator of the Program in Cognitive Science at the University of Toronto. His major research interests are in the areas of memory, problem solving, and decision making.

Jane Roland Martin, a Professor of Philosophy at the University of Massachusetts, Boston, has written numerous articles on education and is the author of *Reclaiming a Conversation: The Ideal of the Educated Woman* (Yale University Press, 1985). Her most recent book is *The Schoolhome: Transforming American Education* (Harvard University Press, 1992).

John E. McPeck is Professor of Education at the University of Western Ontario, and specializes in philosophy of education. He is the author of *Critical Thinking and Education* (St. Martin's Press, 1981), and *Teaching Critical Thinking: Dialogue and Dialectic* (Routledge, 1990).

Stephen P. Norris is Professor of Educational Research and Philosophy of Education at Memorial University of Newfoundland. He has published analyses of the status of critical thinking testing, reports of empirical research on alternative methods for validating critical thinking tests, and arguments for the applicability of philosophy of science to science education. He is co-author (with Robert H. Ennis) of *Evaluating Critical Thinking* (Midwest, 1989), and co-editor (with Linda M. Phillips) of *Foundations of Literacy Policy in Canada* (Detselig, 1990).

Linda M. Phillips is Professor of Reading Research at Memorial University of Newfoundland. Her areas of research are reading, writing, critical thinking, and children's literature. She has published numerous articles and book chapters on these topics, is author of *Ask Me No Questions* (Prentice-Hall, 1990), and co-editor with Stephen Norris of *Foundations of Literacy Policy in Canada* (Detselig, 1990).

David R. Olson is Professor of Applied Psychology at the Ontario Institute for Studies in Education and former Director of the McLuhan Program in Culture and Technology at the University of Toronto. He is co-editor with Janet Astington and Paul Harris of *Developing Theories of Mind* (Cambridge University Press, 1988), and with Nancy Torrance and Angela Hildyard of *Literacy, Language and Learning* (Cambridge University Press, 1985). He is author of some

150 research articles on the topics of language communication and cognition, and is the author of the entry on *Writing* in the *Encyclopaedia Britannica*. His most recent publication is *Literacy and Orality*, co-edited with Nancy Torrance (Cambridge University Press, 1991); he is currently at work on *The World on Paper*.

James Ryan teaches in the Philosophy Department at Memorial University of Newfoundland, and has done research on critical thinking in high school students. He is about to complete a Ph.D. dissertation in the philosophy of science.

Harvey Siegel is Professor of Philosophy at the University of Miami. He works mainly in epistemology, philosophy of science, and philosophy of education. He is the author of *Relativism Refuted: A Critique of Contemporary Epistemological Relativism* (Reidel, 1987) and *Educating Reason: Rationality, Critical Thinking and Education* (Routledge, 1988).

Index